Word and Music Studies

Essays on Music and the Spoken Word and on Surveying the Field

WORD AND MUSIC STUDIES
7

Series Editors

Walter Bernhart
Lawrence Kramer
Suzanne M. Lodato
Steven Paul Scher†
Werner Wolf

The book series WORD AND MUSIC STUDIES (WMS) is the central organ of the International Association for Word and Music Studies (WMA), an association founded in 1997 to promote transdisciplinary scholarly inquiry devoted to the relations between literature/verbal texts/language and music. WMA aims to provide an international forum for musicologists and literary scholars with an interest in interart/intermedial studies and in crossing cultural as well as disciplinary boundaries.

WORD AND MUSIC STUDIES will publish, generally on an annual basis, theme-oriented volumes, documenting and critically assessing the scope, theory, methodology, and the disciplinary and institutional dimensions and prospects of the field on an international scale: conference proceedings, collections of scholarly essays, and, occasionally, monographs on pertinent individual topics as well as research reports and bibliographical and lexicographical work.

Word and Music Studies

Essays on Music and
the Spoken Word
and on Surveying the Field

Edited by
Suzanne M. Lodato
and David Francis Urrows

Rodopi

Amsterdam - New York, NY 2005

The paper on which this book is printed meets the requirements of "ISO 9706: 1994, Information and documentation - Paper for documents - Requirements for permanence".

ISBN: 90-420-1897-6
©Editions Rodopi B.V., Amsterdam - New York, NY 2005
Printed in The Netherlands

Contents

Suzanne M. Lodato
Introduction vii

Surveying the Field

Eric Prieto
Deleuze, Music, and Modernist Mimesis 3

David L. Mosley
Listening to Parsifal
Premodern Romance, Modern Music Drama, Postmodern Film 21

Michael Halliwell
'Opera about Opera'
Self-Referentiality in Opera with Particular Reference to
Dominick Argento's *The Aspern Papers* 51

Jürgen Thym
Schubert's Strategies in Setting Free Verse 81

Suzanne M. Lodato
False Assumptions
Richard Strauss's Lieder and Text/Music Analysis 103

Music and the Spoken Word

Lawrence Kramer
Speaking Melody, Melodic Speech 127

Werner Wolf
Language and/or Music as Man's 'Comfort'?
Beckett's Metamedial Allegory *Words and Music* 145

Stephen Benson
Beckett, Feldman, Joe and Bob:
Speaking of Music in *Words and Music* 165

Deborah Weagel
Musical and Verbal Counterpoint in
Thirty Two Short Films About Glenn Gould 181

Notes on the Contributors 197

Introduction

This volume of essays from the Fourth International Conference of the International Association for Word and Music Studies, held in Berlin in 2003, is published in the wake of Steven Paul Scher's passing on December 25, 2004. Professor Scher, whom Walter Bernhart described as "the mastermind behind establishing and 'defining the field' of Word and Music Studies as a recognized interdisciplinary area of scholarly enquiry" (Bernhart xi), was arguably the central figure in our field during the late twentieth century and the beginning of the twenty-first. I will not attempt to discuss the large body of his work and his legacy to us here. That has already been accomplished by Bernhart in his introduction to volume 5 of Word and Music Studies, which comprises a selection of Professor Scher's essays from the earliest years of his career through the final year of his life[1]. I would simply suggest that Professor Scher's interests in the theory and methodology of interdisciplinary studies and in cultivating "a happy balance between critical theory and interpretive practice" (Bernhart xvi) can be seen in the essays in this volume as well as those representing the activities of our previous three international conferences. These papers also reflect the breadth of Scher's work, which included not only word and music studies, but German literature, Romantic studies, and comparative literature as well. The work in this volume runs the gamut from close musical and textual analysis to postmodern critical theory and deals with a variety of topics such as the lied, the Parsifal tale, opera, radio plays, and film. A few years ago, Bernhart wrote that Professor Scher's ideas "have become starting points for further reflexion and have stimulated other minds to find their own solutions to central issues of the field" (Bernhart xviii). That statement is still true today, more than ever. We will miss Steven Paul Scher, but he will live on in our work as we move forward in advancing the field of word and music studies.

---

[1] Bernhart's essay was first published in volume 4 of the Word and Music Studies series (cf. Lodato). The papers in volume 4, which were given at the Third International Conference of the International Association for Word and Music Studies held at the University of Sydney in 2001, honored Steven Paul Scher in the year of his sixty-fifth birthday.

The first part of this volume, entitled **"Surveying the Field"**, covers recent trends and new outlooks in the constantly changing interdisciplinary area of word and music studies. The volume begins with three essays that employ philosophy and critical theory to explore relationships between music and literature.

First, **Eric Prieto** discusses the attempt of two mid-twentieth-century French postmodernists – Gilles Deleuze and Félix Guattari – to do away with the idea of representation by "overturning the entire edifice of representational thought" [5][2] going back to Plato and Aristotle. According to Deleuze, because representation as a basis for thought arises from Platonic ideas, we cannot experience the world in an unmediated way without abolishing representation. Such direct experience would involve a focus on "differences, becomings, and intensities" – all of which Deleuze and Guattari said characterize music – rather than "identity, being, and metric space" [9], which typify language and prevent us from experiencing time in an unmediated manner. Deleuze and Guattari therefore embraced music, which they viewed as an art that is characterized by constant development, as a model for literature, other arts, and other intellectual endeavors. However, discovering that even music possesses some elements of representation or stability – best exemplified in the musical refrain – they modified their approach to one in which "becoming" and flux are privileged without denying the existence of stability and conceptualization in music.

David L. Mosley also looks at literature and music through the lenses of philosophy and critical theory, this time by exploring three manifestations of the Parsifal tale – Wolfram von Eschenbach's thirteenth-century romance, Richard Wagner's opera, and Richard LaGravanese and Terry Gilliam's film, *The Fisher King*. Mosley sets out to show how, by considering these three very different works within their historical and cultural contexts, the voice of Parsifal is heard to speak through a rich and complex web of "historical implications, generic expectations, and medial limitations" [21] that must be loosened (though not broken) in order to reveal relationships among the works. Martin Heidegger described a web of this sort as the basis for his approach for

---

[2] References for this volume appear in brackets.

interpreting speech. But rather than focusing on the sound of speech, Heidegger focused on what speech signifies. Mosley revises Heidegger's approach by interrogating the **sound** of each work. Following the writings of Friedrich Nietzsche, Walter Ong, and Jacques Attali, he presents his mode of "criticism-as listening" [21] as an alternative to Heidegger's approach. The sound to which Mosley listens might be a musical setting (Wagner's *Parsifal*), an implied mode of performance (Wolfram's *Parzival*), an approach to the realization of the story (the postmodern and parodic *The Fisher King*), or the overall tone of a work. His discussion of Nietzsche's characterization of music as "both logical proof and ontological manifestation of the one impenetrable, primeval ground" [32] recalls Prieto's discussion of the way that Deleuze and Guattari privileged music as a model for other arts.

Michael Halliwell explores postmodern practices in the transformation of a late nineteenth-century short story into a late twentieth-century opera by investigating the self-referential nature of Dominick Argento's *The Aspern Papers*. This work, which concerns itself with opera, its artists, and its customs, in turn reflects the story by Henry James on which the opera is based, for the James tale itself is "self-consciously about the literary life" [56]. Halliwell sees this self-reflexivity in the use of traditional operatic structures and older musical styles with atonality and complex and non-linear narrative techniques; a narrator whose objectivity is in question; Argento's frequent use of song *qua* song in the opera; allusions to operatic rivalries, inside jokes, and other opera trivia; an opera (*Medea*) within the opera; various inter-relationships between *Medea* and *The Aspern Papers*; parodies of older operatic styles and characters; irony; and Argento's "deconstruc[tion] [of] the idea of the integrity and autonomy of the work of art" [64].

The final two essays in this section approach the seemingly straightforward practice of examining text/music relationships in lieder in very different ways. **Jürgen Thym** shows the methods that Franz Schubert used to set free verse poems with metrical, periodically structured music. In rendering free verse metrical during the compositional process, Schubert often suggested meanings that were different from meanings in the original poems. In my own essay, I examine the reverse process: Strauss often set metrical, traditionally structured poetry with flexible, almost speech-like melodies in which the meter was not easily discernible. In other instances, his poetry settings were clearly metrical, but by breaking the poetic lines and stanzas into smaller fragments and setting the fragments to disjunct melodies, he deprived the listener of a clear sense of textual structure. These techniques relate closely to "consistent naturalism" and "necessary rhythm", which were developed by late nineteenth-century German naturalist writers.

Part 2 of the volume comprises four essays on the theme of **"Music and the Spoken Word"**. The WMA's charge to participants was to "explore – in the appropriate historical depth and geographical breadth – the manifold interactions and […] focus on the interpretive potential of both the convergences and the divergences between the two discrete yet conjoined artistic media" (Call for Papers for the Fourth International Conference of the International Association for Word and Music Studies).

Lawrence Kramer's essay, which opens this section, introduces a theoretical basis for thinking about 'singing melody', a melody or motive originally set to a text that is played subsequently without the words. Beginning with two points of departure – Slavoj Zizek's theory of the Real as the manifestation of the relationship between text and images, and the "counterpoint" [127] formed by musical melody, words, and the "melody" [128] of speech intonation – Kramer illustrates by examples from an opera, a film, and two instrumental compositions how singing melody, in recalling but not stating the words, generates new meanings that cannot quite be defined by language. Prieto's discussion of Deleuze and Guattari resonates in this essay, in which Kramer talks about how the world exists prior to being "imprinted" by language, and the process of listening to instrumental music can permit the experience of the world before language defines it, but at the same time allows the listener to perceive the world's "imprintability […] by language" [142].

Next follow two essays on Samuel Beckett's 1962 radio play, *Words and Music*. The first, by **Werner Wolf**, analyzes the play as a "metamedial allegory" [145] of relationships between words and music in which Beckett addresses the question of dominance of one over the other and looks at the functions and limitations of words and music in imitating reality and creating meaning. Wolf also explains Beckett's radio play as a self-reflexive work that deals with the nature of the art work itself, as does Halliwell in his discussion of *The Aspern Papers*. **Stephen Benson**, on the other hand, focuses on Morton Feldman's musical setting of the play in a "sound-oriented reading" [167; also, cf. Mosley's essay] by "uncoupling" [177] music and words. He explores how the sound of Feldman's music, as well as the sound of words, music, and silences (as opposed to their dramatic meanings) experienced by radio listeners, shows larger relationships between words and music as perceived by both Beckett and Feldman. In Benson's analysis, one can see a similarity between the views of Feldman, who eschewed constructs such as plot, language, or rhetoric as the basis for musical composition, and the ideas of Deleuze and Guattari.

Finally, **Deborah Weagel**'s essay, "Musical and Verbal Counterpoint in Thirty Two Short Films About Glenn Gould", also deals with radio works – this time in the form of radio documentaries by Gould seen in the film. Known as "contrapuntal radio" [165], these works employ recordings of spoken voices overlaid so as to form "verbal counterpoint" (181). Weagel discusses how this spoken word counterpoint forefronts the sonic aspects of the words, even though Gould carefully arranged the recorded voices to highlight aspects of semantic meaning.

* * *

The Berlin Conference, held in the fascinating environs of the Musikinstrumenten-Museum on Postdamer Platz, attracted a wide range of scholars from around the world: from Scandinavia to South Africa, and from the heartland of the United States to Russia, Australia, and China. Such a global gathering in the world's first postmodern city brought forth a large number of original and challenging papers and presentations, delivered by scholars at varying stages of development, with differing points of orientation and reference. Some, like those presented in this volume of proceedings, represent important research and thinking among members of the confraternity in a rapidly developing field. Other stimulating papers given were more in the nature of prolegomena – trial balloons sent up experimentally and then hauled back down for analysis and further thought at the end of the four-day congress. The International Association for Word and Music Studies will continue pursuing its mission, and continue to pursue the goals so importantly articulated by the life and work of Steven Paul Scher, at its Fifth International Conference, to be held at the University of California at Santa Barbara in August 2005.

June 2005
                                                        Suzanne M. Lodato
                                                        David Francis Urrows

References

Bernhart, Walter. "Masterminding Word and Music Studies: A Tribute to Steven Paul Scher". Bernhart/Wolf, eds. xi-xxi. Lodato/Aspden/Bernhart, eds. 3-11.

Bernhart, Walter, and Werner Wolf, eds. *Word and Music Studies: Essays on Literature and Music (1967-2004) by Steven Paul Scher*. Word and Music Studies 5. Amsterdam, New York: Rodopi, 2004.

Lodato, Suzanne Marie, Suzanne Aspden, and Walter Bernhart, eds. *Word and Music Studies: Essays in Honor of Steven Paul Scher and on Cultural Identity and the Musical Stage*. Word and Music Studies 4. Amsterdam: Rodopi, 2002.

Surveying the Field

Deleuze, Music, and Modernist Mimesis

Eric Prieto, Santa Barbara

This essay focuses on the role of music in *Thousand Plateaus*, which was written by two of the most radical exponents of the antirepresentational doctrine that became a hallmark of French postmodern theory in the 1960's and 1970's, Gilles Deleuze and Félix Guattari. They use music to reflect upon the means and ends of their 'nomadic', philosophical project, which involves nothing less than overturning the entire edifice of representational thought in the Aristotelian tradition. For them music is an exemplary art, and they initially intend to propose it as a model for the other arts – and indeed for all forms of human inquiry, including philosophy and science – that would eventually supersede all forms of thought in the representational tradition. Surprisingly, however, their analyses of music actually end up having the opposite effect, leading them to reintroduce representation into the heart of their philosophy. It is this surprising reversal – in which music, paradoxically, provokes a return to representational values – that interests me here.

Of all the arts, it is no doubt music that provides the most interesting test case for understanding the role of representation in aesthetic communication. The lack of any stable, codifiable referential mechanism of the kinds found in language and pictorial representation has created a number of well-known but intractable problems for artists and aestheticians interested in understanding how music makes meaning and whether or not it can, or should be able to, teach us anything useful about the extra-musical world. Some, seizing on this referential instability, have gone so far as to claim that music is incapable of making reference to the outside world (as in Igor Stravinsky's often quoted dictum about music being "by its very nature, essentially powerless to express anything at all," 53-54) or that that any attempt to make it do so betrays a grave misunderstanding of music's fundamental nature (as in Eduard Hanslick's anti-Wagnerian treatise *On the Musically Beautiful*). But even for those of us who are unwilling to go to such extremes, it seems clear that music poses the question of referential meaning in a particularly acute form. It is for this reason, no doubt, that references to music often surface in discussions about the various roles allotted to representation in the other arts, including literature.

Modernist writers in particular have found music to provide a useful point of reference in their struggles to break away from more traditional forms of literary representation. Beginning with the French Symbolists and continuing throughout the first half of the twentieth century, many of the most important exponents of literary modernism used music as a way to explain and justify their experiments with literary representation. Most typically, music served for them as a way to think about the representation of consciousness[1]. Thus we find writers as diverse as Stéphane Mallarmé and Thomas Mann, James Joyce and André Gide, Marcel Proust and Aldous Huxley, discussing the workings of the mind, and their attempts to represent it, in terms of polyphony and counterpoint, symphonic orchestration, the leitmotif and motivic development, and the principles of repetition and variation. This link between music and mind continued to play an important role for the generation of writers that came to maturity in the years following World War Two, especially in France, where writers like Samuel Beckett, Michel Leiris, and the French New Novelists would push the representation of consciousness to its furthest limits. Like their predecessors, these post-war writers tend to see in music a reservoir of formal and expressive models useful in the development of new, inwardly directed modes of mimesis able to foreground the workings of consciousness over the objects of consciousness.

Throughout the twentieth century, then, music has been used by modernist writers to suggest, not an alternative to representation, but a number of models for new and better modes of representation, more in tune with the modernist preoccupation with the representation of consciousness. Beginning in the late 1960s, however, there is a surprising new development, an unprecedented desire to move away from this by-now familiar emphasis on the representation of consciousness – not in order to go back towards more traditional forms of representation, but rather to argue for the need to do away with representation altogether. Once again, this movement is especially prominent in France. The *Tel Quel* group, led by Philippe Sollers, founded its entire theory of literature on this anti-mimetic premise, which is summed up nicely in Jean Ricardou's

---

[1] This assertion, which can only be defended in the most schematic way here, is developed more fully in my book *Listening In: Music, Mind, and the Modernist Narrative*.

often cited injunction to write "not the narrative of an adventure but the adventure of a narrative" (cf. Tel Quel). For these writers, theme, character, and indeed all forms of narrative content are considered to be mere pretexts for, secondary by-products of, or outright distractions from the pure play of linguistic signifiers and abstract verbal constructions. The radical challenge that this theory of literary meaning poses to more traditional accounts of literature is clear: literature, the art that has been most closely allied with representation over the entire course of its history, is suddenly being explained as an art that is, like music, fundamentally non-representational in nature. But what is it that led these thinkers to conceive of literary meaning in this way? Why did they consider it so essential to go beyond representation? And how successful were they in their endeavor? In order to answer such questions, it will be useful to focus on the work of Gilles Deleuze and Félix Guattari. Among the primary philosophical exponents of this antirepresentational school of thought, it is their work that most clearly shows what is at stake in this theory of literature.

In *Difference and Repetition*, first published at the height of the countercultural movement and social unrest of 1968, Deleuze lays out the philosophical groundwork for this antirepresentational doctrine, running through a critique of the history of philosophy going back to Plato and Aristotle in order to argue that representation is not only a dull tool that has outlived its usefulness, but that it is linked to modes of thought that are inherently repressive. Twelve years later, in *A Thousand Plateaus*, Deleuze joins forces with Félix Guattari in order to illustrate the radical philosophical project proposed in *Difference and Repetition*, which requires nothing less than overturning the entire edifice of representational thought. Significantly, music plays a prominent role in the argument of *Thousand Plateaus*, serving primarily as a way to reflect upon the means and ends of their larger, 'nomadic', philosophical project.

Music, Deleuze and Guattari assert, provides an instructive model for literature and the arts, and indeed for philosophy, the sciences, and all other forms of human endeavor as well. It suggests to them an alternative mode of inquiry, one able to overcome more traditional forms of understanding dependent on representation. If their ultimate goal is to do away with representational thought entirely, then music seems to them to provide a useful model for understanding the kinds of thinking that might replace it. This antirepresentational use of music clearly runs counter to the modernist approach to music described earlier, which linked music to the development of new modes of representation, not its destruction. Indeed, some have argued that Deleuze's rejection of representation might be taken as a way to define the moment at which modernism flips over into post-modernity. My own research has convinced me, however, that there are important points of continuity between modernism and postmodernism, suggesting that the break between the two cannot be defined so neatly. In order to show how Deleuze and Guattari's use of music does relate to that of their modernist predecessors, I will be focusing on *Thousand Plateaus,* which devotes two full chapters to music. Before turning to *Thousand Plateaus,* it will be necessary to provide a brief overview of Deleuze's critique of representation in *Difference and Repetition,* since it provides the foundation for all that follows. This first part of my analysis will lead us fairly far away from questions relating specifically to music, but is necessary if we are to understand the significance of music as a model for the 'nomadic', 'deterritorialized', 'molecular' mode of thought that Deleuze and Guattari seek to promote in *Thousand Plateaus.*

Antirepresentationalism in *Difference and Repetition*

It is Henri Bergson's philosophy of becoming that provides the initial impetus for Deleuze's critique of representation. Bergson famously noted that language is an inherently spatializing medium, blocking our intuitive understand of time-as-becoming and making it all but impossible to have any direct experience of the passing of time. Music, on the other hand, by asking us to focus on the ebb and flow of intensities experienced qualitatively, could help us to grasp this essential aspect of time and temporality (cf., for example, Bergson's "The Idea of Duration"). Deleuze builds on Bergson's critique of language, but extends it to the entire system of representation, while also drawing a number of political conclusions from it. For Deleuze, representation is inherently oppressive, responsible for the mental habits that allow the many institutionalized forms of political and social injustice that surround us to prosper.

For this reason, he argues, it is necessary to break out of the mental habits associated with representational thought if we are to think freely and effect any real changes in the current social and political order.

The first stages of his analysis in *Difference and Repetition* are fairly classic. Deleuze begins by pointing out that linguistic communication requires the use of concepts, and that concepts work by subordinating individuals (i.e. any objects found in the empirical world) to the generality of the concepts by which they are named. In order to facilitate communication, they disregard the individuality of individuals, subsuming individuals, with all of the differences that distinguish them from each other, into general categories. It would be difficult to dispute him on this point, and few would care to try. But Deleuze then goes a step further, equating this conceptual subordination of the individual to the general with Platonic Idealism: just as (he argues) Plato considered all actual beings to be mere copies of originals found only on the plane of Ideas, concepts treat individuals as if they were merely examples of general categories. Deleuze argues that there is, consequently, an implied ontological hierarchy in the very use of concepts, which accords primacy to the general category, as if concepts were somehow more real or perfect than the individual members of the categories they define.

This is a delicate point, philosophically, and to make his case Deleuze zeroes in on Aristotle's theory of difference, as formulated in Book X of the *Metaphysics*. This is one of the most difficult and rewarding passages of *Difference and Repetition*. By paying special attention to the taxonomical procedures that characterize Aristotelian thought (where every individual is a member of a conceptual category and every category a member of a still more general category), Deleuze is able to show that Aristotle is unable to conceive of difference on its own terms: individual differences are always conceived of as a function of the categories to which the individuals belong; difference itself is defined as a function of identity. Deleuze then argues that this inability to conceive of difference without reference to identity has distorted the entire history of rational thought in the Western tradition, leading us to seriously misunderstand the very nature of individuality and difference, notably by leading us to undervalue the particularity of direct experience, which is always lost in the system of representation because it is subordinated to the generality of concepts.

There are a number of points on which we could contest this conclusion, but the main sticking point of Deleuze's argument is that Aristotle and his successors describe the generalizing function of concepts in strictly logical terms. Unlike Plato's conception of the Ideas, which explicitly subordinates empirical experience to the superior ontological plane of Ideas, Aristotle's descriptions of conceptual thought avoid making any explicit metaphysical or ethical claims. But Deleuze, who is aware of this objection, argues that Aristotle's logic is, if anything, even more insidiously oppressive than Plato's metaphysics, because it has, over the centuries, conditioned us to accept general categories as the primary data of thought, to substitute, at some subconscious level, concepts for the direct experience of individuals, thereby restricting and limiting every aspect of our relation to the world around us. For this reason, Deleuze actually finds Platonic metaphysics more palatable than Aristotle's logic:

> With Plato the outcome is still in doubt; the process of mediation has not yet been automated. The Idea is not yet an object-concept that subordinates the world to the needs of representation, but rather a *brut* presence, which can only be evoked in the world by referring to what is not 'representable' in things. Moreover the Idea has not yet chosen to subordinate differences between individuals to the identity of a concept in general (*Difference and Repetition*, 83).

For Deleuze, then, the problem with representation is that it has become so entrenched in our thought patterns that it has become all but impossible for us to think about individuals directly, without the mediation of the concept. As a result, all direct experiences of becoming and difference melt away before the abstractive, generalizing work of conceptual, representational thought.

Deleuze's analysis leads him to conclude that it has become necessary to undertake a complete renovation of our epistemological attitudes if we are to regain a more direct, unmediated relationship with the world around us. This, he believes, will require tearing down the entire edifice of representation in the Aristotelian tradition and replacing it with a mode of thought emphasizing the perceptual realm, which he describes in the Bergsonian terms of differences, becomings, durations, intensities, and individuals. It is not clear, however, exactly how we are supposed to do this – even to Deleuze – and so we're left at the end of *Difference and Repetition* in the uncomfortable position of having to develop a whole new arsenal of tools that would enable us to think productively while also avoiding the temptation to structure the world according to the hierarchical categories of conceptual thought. Indeed, we might well ask if such a thing is even possible. How might we go about bringing such a non-representational regime into existence? Is it possible to think without representation? And even if we can imagine ourselves acquiring non-representational knowledge of the world, how would we go about communicating that knowledge to others? Indeed, given that language is an inherently representational medium, doesn't the very use of language by Deleuze and Guattari seem to imply a contradiction at the heart of their philosophical project? These are some of the questions that Deleuze and Guattari attempt to answer in *Thousand Plateaus*. And it is their attempts to answer these questions that will lead them to reflect upon the production of meaning in music.

Molecules, Moles, and Music in *Thousand Plateaus*

The stated goal of *Thousand Plateaus* is to revolutionize the field of 'perceptual semiotics' (23), that is, to teach people to re-envision the world, to see it in new ways, by changing the cognitive tools with which they think. The epistemology Deleuze and Guattari promote there grows directly out of the Bergsonian ontology promoted in *Difference and Repetition*, with its emphasis on differences, becomings, and intensities over identity, being, and metric space. They also reject, or at least try to overcome, the use of hierarchical categories of conceptual thought in the Aristotelian tradition. It is for this reason that they call their way of doing philosophy 'nomadic'. In the Aristotelian tradition, as they explain it, the world is organized conceptually, into plateaus or strata of analysis, where each stratum is defined by a small set of concepts related hierarchically to each other, according to the 'arborescent' logic of family trees, corporate power structures, military rank, and, of course, Aristotle's own taxonomies. What they propose instead is to focus attention on the creation of transversal lines that move freely between strata, making often unexpected connections between them. They call these transversal lines 'planes of consistency' and make them one of the central features of their methodology.

This kind of nomadic conceptual wandering between conceptual strata is at the heart of their philosophical technique, and is responsible for much of what is most exciting and interesting – but also at times exasperating – about that technique. Deleuze and Guattari are not systematic thinkers. On the contrary, they are self-consciously a-systematic thinkers: refusing to stay put in one field or metaphorical register, they roam constantly from one to the next, often without much in the way of explanation, and often within the space of a single sentence. This is what makes their work so difficult and so provocative. By considering, for example, biological phenomena in geological terms, or social interactions in terms of chemical reactions, they hope to provoke new insights, to energize new modes of thought that would make it possible, eventually, to escape from the hierarchically structured world of Aristotelian epistemology. In this sense, 'nomadic' philosophy refers to a kind of interdisciplinarity gone wild. They do not simply disregard established disciplinary boundaries, they work consistently against the grain, always cutting through established generic and disciplinary boundaries in order to create hybrid analytic tools, to which they give odd, anti-Aristotelian names like rhizomes, assemblages, the Body Without Organs, and planes of consistency.

So where does music come into all of this? For Deleuze and Guattari, music is an exemplary art, providing the clearest practical example of the kind of nomadic thought they seek to promote. A temporal art, it puts the emphasis on the Bergsonian dynamics of flux and becoming; a non-representational art, it puts our perceptual faculties in touch with our intellectual faculties in a way that does not require the mediation of concepts and representation. But above all, they argue, it is nomadic, it brings together different levels of analysis, enabling them to be contained within a single thought. By liberating us from the limitations of representational thought in the Aristotelian tradition, which requires that we work on one conceptual plane at a time, music helps us to understand how, from the interstellar to the sub-atomic level, everything is in touch with everything else. In this sense, we could say that the musical experience described by Deleuze and Guattari involves a postmodern update of the Pythagorean harmony of the spheres.

> By placing all its components in continuous variation, music [...] enters the service of a virtual cosmic continuum [...]. This ferment came to the forefront and made itself heard in its own right; and, through the molecular material thus wrought, it made audible the nonsonorous forces of the cosmos that have always agitated music – a bit of Time in the pure state (Proust), a grain of absolute Intensity [...]. Music is not alone in being art as cosmos and in drawing the virtual lines of an infinite variation. (95-96)

Their primary reference in this passage is to twelve-tone music, but all music, they argue, or at least all true music, has this ability to put us in touch with all of the various links in the great chain of being – whether human, animal, vegetable, mineral, or otherwise – and to help us understand how these different levels interact with each other. Thus:

> The properly musical content of music is plied by becomings-woman, becomings-child, becomings-animal; however, it tends, under all sorts of influences, having to do also with the instruments, to become progressively more molecular in a kind of cosmic lapping through which the inaudible makes itself heard and the imperceptible appears as such: no longer the songbird, but the sound molecule. (248)

It is this 'molecular' scale of infra-conceptual relations, which is opposed to the 'molar' scale of conceptually defined resemblances, that interests them[2]. When we are concerned with understanding bird-song on the molecular level, what counts is not the bird or the song (i.e. the molar units, which are thought of as indivisible), but bird molecules and sound molecules, which can be shown to function in ways that are independent from conceptual units like 'bird' or 'song'. It is clear, for example, that the sound molecules that make up bird-song interact in accordance with laws that exist on numerous planes, including (to name only a few out of a potentially infinite number) the laws of acoustics and of natural selection, and the various neurological and physiological laws that govern the production and reception of sound. Music helps us to understand such interactions because it forces us to make better use of our perceptual

---

[2] This opposition between the 'molar' and the 'molecular', which is central to the arguments of Deleuze and Guattari, deserves a bit of clarification here. It is an opposition borrowed from chemistry, where a mole is a standard scientific unit used to measure large quantities of very small entities such as atoms and molecules. For the purposes of this article, all we need to retain is that the concept of the mole helps chemists put quantitative information about what happens to molecules on a macroscopic level subject to empirical measurements like weighing. Deleuze and Guattari use the term molar pejoratively, as a way to emphasize what they see as the Aristotelian tendency to base representations on macroscopic appearances visible to the naked eye, and to ignore the molecular level, which is, however, where the real (i.e. individual) interactions take place. Nomadic philosophy, in this sense, is an attempt to pierce the epiphenomenal crust of representation (identified with 'mere appearances') in order to work on the microscopic level of individual, infra-conceptual relationships.

faculties, encouraging us to free ourselves from the cognitive barriers of molar thought erected by concepts such as 'bird' and 'song'. This is the first major point to retain from the account of musical communication given in *Thousand Plateaus*: music helps us to think on the molecular level of infra-conceptual relations.

Music as a Nomadic Art

This 'molecular', nomadic, quasi-Pythagorean theory of music, it should be noted, is rooted in a view of music history that is borrowed largely, and often uncritically, from the writings of Pierre Boulez. Like Boulez, they see the advent of the twelve-tone system as a key moment in the history of music. Significantly though, for Deleuze and Guattari, as for Boulez, twelve-tone music should not be understood as a radical break with the traditional syntax of diatonic tonality, but as a logical development in the much vaster project that Webern called the "ongoing conquest of the tonal field" (cf. *Path to the New Music, passim*). Deleuze and Guattari run through the history of music on several occasions – citing innovations ranging from medieval polyphony to Romantic-era chromaticism to Darmstadt-era serialism – in order to argue that the entire history of music shows that the art is most tellingly defined by a process of constant renewal, of which the advent of twelve-tone music is only a particularly revealing turn.

> The Viennese school is exemplary of this kind of diagonal, this kind of line-block. But [...] [t]he important thing is that all musicians have always proceeded in this way: drawing their own diagonal, however fragile, outside points, outside coordinates and localizable connections, in order to float a sound block down a created, liberated line, in order to unleash in space this mobile and mutant sound block, a haecceity (for example, chromaticism, aggregates, and complex notes, but already the resources and possibilities of polyphony, etc.). (297)

For them, music is an exemplary art because it is constantly reworking its own materials from within, in a quest to understand the fundamental principles and deep structures that govern the art. They situate these principles on the 'molecular' level and oppose them to the 'molar' units of music that are defined by whatever local conventions – such as the diatonic system of tonality – might be in effect at any given moment. Ultimately, they argue, twelve-tone music simply enabled us to understand a tendency that had always been present in music: the nomadic tendency to constantly call into question the existing codes as part of its quest to reveal its underlying structures.

> the important thing is certainly not to establish a pseudobreak between the tonal system and atonal music; the latter, on the contrary, in breaking away from the tonal system, only carried temperament to its ultimate conclusion (although no Viennese stopped there.) The essential thing is almost the opposite movement: the ferment in the tonal system itself (during much of the nineteenth and twentieth centuries) that dissolved temperament and widened chromaticism while preserving a relative tonality, which reinvented new modalities, brought a new amalgamation of major and minor, and in each instance conquered realms of continuous variation for this variable or that. (95-96)

This, then, is the second point to retain from their account of musical communication: for them, music is of all the arts the one that has most consistently devoted itself to the work of nomadism. Music is constantly creating new planes of consistency, whose primary value is in the way they cut across existing boundaries, breaking down barriers between different levels of thought and establishing new and unforeseen connections. That which most tellingly distinguishes music from the representational arts, as they see it, is its commitment to bringing to light the underlying codes that govern its expressive language, its willingness to constantly call into question accepted conventions, categories, and compositional techniques. And this, they argue, is precisely what nomadic philosophy has to offer more established forms of scientific inquiry: an ongoing, self-perpetuating critique of established conventions that will make it possible to better understand phenomena at the microscopic, molecular level by deconstructing the accepted categories of molar thought.

Music, the Refrain, and Representation

Before going any further, it is important to recognize that Deleuze and Guattari do not present music as an abstract, contentless, or non-representational art. On the contrary, they insist that all music has thematic content, of a kind that is indissociable from its form, but that is not different in any essential sense from the sorts of content found in literature. They identify this content with the *refrain* in music.

> What does music deal with, what is the content indissociable from sound expression? It is hard to say, but it is something: a child dies, a child plays, a woman is born, a woman dies, a bird arrives, a bird

> flies off. We wish to say that these are not accidental themes in music [...] much less imitative exercises; they are something essential [...]. We would say that the *refrain* is properly musical content, the block of content proper to music. (299)

It is with the concept of the refrain that their theory of musical meaning begins to resonate most interestingly with their antirepresentational philosophical stance. Because for Deleuze and Guattari the refrain marks the representational moment in music, that moment at which the thematic content of the work expresses itself most clearly. And for Deleuze and Guattari what makes music a model for the arts, philosophy, and the sciences is neither its apparently abstract tonal surface nor its foregrounding of the temporality of performance, but the nomadic manner in which music develops the refrain. Since this is the key point that comes out of their account of musical thought, it will be worth examining in some detail.

Again: for Deleuze and Guattari the refrain marks the representational moment in music. If we think of the role of refrains in song – from primitive chants to nursery rhymes to the art songs of Franz Schubert and Robert Schumann – we can see what they mean: the refrain marks the moment of greatest stability in a song. When we ask ourselves what a song is about, we begin by humming the refrain. When we have forgotten all the other lyrics of a song, we return to the refrain. Significantly, however, the particularity of musical thought for Deleuze and Guattari is that music does everything in its power to destabilize the refrain, to 'deterritorialize' it, as they say. Indeed, for them, music owes its exemplary status to its tendency to subordinate the refrain to the various processes of musical development. This is the third crucial point to retain from their account of music: the refrain may be the most basic, easily recognized feature of a work of music, but, for precisely this reason, it is an obstacle to the kind of meaning that interests Deleuze and Guattari. The refrain, in other words, is precisely that which must be overcome for truly musical communication to take place.

> We are not at all saying that the refrain is the origin of music, or that music begins with it. It is not really known when music begins. The refrain is rather a means of preventing music, warding it off, or forgoing it. But music exists because the refrain exists also, because music takes up the refrain, lays hold of it as a content in a form of expression, because it forms a block with it in order to take it somewhere else [...]. Music is a creative, active operation that consists in deterritorializing the refrain. Whereas the refrain is essentially territorial, territorializing, or reterritorializing, music makes it a deterritorialized content for a deterritorializing form of expression. (300)

This idea of deterritorializing the refrain leads them to conclude that the essence of music is not to be sought in song, the voice, or the refrain itself but in the use of all the processes of development and variation characteristic of instrumental music in the art music tradition. Here again, it is easy to see what Deleuze and Guattari mean: in the development section of a sonata, the contrapuntal development given to fugal subjects, the progressive transformations of the variations-on-a-theme format, the idea of continuous development dear to Boulez and the serialists, and even the shifting patterns of repetition used by minimalists like Philip Glass and Steve Reich, art music tends to submit its refrains to ever more complex processes of development and variation, moving the work ever further afield from the starting point provided by the refrain.

It is this musical emphasis on the processes of variation, identified with becoming, that they would like to reintroduce into philosophy and the sciences. It comes as no surprise, then, that Deleuze and Guattari go on to generalize from this basic insight, using the metaphor of musical deterritorialization as a way to justify and explain their own practice of nomadic philosophy. Indeed, for those who know the work of Deleuze and Guattari, it will already be apparent that their descriptions of music could serve equally well as descriptions of the kind of philosophizing they do. Their chapters are organized around recurrent motifs that function much like refrains, but their analysis shifts constantly from one conceptual level to another and from one subject to another, often without clearly signaling the transition points or overarching themes that might explain the shift from one development to the next. Rather than progressing systematically from point to point, in hierarchical fashion, as philosophers in the Aristotelian tradition do, Deleuze and Guattari proceed by a process resembling free association. They are constantly deterritorializing their refrains, allowing momentary associations, rather than a systematic argument or global theme, to determine the shape of their chapters. And the history of music seems to them to provide justification for this choice. Works in the classic, Aristotelian, representational tradition, they argue, tend to cling desperately to their refrains. In this, they are like the more elementary song forms, which treat variation, development, and exploration as if they were necessary evils, no-man's-lands that must be traversed in order to arrive at the next statement of the refrain. But Deleuze and Guattari place themselves on the side of continual development. Their mode of philosophizing puts the emphasis on deterritorialization, conceiving of the refrain as a necessary but somewhat dull resting point on the journey of nomadic thought. For this reason, nomadic philosophy is more apt at affirming the importance of becoming over being. Whereas thinkers in the Aristotelian tradition tend to put the emphasis on being and stasis, on the refrain itself, thinkers in the tradition espoused by Deleuze and Guattari use their a-systematic, improvisational, associative style to emphasize the importance of flux and becoming.

Given the preceding analysis, it seems clear that music can be said to serve for Deleuze and Guattari much the same purpose as it did for the modernist writers evoked in my preamble: as a model for the representation of a mode of thought. In this case it serves as a metaphor for their way of doing philosophy, which is opposed to the more systematic analyses characteristic of philosophy in the Aristotelian tradition. This should not, of course, be taken to imply that there is something inherently musical about the way Deleuze and Guattari do philosophy. On the contrary, it would be more accurate to say that their descriptions of music are largely overdetermined – one might even say distorted – by their practice of philosophy. They simply emphasize those aspects of music that can be shown to be analogous to their preferred mode of philosophy, ignoring or downplaying all the rest. In this sense, music serves primarily as an oppositional marker, a handy metaphor for explaining what they see as distinctive and noteworthy about their brand of philosophy.

Does this imply that we should discount their protracted analyses of music in *Thousand Plateaus*, on the grounds that the chapters-long developments on music provide little more than rhetorical maneuvering, strategic metaphors whose only function is to help them make their polemical point? Not necessarily. But in order to overcome such an objection, it should be possible to show that music makes some positive contribution to their philosophy, that it has enabled them to say something that they would have been unable to say otherwise. Does music make such a contribution to their argument? Yes, but it is not exactly what one might have thought, given their antirepresentational point of departure. In fact, I would argue that the clearest sign of music's influence on their philosophical system is that it leads them to renounce the antirepresentational aspects of their original project. For if their initial intention in introducing music into their argument was to buttress their claims for nomadic philosophy as an antirepresentational alternative to philosophy in the Aristotelian tradition, music actually ends up having the exact opposite effect, leading them to abandon the very position they were trying to defend. I would like to conclude, then, by showing how the analysis of music in *Thousand Plateaus* leads them to retreat from their initial antirepresentational position.

Music and the return to representation

Towards the end of their discussion of music, Deleuze and Guattari come to realize that if even music has a territorializing, content-oriented, representational dimension – that of the refrain – then there is no doubt something necessary about representation and territory that even their militantly nomadic form of philosophy cannot do without. This leads them to add a significant qualification to the attacks on representation found elsewhere.

> The fact that there is no deterritorialization without a special reterritorialization should prompt us to rethink the abiding correlation between the molar and the molecular: no flow, no becoming-molecular escapes from a molar formation without molar components accompanying it, forming passages or perceptible landmarks for the imperceptible processes. (303)

This is a way of saying that we cannot do without representation. Yes, music allots a much smaller role to representation than the other arts, but even music cannot do without it entirely. We must always reintroduce representation at a certain point, if only so that we can explain to others what we think is going on in a work. It can then no longer be a matter of bringing about "the ruin of representation" (as Dorothea Olkowski titled her study of Deleuze) in order to open up a utopian realm of pure difference and becoming. Instead, Deleuze and Guattari find themselves forced to fall back on a much more moderate position, that of merely reversing the traditional hierarchy between representation and difference, putting the emphasis on the differential moment while allowing that there must always be an eventual reterritorialization, a moment of return to representational values. Thus, although they continue to insist that "becoming is never imitating", they immediately concede that imitation nevertheless plays an essential role in becoming: "One does not imitate; one constitutes a block of becoming. Imitation enters in only as an adjustment of the block, like a finishing touch, a wink, a signature." (305) This is a highly significant formulation. For even if imitation is considered to add only an "adjustment", a "wink", or a "signature" to the work of becoming, and even if they immediately add that "everything of importance happens elsewhere", it is nonetheless imitation that brings closure to the work, providing the "finishing touch", the "signature", without which the work would not be complete. Imitation, in other words, not only plays a role; it has the final word, even in music.

In light of the hyperbolic claims made against representation in *Difference and Repetition*, this is a major concession. And we find similar concessions throughout *Thousand Plateaus*, which eventually lead them to a drastic reduction in scope of their philosophical project. Indeed, towards the end of *Thousand Plateaus* Deleuze and Guattari allow that the entire theory of nomadism should be understood, not in opposition to mainstream science and traditional modes of representation and analytic thought, but within the field of representation, as a moment of instability that participates in scientific inquiry and conceptual thought in the territorial tradition of 'royal' science.

> What becomes apparent in the rivalry between the two models is that the ambulant or nomad sciences do not destine science to take on an autonomous power, or even to have an autonomous development. They do not have the means for that because they subordinate all their operations to the sensible conditions of intuition and construction – following the flow of matter, drawing and linking up smooth space [...]. However refined or rigorous, 'approximate knowledge' is still dependent upon sensitive and sensible evaluations that pose more problems than they solve: problematics is still its only mode. In contrast, what is proper to royal science, to its theorematic or axiomatic power, is to isolate all operations from the conditions of intuition, making them true intrinsic concepts, or 'categories'. That is precisely why deterritorialization, in this kind of science, implies a reterritorialization in the conceptual apparatus. (373)

In passages like this one, we can see that Deleuze and Guattari have abandoned their initial project of going beyond representation, falling back on the much more moderate project of enacting a reform of representation from within, a reform that works by taking the emphasis off of conceptual stability, which they see as a brief moment in the thought process, and placing it on the inherent instability and flux of the becoming of ideas. In this sense, despite the more radical rhetoric of *Thousand Plateaus*, it is actually a much more conservative, more representational text than *Difference and Repetition*.

Paradoxically, then, *Thousand Plateaus* might be said to confirm the fundamental strength of the representational model Deleuze and Guattari had initially set out to destroy: by subjecting it to the most severe of critiques and then retreating in the face of incontrovertible evidence, they give us all the more reason to have confidence in representation and conceptual analysis in the Aristotelian mold. And it is their analysis of the refrain in music that plants the seed that will eventually lead them to this conclusion.

It is not necessary, however, to see this defeat of antirepresentationalism as a defeat for the philosophy of Deleuze and Guattari. Although they were wrong in predicting the imminent demise of representational thought, they were no doubt correct in pointing out the need to continue to refine and reform representational practices. Their work contributes significantly to this process of reform, but it does so from within rather than without, adopting the critical, oppositional stance of the loyal adversary rather than the destructive, homicidal stance of the revolutionary insurgent. The very fact that they are willing to concede the fundamental strength of representational thought, despite having set out to prove the contrary, is a sign of their desire to make a genuine contribution to the slow march of philosophy towards true understanding and fundamental truths.

Even more important than this, though, are the very real conceptual and methodological contributions they make to the repertoire of representational thought. By developing new kinds of concepts – such as the rhizome, the simulacrum, the assemblage, the plane of consistency, and all the rest of their transversal, hybridizing concepts, which work by cutting across established conceptual boundaries – their work has made it possible to see the world in new ways, enabling us to discern objects that would not even have been recognizable as such using the more established categories of traditional philosophy. In this way, their work has made important contributions to the analytic work of representation, improving its range and depth and the fineness of the distinctions it is able to make. And ultimately it is the nomadic structures of their analyses, inspired in large part by the way music uses variation and development to deterritorialize its refrains, that makes this kind of hybrid, boundary crossing vision possible.

References

Bergson, Henri. "The Idea of Duration". *Philosophers of Process.* Douglas Browning, ed. New York: Random House, 1965.
Deleuze, Gilles. *Différence et répétition.* Paris: Presses universitaires de France, 1968.
Deleuze, Gilles, and Félix Guattari. *Mille Plateaux.* Paris: Éditions de minuit, 1980.
—. *A Thousand Plateaus: Capitalism and Schizophrenia.* Brian Massumi, trans. Minneapolis: Univ. of Minnesota Press, 1987.
Hanslick, Eduard. *On the Musically Beautiful.* Geoffrey Payzant, trans. Indianapolis: Hackett, 1986.
Olkowski, Dorothea. *Gilles Deleuze and the Ruin of Representation.* Berkeley: Univ. of California Press, 1999.
Prieto, Eric. *Listening In: Music, Mind, and the Modernist Narrative.* Univ. of Nebraska Press, 2002.
Stravinsky, Igor. *An Autobiography.* London: Calder and Boyars, 1975.
Tel Quel. *Théorie d'ensemble.* Paris: Seuil, 1968.
Webern, Anton. *The Path to the New Music.* Willi Reich, ed. Leo Black, trans. New York: Theodore Presser/Universal Edition, 1960.

Listening to Parsifal

Premodern Romance, Modern Music Drama, Postmodern Film

David L. Mosley, Louisville

This article examines three versions of the quest for the holy grail: Wolfram von Eschenbach's *Parzival*, Richard Wagner's *Parsifal*, and *The Fisher King* of Richard LaGravanese and Terry Gilliam. Each inhabits a different socio-historical context, conforms to the expectations of a different genre, and employs different artistic media. The article contends that listening to the tone of voice with which each of these articulations of Parsifal speaks constitutes the most adequate way to understand and evaluate Parsifal as a premodern romance, a modern music drama, and a postmodern film. The author develops and applies a mode of criticism-as-listening, derived from Friedrich Nietzsche's idea of "philosophizing with a hammer", and argues that this approach offers an alternative to the speculative bent of much contemporary criticism.

> [...] but I will promise that I do not attribute to Nature either beauty or deformity, order or confusion. Only in relation to our imagination can things be called beautiful or deformed, ordered or confused.
>
> Baruch Spinoza

Each of the three articulations of the tale of Parsifal examined in this article – Wolfram von Eschenbach's *Parzival*, Richard Wagner's *Parsifal*, and *The Fisher King* written by Richard LaGravanese and directed by Terry Gilliam – inhabits a different socio-historical context, conforms to different generic expectations, and employs different artistic media. Thus Parsifal's voice, as heard in the premodern romance, the modern music drama, and the postmodern film, is entirely enmeshed in a complex web of historical implications, generic expectations, and medial limitations. Martin Heidegger describes such a web in his 1959 essay "The Way to Language", where he asserts his intention to "speak about speech *qua* speech":

> A web compresses, narrows, and obstructs the straight clear view inside its mesh [...] we may not disregard the web which seems to crowd everything into a hopeless tangle [...]. Rather [we must] urge

our reflection to attempt, not to remove the web, of course, but to loosen it so that it allows us a view into the open togetherness of the relations [...]. (113)

It would seem that Heidegger's approach shows some promise for the examination of these three works and their various relations to one another; yet building on this prospectus, Heidegger soon turns his attention to the 'design' ("Aufriss") of language, and the way that design implies the cutting of a 'trace' ("Riss") or tear. As a consequence the philosopher focuses on what is shown by speaking:

> To be sure, speaking is vocalization. Also, it can be considered a human activity. Both are correct views of language as speaking. Both will now be ignored [...]. To speak to one another means: to say something, show something to one another, and to entrust one another mutually to what is shown." (121-22)

By bracketing the acoustic properties of speech, turning a deaf ear to vocalization and intentionally ignoring the human dimension of speech, Heidegger precludes the possibility of listening as a hermeneutic activity.

Like Heidegger, I wish to clear a space for these three very different articulations of the Parsifal story. However, once in this clearing I propose to listen to the voice of *Parzival*'s embodied and culturally situated premodern narrator, the operatic voices of Parsifal and Kundry as they perform Wagner's modern revision *Parsifal*, and the parodic voice(s) of the postmodern *Fisher King*. Some will hasten to point out that Heidegger's decision to privilege the manner in which speech shows at the expense of the way it sounds is a methodological necessity if he is to advance his phenomenological project. Be that as it may, both Heidegger's willed deafness and his denial of vocalization as a human activity have been of great consequence for contemporary criticism. His decision to look rather than listen contributes directly to today's textualist hermeneutics and its almost exclusive focus on the design of language and its traces, so much so, that when Jacques Derrida (in)famously declares, at the beginning of *Of Grammatology*, that "there is no linguistic sign before writing", he reenacts Heidegger's deafness to what might be learned by listening and initiates a speculative critical trajectory that today veers ever further from what might be learned by listening (14).

While Heidegger's phenomenology and Derrida's literary theory prove inadequate to the task at hand, there are those who have explored the act of listening and recognized the significance of speech as a human activity in rewarding theoretical ways. The approach developed below owes most to Friedrich Nietzsche's exhortation to "philosophize with a hammer". Too often accepted at first glance as exclusively aggressive and anarchic, this metaphor resonates with artistic, expressive, and even diagnostic overtones[1]. As Nietzsche explains in the foreword to his *Twilight of the Idols*, subtitled "How to Philosophize with a Hammer", he intends to, "[...] sound out ["aushorchen"] the idols [...]. For once to pose questions here with a hammer – what a delight for one who has ears behind his ears." (31) And a few lines later, Nietzsche announces his plan to touch these idols "with the hammer as with a tuning fork". In addition to the iconoclastic hammer used to shatter idols, Nietzsche's hammer might also be imagined as: 1) the tool of the sculptor, 2) a part of the piano's striking mechanism, or 3) the percussion hammer employed by physicians in the nineteenth century to strike, or percuss, the abdomen of patients and make diagnostic judgments based on the acoustic qualities of the sounds produced[2]. When Nietzsche's penchant for playing the part of cultural physician is recalled, the diagnostic aspect of philosophizing with a hammer is further reinforced. Similarly, the otherwise opaque designation "one who has ears behind his ears" becomes clear if read as a reference to the philosopher-as-physician diagnosing the integrity of idols with the aid of a stethoscope. In the same way that Nietzsche wishes to sound out the idols of philosophy, what follows is a sounding out of three articulations of Parsifal. The intention is to allow the resonance of each, – i.e., its characteristic voice – to be heard.

In a similar vein, Walter Ong's *Orality and Literacy: The Technologizing of the Word* speaks to the significance of sound and our auditory sense. Ong suggests that the

---

[1] Both Heidegger and Derrida have written extensively about Nietzsche and often use his ideas to buttress their own arguments; yet neither treats the central role music played in Nietzsche's life and thought. Similarly, neither seems to understand the significance of Nietzsche's idea of philosophizing with a hammer – sounding out philosophical ideas or aesthetic expressions and listening to their resonance as a means of analysis and evaluation. Cf. Heidegger's *Nietzsche* and Derrida's *Spurs*.

[2] Blondel's discussion of auscultation opened up this metaphor of philosophizing with a hammer for me for the first time.

principle characteristic of sound is its unique relationship "to interiority when compared to the rest of the senses. This relationship is important because of the interiority of human consciousness and of communication itself [...]. Hearing can register interiority without violating it [...]." (70) As to the significance of the voice, Ong states, "Above all, the human voice comes from inside the human organism which produces the voice's resonances." He concludes, "Sight isolates, sound incorporates." (71)

Likewise, Jacques Attali addresses the significance of sound and the importance of listening. While his interest is more cultural and less anthropological than Ong's and the political ideology that informs his *Noise: The Political Economy of Music* is dated, the central thesis of the work seems still to be of consequence. Attali claims: "Western knowledge has tried to look upon the world. It has failed to understand that the world is not for the beholding. It is for the hearing. It is not legible, but audible [...]. Nothing happens in the absence of noise [...]." (3) By listening to a culture, we understand it more fully, especially its judgments about noise, i.e., non-sense sounds versus the significant sounds comprising music. For Attali, "music is prophetic", inasmuch as it "makes mutations audible". Moreover, "music is more than an object of study, it is a way of perceiving the world. A tool of understanding" (4).

Neither Ong nor Attali pay much attention to Nietzsche in the works mentioned above. Attali's two citations of Nietzsche in *Noise* serve to establish context for his argument and neither provide material essential to his thesis. Also, there are no explicit references to Nietzsche in Ong's *Orality and Literacy*. However, Ong's contention that sound – especially the sound of the human voice – tells us more about interiority than does sight, and Attali's understanding of music – as both a cultural indicator and an analytical tool – are crucial elements of the following attempt to listen to Parsifal.

Parzival as Premodern Romance

Wolfram's *Parzival* is thought to have been written some time after 1200 CE. In this version of the tale, Parzival is a beautiful and courageous young man whose destiny is to travel from isolated ignorance, through a process of chivalric refinement, to spiritual enlightenment. His quest for the grail can be understood as an attempt to bridge the chasm between the worldly kingdom of Arthur's court and the otherworldly realm of Munsalväsche, with its wounded King, Anfortas. Once this bridge is built, Anfortas will be healed and the grail community will return to prosperity.

In his insightful monograph *Romancing the Grail*, Arthur Groos convincingly shows that Wolfram's *Parzival* is a polyvocal narrative involving elements of epic, lyric poetry (specifically *Minnesang*), saint's life, and dynastic chronicle. Groos finds in Wolfram a narrator willing to "immerse us in a discourse that is not so much authorial or monologic as fundamentally decentered and pluralistic" (17). While I have no argument with Groos's discussion of Wolfram's *Parzival* as a text, I confess discomfort with the way his Wolfram becomes a kind of Middle High German Mikhail Bahktin, more concerned with *heteroglossia*, *chronotope* and *carnival* than with a good cause, a good fight, or a good kiss. By contrast, the Wolfram I encounter is a former knight with a particular grudge against what he perceives to be the inconstancy of women and an ambivalence toward the relatively new code of courtly love. He is eager to inundate his audience with the minutiae of Parzival's armor and to show that he values the fine points of a worthy horse as much as those of a beautiful woman. As a storyteller – the one whose voice articulates the tale and embodies all of its characters – Wolfram thrills to the bodily aspects of the chivalrous life and, at the same time, exhibits a kind of paternal concern for the fate of his hero.

Indeed, Wolfram takes care to distance himself from his *Parzival* as a text; he exhibits skepticism toward the written word and revels in the telling of the tale. At the conclusion of book 2, Wolfram states:

> If the women would not take it for flattery, I would add further unknown words to this story for you, I would continue the adventure for you. But if anyone requests me to do so, let him not consider it a book. I don't know a single letter of the alphabet. Plenty of people get their material that way, but this adventure steers without books. Rather than have anybody think it is a book, I would sit naked without a towel, the way I'd sit in a bath – if I didn't forget the bouquet of twigs. (2: par. 15)

Much interpretive ink has been spent on this passage, and I can offer no informed contribution to the ongoing discussion of Wolfram's literacy, or the lack thereof. Yet this statement does prompt me to consider the scenario of Wolfram performing this poem for an audience – that is, incorporating the tale and embodying its action while accompanying himself on a musical instrument[3]. Moreover, Wolfram's skepticism toward the written word, his unwillingness to accept the authority of a written text, and his assertion that his "adventure steers without books", followed immediately by reference to his body, suggests the possibility of a reading of *Parzival* informed by the shadows and echoes of an imagined performance. In such a reading the spoken word, the physical gesture, and the musical event form a constellation making patent the gestural and acoustic potential only latent in the tale as a text. While it is clear that *Parzival* owes much to his familiarity with Chretien's seminal *Le Conte du Graal*, Wolfram also makes six references to the *l'enchanteur* or *le chanteur* Kyot, whose "skill would not allow him to do other than sing and recite" the tale (8: par. 416)[4]. While there is disagreement about whether Kyot was an actual acquaintance or simply a useful narrative invention, Wolfram's insistence on oral transmission and a sung performance is of paramount importance for the reading here proposed.

With this orientation in mind, we may entertain, with renewed interest, those references to physical activity and the manipulation of objects that might recommend themselves to the performance of *Parzival*. Two, in particular, are quite compelling: the gesture of throwing dice and the gesture of drawing a bow and letting loose an arrow. If we assume, for the sake of this reading, that a musical instrument might also have

---

[3] That *Parzival* was intended for oral performance is a long-standing and generally accepted premise in medieval literary scholarship. One among the many assertions supporting this position comes from the introduction to an English translation by Mustard and Passage:

> The poem reads like an oral work. The scenes, the pauses, the transitions, and above all the asides, convey the impression of oral delivery caught, as it were, by an agile taker of shorthand. Gradually we form a concept of Wolfram, not as a poet or author, but as a public reciter and entertainer who delivered his recitation for the sheer love of the story and the glorification of the knightly class. (xxi)

[4] Wolfram's word is *laschantiure*, thus it might be construed as *l'enchanteur* ('magician') or *le chanteur* ('singer'). In a note at this point in the text, Mustard and Passage acknowledge that both interpretations are possible; however, *le chanteur* or 'singer', is a better fit given the context. (224)

accompanied the performance of this tale – for example, a small harp, as is typically assumed – these gestures become all the more significant[5].

Assuming the performer plucks specific strings in a manner that complements and reinforces the rhymed couplets of the romance with consonant pitches or pitch-complexes, then the gestures of throwing dice and drawing a bow offer the opportunity for a disruption of the intentional rhythmic and musical accompaniment by a glissando-like wash of sound. The gesture of throwing dice presents the opportunity for a sweeping movement of the hand away from the chest, in which the nails of the fingers run across the strings of the harp (cf. 2: pars. 88 and 112; 5: par. 248; and 6: pars. 289 and 292). Conversely, the gesture of drawing a bow offers the opportunity for a sweeping motion toward the chest in which the pads of the fingers run across the strings of the harp (cf. 3: par. 140, 4: par. 180, 5: par. 241, and 16: par. 805). In both cases, the musical effect of this glissando-like wash of sound introduces a random dissonance that contrasts with the intentionality and consonance of the plucked pitches.

There is also a significant passage in which the harp might be used as more than a musical instrument. The setting is the birth of Parzival at the conclusion of book 2. Wolfram recounts the ways Herzeloyde, Parzival's mother, first holds the baby boy:

> When the queen recovered consciousness and took her baby into her arms, then she and the other ladies intently observed the tiny pizzle between his legs. He could not be other than fondled and cherished [...]. It was the queen's delight to kiss him over and over again, and always she kept calling him *Bon fils, cher fils, beau fils* [...]. Directly the queen took those little brownish-pink buds of hers – I mean the tips of her breasts – and pressed them into his tiny mouth. (2: pars. 111-112)

If at this point the performer ceases playing the harp and begins to handle and regard it as if it were an infant, then the harp, as a kind of theatrical prop, is identified with Parzival. Thus the performer and his harp enact the motherly care shown by Herzeloyde for her son as recounted in the text. It is this sense of care – of paternal concern – that most marks the storyteller's attitude toward his young hero. For Parzival's sake, he constantly calls attention to the fickleness of women, the complications of courtly love, and the dangers of battle.

---

[5] Such assumptions are authorized by recent scholarship from the fields of literary criticism, musicology, and linguistics. Cf., e.g., Green, Page, and Zumthor.

Wolfram's ambivalence about the theme of 'constancy' ("Stӓte") in love pervades the prologue to *Parzival* and colors much of his commentary on women throughout the romance. Indeed, it seems that Wolfram has personal and painful experience with the 'inconstancy' ("unstӓte") of the opposite sex. Wolfram states:

> If there is anyone who praises women better than I, I will surely not be the one to hold it against him. I would be glad to hear their joys spread far and wide. For only one of them am I unwilling to do loyal service, and against her my anger is still fresh – ever since I found her in disloyalty [...]. Why, alas! do they do so. (2: par. 114)

Wolfram's distrust of women's constancy, his ambivalence about their half of the courtly contract involving love ("Minne") and battle ("Strît"), humanizes him. In addition to his particular concern for Parzival, Wolfram's attitude can also be read to address more generally an apprehension about the possibly pernicious and destabilizing influence the new code of courtly love may present for his community. In both these regards, Wolfram becomes socially situated and emotionally vulnerable; consequently he enters into a richer and more complex relationship with his audience (albeit one that is markedly different for its male and female members).

In his book *After Virtue*, philosopher and political scientist Alasdair MacIntyre speaks of the reciprocal relationship between individual and social identity that characterizes premodern thought.

> In many premodern societies it is through his or her membership in a variety of social groups that the individual identifies himself or herself and is identified by others. I am brother, cousin, and grandson, member of this household, that village, this tribe. These are not characteristics that belong to human beings accidentally, to be stripped away in order to discover the 'real me'. Individuals inherit a particular space within an interlocking set of social relationships, lacking that space, they are nobody, or at least a stranger or an outcast. To know oneself as such a social person is however not to occupy a static and fixed position. It is to find oneself at a certain point on a journey with set goals; to move through life is to make progress – or to fail to make progress – toward a given goal. (33-34)

Wolfram von Eschenbach, former knight in the employ of Landgrave Hermann of Thuringia, still smarting over the infidelity of his lover and longing for the thrill of battle instead of the niceties of the court, is such a premodern narrator. Likewise, his Parzifal is a work in progress. Parzival's father is the warrior Gahmuret and his mother, Herzeloyde, is the sister of Anfortas, the wounded king. Thus Parzival's very being constitutes a bridge between chivalry and spirituality mentioned above. Wolfram's tale is an account of the construction of this bridge between worldly activity and spiritual understanding – a status report on the "brave man slowly wise" ("er küene, träclîche wîs") (1: par. 4).

The tone of voice that characterizes Wolfram's *Parzival* is exceptionally ardent. Perhaps as a consequence, when listening to this articulation I am also struck by its alternation between ferocity and gentleness. The voice is sometimes impetuous and at others solicitous, yet it is always impassioned. Part of what makes this alternation so striking is that a single voice embodies so many characters and conveys so many moods in such an extended text. Wolfram's singular voice, and the interiority of *le chanteur* from which it originates, resonates with a dazzling diversity. His voice ignites the material of the story and fires its 'infabulation' – its transformation into a tale.

Parsifal as Modern Music Drama

An 1880 issue of the *Bayreuth Blätter*, the official organ of all things Wagnerian, was given over in its entirety to Wagner's work on *Parsifal*. In it the composer states:

> So long as we have to fulfill the work of the Will, that Will which is ourselves, there is in truth nothing for us but the Spirit of Negation, the spirit of our own will that, blind and hungering, can only plainly see itself in its unwill toward whatsoever crosses it as an obstacle or disappointment. Yet that which crosses it is but itself again; so that its rage expresses nothing save its self-negation: and this self-knowledge can be gained at last by Pity born of suffering. (qtd. in *Religion and Art* 244)

In metaphysical terms, this somewhat confused embrace of Arthur Schopenhauer and its expression in *Parsifal* constitutes the proximate cause for Nietzsche's final break with Wagner. Such self-knowledge "gained by pity and born of suffering", especially when cast within the context of the Christian doctrine of redemption, was, for Nietzsche, nothing more than the unpleasant echo of a thoroughly decadent moral convention. Many have written about this aspect of the relation between Nietzsche and Wagner, and it seems that no more need be said[6]. Aesthetically speaking, however, Nietzsche could not countenance what Wagner had done to music. This aspect of the relation between the composer and the philosopher has received far less critical attention and is addressed in what follows[7].

Nietzsche's first contact with Wagner came in 1868, four years prior to the publication of his *Birth of Tragedy from the Spirit of Music*. His final written treatment of the composer and his music, *The Case of Wagner*, was published in 1888, the year before the philosopher's collapse into insanity. During these years, which comprise almost all of Nietzsche's adult, professional life, much of his thinking went through surprising, often kaleidoscopic, transformations. While Nietzsche first questioned Wagner's so-called "art work of the future" early in this twenty-year span, he continued to write with both frequency and sometimes ferocious invective about the composer and his music dramas. What can account for Nietzsche's preoccupation?

Many of the most pointed of Nietzsche's barbs in *The Case of Wagner* have less to do with philosophy or religion, the abstractions upon which most critics focus when addressing the matter, than they do with the violence the composer had done to music. According to Nietzsche, Wagner has infected music:

> To the artist of decadence: there we have the crucial words. And here my seriousness begins. I am far from looking on guilelessly while this decadent corrupts our health – and music as well. Is Wagner a human being at all? Isn't he rather a sickness? He makes sick whatever he touches – he has made music sick. (164)

Moreover, Wagner has turned music into an abstraction:

> Let us remember that Wagner was young at the time Hegel and Schelling seduced men's spirits; that he guessed, that he grasped with his very hands the only thing Germans take seriously – "the idea" [...]. Hegel is a taste. – And not merely a German but a European taste. – A taste Wagner comprehended – to which he felt equal – which he immortalized. – He merely applied it to music – he invented a style for himself charged with "infinite meaning" – he became the heir of Hegel. – Music as "idea". (177-78)

---

[6] An especially insightful teasing-apart of the philosophical nexus that entangled Wagner and Nietzsche with Schopenhauer is found in Safranski.

[7] The works of Janz and Higgins are noteworthy exceptions.

Nietzsche was enough of a musician, both a skilled pianist and would-be composer, to understand the means of Wagner's transgression, namely, his use of the *Grundthema*.

> Wagner was not a musician by instinct. He showed this by abandoning all lawfulness and, more precisely, all style in music in order to turn it into what he required, theatrical rhetoric, a means of expression, of underscoring gestures, of suggestion, of the psychologically picturesque. Here we may consider Wagner as an inventor and innovator of the first rank – he has increased music's capacity for language to the point of making it immeasurable: he is the Victor Hugo of music as language [...]. Finally, as far as the Wagnerian "leitmotif" is concerned, I lack all culinary understanding for that. If pressed, I might possibly concede it the status of an ideal toothpick, as an opportunity to get rid of the remainders of food. (173-74)

For Nietzsche, Wagner's use of musical motives to illustrate characters, ideas or objects – and the manner in which these motives interact, evolve, and acquire an ever more complex significance – constitutes an attempt to enhance artificially music's semantic potential, i.e., to turn it into a language. Nietzsche's objection is not that Wagner uses music as a means rather than an end. Indeed, such an objection appeals to the kind of abstraction Nietzsche wishes to transvalue. Rather, Nietzsche could not stomach Wagner's willingness to violate the fundamental nature of music.

As I have argued elsewhere, Nietzsche's attitudes toward music are inextricably bound to his ideas about language. In an unpublished essay titled "On Music and Words" from 1871, Nietzsche lays out his ideas about the ontological and phylogenetic relationships between music and language in a relatively straightforward manner. The three most important claims in this essay are: 1) that music and language arise from an essential duality that remains embedded in language; 2) that the members of this essential duality are the "tone of the speaker" ("Tone des Sprechenden") and his or her "gesture-symbolism" ("Geberden-Symbolik"); and 3) that the acoustic properties of language, which Nietzsche refers to as its primeval melody, antedate and supercede the conceptual powers of language. Further on in this essay, Nietzsche states:

> All degrees of pleasure and displeasure – expressions of one primeval ground that we cannot see through – find symbolic expression in the tone of the speaker, while all other representations are designated by the gesture-symbolism of the speaker. In so far as this primeval ground is the same in all human beings, the tonal background is also universal and intelligible despite the differences between languages. Out of this develops the more arbitrary gesture-symbolism that is not wholly adequate to its foundation, and with this begins the multiplicity of languages whose variety we may consider metaphorically as a strophic text for this primeval melody of the language of pleasure and displeasure. (Nietzsche, "On Music and Words" 21)

He continues, "[This] scale of sensations of pleasure and displeasure gains an ever more adequate symbolic expression in the development of music." (22) Thus music, as a human activity and cultural artifact, is both logical proof and ontological manifestation of the one impenetrable, primeval ground (cf. Higgins 663).

According to Nietzsche, when Richard Wagner employs music as a means of expression, he confuses the proper relation between music and language. Already in the 1871 fragment "On Words and Music", Nietzsche contemplates such a situation:

> Imagine [...] what an undertaking it must be to write music for a poem, that is, to wish to illustrate a poem by means of music, in order to secure a conceptual language for music in this way. What an inverted world! An undertaking that strikes one as if the son decided to beget the father! [...]. While it is certain that a bridge leads from the mysterious castle of the musician into the free country of images – and the lyric poet walks across it – it is impossible to proceed in the opposite direction, although there are said to be some people who have the delusion that they have done just this. (22)

Only three years into his friendship with Richard and Cosima Wagner, and a year prior to the publication of *The Birth of Tragedy*, Nietzsche the psychologist has already diagnosed Wagner as delusional. By the time Nietzsche composes his case history of Wagner in 1888, the diagnosis will be more severe: Wagner is an illness and perhaps other than human.

Music was indispensable for Nietzsche, both personally and philosophically. For Nietzsche, to sing was to give voice to conditions more veritable than the so-called truths mediated by language. To sing was, in the words of Section 15 of *The Birth of Tragedy*, to be a "Socrates who practices music" – one who both gives voice to the primeval ground of existence and by doing so subjects it to the most careful criticism (75). This is what Nietzsche means when, in the preface to the 1886 edition of *The Birth of Tragedy*, he laments, "[i]t should have **sung**, this new soul – and not have spoken!". So far as Nietzsche is concerned, Wagner does not sing; instead he writes. Worse still, he writes 'infinite melody' ("unendliche Melodie"). Wagner's music is so far removed from the primeval melody that it requires a literature to explain it (*Case of Wagner* 177), and it can be sung only with a ruined voice (*Case of Wagner* 180). These objections lead Nietzsche to the three demands with which he closes his *Case of Wagner*:

That the theater should not lord it over the arts.
That the actor should not seduce those who are authentic.
That music should not become the art of lying. (180)

Wagner intended his music dramas to be at once a reformation of operatic practice in the nineteenth century, a presentation of the ineluctable spirit of the German *Volk*, and a renaissance of ancient Greek drama in which religion and art were coextensive. In addition to reflecting these admittedly grandiose general objectives, *Parsifal* is also a special case in Wagner's *oeuvre*. In this his final opera Wagner: 1) replaces his alliterative *Stabreim* with an epic end-rhyme technique, 2) labels it a Sacred Festival Drama in three acts ("Ein Bühnenweihfestspiel in drei Aufzügen"), and 3) states his desire to restrict its performance exclusively to the Festspielhaus at Bayreuth.

In an 1859 letter to Mathilde Wesendonck, the composer describes his reactions to Wolfram's romance and what will be required to refashion it into an artwork of the future:

> Wolfram is a thoroughly immature phenomenon [...] [I am] utterly repelled by the poet's incompetence. I would have to make a completely fresh start with Parzival! For Wolfram didn't have the first idea what he was doing [...]. I would have to invent everything here [...]. Parzival's development and the profound sublimity of this purification although entirely predestined by his thoughtful and deeply compassionate nature, must again be brought to the foreground [...] I have to compress everything into three climactic situations of violent intensity, so that the work's profound and ramified content emerges clearly and distinctly; for my art consists in working and presenting things in this way. (*Selected Letters* 459-60)

Obviously Wagner was impatient with the many digressions and obscure complications that mark Wolfram's narrative. It seems, at least according to Wagner's taste, wisdom came too slowly to Wolfram's Parzival.

Wagner's treatment of Wolfram's premodern text is a modernist distillation. He purifies and condenses the romance in a number of significant ways: 1) he jettisons Wolfram's epithet describing Parzival as a "brave man slowly wise" and replaces it with the "pure innocent made wise by pity" ("Durch Mitleid wissend, reine Tor"); 2) the grail king's illness arises when Amfortas violates a vow of chastity imposed upon him by the composer as librettist; 3) the delights of Klingsor's garden are no longer simply magical, but overtly sensual; 4) all of Parsifal's adventures, save his encounter with Kundry, are banished from the stage and, instead, performed by the orchestra during the agitated prelude to Act II; and 5) Wagner dispenses with Parzival's wife, Cundwiamurs, and instead swears Parzival, along with all the other Grail knights, to celibacy.

Wagner constructs *Parsifal* with an emphasis on binary oppositions, thus placing an unprecedented premium on symmetry when compared with his other works. It is the only one of his operas to begin and end in the same key, and this harmonic symmetry, along with the sense of closure it creates, is echoed in the overall ABA structure of the work[8]. As many commentators have observed, the musical material of the opera is driven by a basic opposition between diatonicism, exemplified by the motives of Parsifal and the Holy Grail, and chromaticism, identified with Kundry and the realm of Klingsor[9].

When viewed through the lenses of Bruno Latour's ideas of purification and hybridity outlined in his *We Have Never Been Modern*, Wagner's own modernist attitude and aesthetic come clearly into focus[10]. The composer's purification of Wolfram's *Parzival* begins with the opposition of the kingdoms of Amfortas and Klingsor, whereby Wagner creates the distinction – crucial according to Latour's account – between the ontological zones of culture and nature. The kingdoms are distinguished by the vow of celibacy that marks the knights of the grail in the zone of culture and the attractions of sensuality that characterize the kingdom of Klingsor in the zone of nature. Latour argues that such artificial purification typically necessitates the designation of "entirely new types of beings, hybrids of nature and culture" (10-11).

---

[8] Act I, dominated by the key of A-flat, is situated in the elevated hall of the Grail knights. In Act II, the action is removed to a garden in the kingdom of Klingsor and characterized by the key of B. With Act III, the action returns to the hall of the Grail knights and to the key of A-flat. As is often the case when dealing with Wagner, the danger of statements like this one is oversimplification. The reader is directed to Beckett's *Parsifal* for a more nuanced discussion of coherence and symmetry in regard to dramatic action, setting, and harmony (cf. 87-102).

[9] Among those making this assertion are Dahlhaus in his *Music Dramas of Richard Wagner* and Whithall.

[10] I am aware that Latour's ideas are not enthusiastically endorsed in all quarters; however, it does seem that, in general, his characterization of modernism is especially felicitous for the analysis of aesthetic expressions.

Klingsor's garden is populated with such hybrids. We meet them first in the form of flower maidens. Early in Act II, Parsifal addresses them: "How sweetly you smell! Are you then flowers?" ("Wie duftet ihr hold! Seid ihr denn Blumen?"), to which they reply:

> Our garden's pride / and pleasant aroma! / Our lord plucked us in springtime! / We flourish here / in sunlight of summer, / thus blooming for our newcomer. / Now be our sweetheart true, / begrudge not the flowers their due! / Sweetly must you love us and cherish, / or else we will wither and perish.

More troubling, however, than these more or less harmless conflations of plants and people, is the character of Kundry.

Wagner invests Kundry with much that was ardent and impetuous in Wolfram's *Parzival*, including the suffering Sigune and the fickle Orgeluse. Moreover, in Wagner's hands she is imbued with features of Herodias, who procured the head of John the Baptist on a platter; Gundryggia, the wandering spirit of Nordic mythology; and a female incarnation of Ahasuerus, the Jew whose laughter at Christ on the cross destined him to wander the earth in permanent exile. This last association – Kundry as wandering Jewess – is the most potent of all the associations for Wagner the anti-Semite. Whereas Wolfram's narrator was ambivalent about women's fidelity, Wagner's modern music drama shows him to be both xenophobic and misogynistic.

In Wagner's *Parsifal*, Kundry has seduced Amfortas. Thus she is partially responsible for his disability and the deteriorating state of the Grail kingdom. For this she is banished to the kingdom of Klingsor and subjected to a curse compelling her to seduce any man she meets. Kundry is thus condemned to lead a life of desire until her advances are rejected by a "pure man". As Carl Dahlhaus has observed, Kundry embodies a tragic paradox: she "desires absolution but seeks it in Parsifal's arms, which is precisely what would bar her from absolution" (151). Once Kundry is rejected, she will be free of the curse and rewarded with a peaceful death. Of course Parsifal, the *reine Tor*, meets with Kundry, withstands her advances, secures healing for Amfortas and the kingdom, and ultimately ascends to the Grail kingship.

When first encountered in Act I, Kundry has recently returned from a magical trip to the Orient to procure medicinal herbs and spices that may alleviate the suffering of Amfortas. At this point, we are unaware of her earlier liaison with Amfortas. Wagner's instructions for her character are as follows: "Kundry rushes in, almost reeling; wild garb fastened high; girdle of snakeskin hanging; long black hair flowing in loose locks; dark brownish-red complexion, piercing black eyes, sometimes wild and blazing, but usually fixed and glassy." When she appears in Act II, during which she attempts to seduce Parsifal, Wagner describes her as a "young woman of the most surpassing beauty [...] lying on a flowery couch in diaphanous drapery of somewhat Arabian fashion".

As a hybrid, Kundry embodies the mixture of nature and culture that Wagner's modernist Grail Kingdom must deny. Marc Weiner argues in *Richard Wagner and the Anti-Semitic Imagination* that Kundry embodies the Other. This is the otherness of the hybrid that Latour believes must be posited for the modernist constitution to exert its authority over matters of legitimacy. Weiner's discussion includes both musical analysis and reference to fascinating photographs of the first Kundry from the 1882 Bayreuth production. According to Weiner, Kundry's appearance is reptilian, pagan, and perhaps syphilitic. She is associated with Eve's original sin, Arabic sorcery, and the Jewish Kabbalah (29-35). Following the ideas of Julia Kristeva, the Finnish scholar Anne Sivouja-Gunarantnam has convincingly argued that Kundry is an operatic abject: "something threatening and disgusting which an individual, a society or a culture must push away, exclude [...] in order to define its own boundaries and continue its existence" (1).

Nowhere is this hybridity more apparent than in Kundry's vocalizing, the sign of her operatic existence. Her exceptionally chromatic *Grundthema* covers a treacherously wide range. Moreover, in much of her 'singing' during Act II, Wagner denies Kundry the coloratura register of feminine operatic legitimacy and, instead, casts her voice into the low mezzo range with the instructions "hoarsely and brokenly" ("rauh und abgebrochen"). Finally, it is in Kundry's uncontrollable laughter – a hybrid form of vocalization somewhere between singing and screaming – that we experience the essence of her psychological suffering and the epitome of her musical rejection. Here Wagner musically inscribes her absolute otherness.

Patrick McCreless has written cogently and with insight about Parsifal's heroic renunciation of Kundry:

In Act II Parsifal learns from Kundry of the suffering that he caused his own mother, and this realization leads quickly to his central revelation in the entire opera. Kundry's seductive words cleverly bring together his newly awakened sense of guilt regarding his mother's grief and his first experience of sensual passion: [...] *sie beut dir heut' als Muttersegen's letzten Gruss der Liebe ersten Kuss*. Kundry's words and her kiss – her artful merging of herself and Parsifal's mother, and her suggestive interweaving of guilt and eroticism – trigger in Parsifal a sudden and shocking vision of Amfortas' wound, a shudder of revulsion and thus his first feeling of pity. His inner recognition of his own sin and his pity for Amfortas articulate the turning point of the drama: through his *Mitleid* he has become *wissend*, and now he instinctively fixes his eye on the Grail [...]. [I]t is only through his own renunciation of those advances that he can achieve salvation for himself, for Kundry and for Amfortas and the brothers of the Grail. (228-29)

Thus Parsifal's dramatic act of renunciation – the assertion of his Wagnerian purity, or perhaps the inscription of Wagner's own obsession with purity – can be heard as the composer's own final embrace of Schopenhauer's philosophy of the denial of the will.

To conclude this discussion of Wagner's *Parsifal*, a final word needs to be said about the theme of redemption that figures so prominently in this work and Wagner's insistence that performances of *Parsifal* be restricted to Bayreuth. Both of these are extensions of Wagner's modernism. Upon Parsifal's return to the Grail Castle in Act III, his first encounter is with the aged hermit Gurnemanz, who informs him of the decline in health and faith in the kingdom of Amfortas. Although it is now Good Friday, the holiest of days, the faith of the Grail Knights is beginning to fade. Gurnemanz tells Parsifal, "The cross is lofty, so they cannot view it" ("Ihn selbst am Kreuze kann sie nicht erschauen"). Yet the hopes of the Grail knights might still be fixed on a less lofty exemplar, "But still their gaze can reach to a man redeemed" ("Da blickt sie zum erlös'ten Menschen auf"). In Parsifal they have their man.

Already in his encounter with Kundry in Act II in Klingsor's garden, this potential is intimated. Immediately after Parsifal rebukes Kundry and her kiss – as his thoughts surprisingly turn to Amfortas, his wound, and the spear – Parsifal sings in a trance-like state: "I hear the voice of our Redeemer, ah lamenting, lamenting for the polluted sanctuary. 'Redeem me! Rescue me from the hands that guilt have tainted!' So calls the voice from heaven, fearful, loud, piercing my being."[11] At the opera's conclusion, in the

---

[11] Des Heiland's Klage da vernehm' ich, die Klage, ach! die Klage um das entweihte Heiligtum. "Erlöse, rette mich aus schuldbefleckten Händen!" So reif die Gottesklage fruchtbar laut mir in die Seele.

sacred space of Amfortas's castle, Parsifal heals the wound of Amfortas and holds the spear aloft while the chorus sings "Highest healing's wonder! Redemption to the Redeemer!" ("Hoschsten Heiles Wunder! Erlösung dem Erlöser!")

In Wagner's *Parsifal*, we witness a thoroughly modern negotiation with divinity as an abstraction: God is both too great and too distant for humanity to comprehend, yet through our own efforts and acts of personal piety, we can achieve God-like status. Latour refers to this theological end run as the final guarantee of the modernist constitution: "God becomes the crossed-out God of metaphysics [...]. His transcendence distance[s] Him infinitely [...]. A wholly individual and spiritual religion [is] made possible [...]. Moderns [can] now be both secular and pious at the same time." (33) It is Parsifal's act of renunciation that powers the redemption of the redeemer, not the embrace of a God who created both heaven and earth, and whose love inexplicably rains down upon saint and sinner alike.

Wagner insisted that his articulation of Parsifal could only be appropriately presented and rightly experienced only in the Festspielhaus in Bayreuth – this new temple consecrated to the religion of art over whose sacramental music-dramas the artist *cum* priest presided. After the composer's death, Cosima Wagner continued to cultivate this exclusivity. Just before the copyright on *Parsifal* expired, she proposed that the Reichstag make a special allowance limiting performances to Bayreuth in perpetuity. The proposal was rejected, yet until 1913 the only European performances of *Parsifal* outside Bayreuth were for Wagner's patron, King Ludwig, who attended eight performances of *Parsifal* between 1884 and 1845 at the Munich Court Opera, where he was the sole audience member (Beckett 94)[12].

When I listen to Wagner's *Parsifal*, not only its music but the work's general tone, I hear an expression typified by fatigue. Compared with Wolfram's *Parzival*, the voice of Wagner's articulation of the tale is faint – weak for want of passion. Parsifal has withstood the exotic wiles of Kundry, but Wagner's transformation of the knight from

---

[12] In his article on Wagner in *New Grove*, Dahlhaus observes that "Bayreuth was the institutionalization in musical practice of a principle that the musical scholarship of the same period was documenting in the first musico-historical editions". Beckett argues that a similar 'conservatism' informs some of the more narrowminded perspectives in today's performance-practice movement and its cult of historical authenticity (92).

an existential question into a theological conclusion has diminished the man. In fact both premodern knights, Parzival and Wolfram, have been hushed, the way parents try to silence their children when they talk too loudly in church.

Parsifal as Postmodern Film

The history of Parsifal's cinematographic treatment begins early in the twentieth century and shows close ties to Wagner's Puritanism. The Metropolitan Opera staged one of the first productions of Wagner's music drama outside of Bayreuth and beyond Cosima's control in 1903. The production was such a success that in 1904, Thomas Edison commissioned Edwin S. Porter to produce a film comprising eight scenes from the opera with one of the earliest motion picture cameras. Of course the early film was silent; however, it can be assumed that showings featured some sort of musical accompaniment, either by organ or house orchestra. The film was soon withdrawn from distribution when Edison was sued for using the opera's libretto in the film without permission. In 1917, Edison participated in another film version, this time in association with the Boy Scouts of America, that told the tale as a model for the character formation of adolescent boys.

According to Kevin Harty, the first Arthurian art film was *L'Eternal retour* (1943), a retelling of the Tristan story "suggesting, almost Nietzsche-like, that legends live on [...] reborn without the knowledge of their principals" (12). Jean Cocteau wrote the screenplay, and the French Legion of Decency eventually banned the film for its "glorification of immoral actions" and "suggestive sequences" (*New York Times* 29 March 1948, qtd. in Harty 14). Other cinematographic versions include Bruce Baillie's *To Parsifal* (1963), which sets the story in San Francisco and exhibits a decidedly environmental agenda; the 1975 parodic classic *Monty Python and the Holy Grail*; and Hans-Jürgen Syberborg's controversial *Parsifal* (1982), in which the opera is performed within a giant death-mask of Wagner and the character of Parsifal is alternately male and female (Harty 14-15).

The postmodern retelling of the tale in LaGravanese's and Gilliam's *The Fisher King* of 1991 locates the quest for the Holy Grail in contemporary New York City. In it aspects of Parsifal are shared by both Jack Lucas, a New York City shock-jock, and Parry, a schizophrenic homeless man who once taught medieval studies at Hunter College. Likewise, elements of Cundwiamurs, Parzival's wife, are shared by Jack and Parry's love-interests, the characters Anne and Lydia. Jack, played by Jeff Bridges, and Parry, played by Robin Williams, come together as the result of Jack's gratuitous and self-indulgent diatribe against Yuppies on his late-night call-in show. This rant results in the shooting of several clients at a swank Manhattan nightclub, among them Parry's beautiful young wife. Jack subsequently retires and enters a prolonged state of alcohol abuse and depression during which he feels he is being punished for his irresponsibility. At the same time, Parry's life unravels in an even more precipitous fashion. He becomes delusional and takes on the persona of a contemporary Grail Knight, performing good deeds among the homeless on the bleak streets of a very sinister New York City. The trajectory of the film follows Jack and Parry as they become friends, assist one another in their romantic lives, eventually rescue the 'Holy Grail' – in the form of a child's sport's trophy stored on the shelf of an aging millionaire – and ultimately work together to heal one another's psychological 'wounds'.

Among the many postmodern strategies employed in the film are: 1) a blending of genres, including comedy, tragedy, epic, farce and Broadway musical; 2) the presentation of a pastiche of artifacts from both high and low culture; 3) an overlapping of aesthetic, economic, and psychological codes; and 4) the exploitation of a decentered and fragmented relationship between subjectivity and objectivity. This final strategy represents the film's greatest modification of the Parsifal plot.

Both screenwriter and director confess to identifying with the project and its production in personal and professional ways. Reflecting on the many years of effort it took to sell his story and the numerous versions of the script involved, LaGravanese states, "In a way the script acted as its own Grail for me – healing the wounds of self-doubt." (137) In an interview conducted on location in New York City, Gilliam confessed that he often lives out the problems of his characters during filming. Following is an excerpt of that interview with David Morgan.

Morgan: How is the film meeting your expectations?
Gilliam: We'll find out when I stick it all together. I don't know. This is the stage when I've lost what I set out to do.
Morgan: Lost?
Gilliam: This is the Parsifal myth; the whole thing is about Parsifal.
Morgan: You're living the dilemmas of your characters again?
Gilliam: Always, yeah. But the difficulty in this film is that I'm two characters – I'm Jack and Parry. And this is really difficult.
Morgan: You're the Fisher King and the Fool?
Gilliam: Well, they both are; both of them is a Fisher King and both of them a Fool. But specifically I know both those characters, Parry and Jack, and I'm both of them; normally I'm just one character in the film. In this one I'm both, and it really throws me ... Its like in the Parsifal myth: as a boy he sees the Grail, but when he gets to the Grail Castle he doesn't do the right thing. There is a clarity of vision when you are young and then you lose it as you go on, and then you find it at the end hopefully; that's what making this film is like. It was really clear in my mind early on, and now that I'm into it I've lost it, so I am stumbling through the forest blind at the moment. I'm doing alot of it by instinct. Its true, that actually is what happens. (LaGravanese 156-57)

Thus, both writer and director seem to experience a fusion of lived experience and artistic expression.

The most striking visual element of the film is its depiction of the Red Knight from Wolfram's *Parzival*. In Wolfram's tale, the slaying of the Red Knight by Parzival is the first act of the young man's journey toward wisdom, and Parzival wears the red armor of his fallen opponent through much of Wolfram's narrative. In the film version of LaGravanese and Gilliam, the Red Knight exists solely in the imagination of the schizophrenic Parry, and the audience sees the apparition through Parry's eyes in three crucial and terrifyingly surreal cinematic moments. In each case, the Red Knight appears when Parry comes close to stepping out of his world of delusional madness, facing the pain of his loss, and daring to experience an authentic emotional life.

Mounted on an imposing red horse, the Red Knight is armed with a red lance and shield, and plumes of yellow flame – flashing forward toward the camera – frequently surround his head. Set in the more or less gray monochrome of an urban landscape, the scenes with the Red Knight are striking in their colorful contrast to the impersonal wasteland of the city. The red of the rider and horse and the yellowish gold of the flames are ubiquitous throughout the film, appearing in scenes too numerous to mention. While in one scene it is possible to construct a logic for the symbolism of the colors, such a reading is undercut or subverted in the next. These colors operate as floating or empty signs able to attach themselves, for a time, to any number of semiotic codes, but they refuse to commit to any sustained and predictable significance. Sometimes red is associated with blood, rage, passion, etc., but as soon as this seems to operate in a predictable manner, the associations change. Similarly, yellow is sometimes associated with things of value and at others identified with taxi cabs, warning signs, and traffic lights.

In the same way that he has used the ubiquitous red and gold colors as open signs, Gilliam explores and exploits as many three-dimensional openings and passages as possible in the background of the film. In virtually every scene of any significance to the story, characters stand in doorways, pass through archways, walk beneath highway overpasses, or converse in front of walls covered by framed pictures. These liminal sites are at once part of a boundary and devoid of intrinsic significance. In this way, Gilliam suggests the transitional nature of his characters and their motives, implying that any purchase they may have on themselves or their world is capable of only partial realization. At the same time, this use of openings and passages provides a self-referential commentary on the genre of film itself.

A final aspect of *The Fisher King*, one that is less visual and more thematic, is Gilliam's interest in the difficult-to-negotiate relation between the body and the book. Jack's girlfriend, Ann, is a purveyor of narratives: she owns a video-rental shop with a well-stocked and popular pornography section. Parry's idealized beloved, Lydia, works for a publishing house specializing in romance novels. When we first meet Ann, she is framed against a wall of video boxes. In Lydia's first appearance, she stops to peruse an outdoor carousel of novels.

Early in the film, when Jack is still a successful and self-absorbed radio personality, he prepares to audition for the starring role in a situation comedy. In a moment of unembarrassed narcissism, anticipating the success of the venture and its benefits for his career, Jack states: "I used to think my biography would be JACK LUCAS – THE FACE BEHIND THE VOICE, but now it can be JACK LUCAS THE FACE 'AND' THE VOICE [...] or maybe just JACK – EXCLAMATION POINT [...]" (LaGravanese 11). In the next scene, Jack soaks in the bathtub while practicing lines for the pilot. As he does so, he applies a thick, blue cleansing cream to his face, effectively masking his physical identity, and repeats the tag line for his character, a sarcastic and insincere "Hey! Forgiiiive ME!" (LaGravanese 12)

Both Parry and Jack wear the narrative in the form of physical injuries – the flesh-wounds sustained in the course of their adventures. Significantly, both characters have matching abrasions on their foreheads through much of the film. And at the conclusion of a magical, almost ritual meal at a Chinese restaurant, Parry serenades Lydia while Jack and Anne look on approvingly. With troubadour-like earnestness, Parry sings "Lydia the Tattooed Lady" from the 1939 Marx Brothers film *At the Circus*:

> Oh Lydia, oh Lydia, say, have your met Lydia?
> Lydia the Tattooed Lady.
> She has eyes that folks adore so,
> and a torso even more so.
> Lydia, oh Lydia, that encyclo-pidia.
> Oh Lydia The Queen of Tattoo ...
> You can learn a lot from Lydia! ...
> When her robe is unfurled she will show you the world,
> If you step up and tell her where ...
>
> (music by Harold Arlen and lyrics by E.Y. Harberg)

All of these scenes speak to a close and often confused relation between physicality and textuality that Gilliam obviously finds fascinating[13].

In their article "Filming: Inscriptions of *Denken*", Wilhelm Wurzer and Hugh Silverman suggest that the art of filming represents a distinctively postmodern epistemology. They describe this mode of thought as one that is "nonlogocentric [*sic*] yet critically imagistic" (173). Derived from the interplay between Heidegger's notions of thought ("Denken") and imagination ("Einbildungskraft"), Wurzer and Silverman describe filming as "a thinking that can be neither metaphysics nor science" (174). For them, filming is "technology's own ironic upheaval of the metaphysical text" and the "continual attempt to free imagination from the transcendental constraints of *Verstand* and for a more privileged play of *Vernunft*" (175). Thus, to make a film is both "ontological thinking and ontic doing" (180). The manner in which the colors red and

---

[13] In her excellent editing of this manuscript, Suzanne Lodato observed that matters of physicality and textuality were also important in Wolfram's *Parzival*.

gold operate as open signs in search of partial or temporary significance; the way in which openings and passages create a liminal space where characters, their actions, and their motives may be filled with meaning; and especially the way in which the relationship between the body and the book is complicated in *The Fisher King*, conflate conception and action. LaGravenese and Gilliam have not only made a film rearticulating the story of Parsifal's quest, but one that thematizes the kind of thinking that Wurzer and Silverman designate as filming.

Tellingly, the film is most arresting when the techniques of cinematography fade into the background and a more decidedly theatrical style surfaces. The most compelling examples of the success of this strategy are two quite moving monologues. In one, a morose and inebriated Jack refers to himself as one of the "bungled and the botched" of Nietzsche's master-slave morality and concludes with the question, posed to a small wooden Pinocchio doll he has been given, "Do you ever feel like you are being punished for your sins?" While it is unclear whether Jack is asking important questions in a sincere fashion or simply indulging in self-pity, the fact that he asks such a question of the boy whose nose for the truth is already suspect presents a wonderfully ironic moment. In another striking example of theatricality, the singer Tom Waits gives an inspired performance as a disabled Vietnam veteran who spends his days panhandling in Union Station. In this brief, cameo appearance, he explains to Jack and Parry how his existence is a service to society. Whenever some driven and ambitious professional is denied a promotion or bonus and is tempted to question the meaning of life, to walk away from it all or to tell off the boss, the memory of this man they pass each day on the way to and from work acts as a warning signal. He stops them from asking existential questions with potentially deleterious answers. He tells them to hold their tongue before all is lost – before they end up like him.

These two theatrical moments aside, when assessing the tone of this film, I am alarmed by its excesses. The voice of this version of Parsifal is strident, sometimes shrill, and almost always confused. Both writer and producer are anxious to prove how much they know about previous versions of Parsifal and equally determined to show their cleverness by recasting this knowledge in surprising ways. Thus, there is frequently more posturing than playfulness in this parodic treatment of the Parsifal legend.

Parsifal's Resonance and Permission to Listen

Those who follow in Heidegger's path might wish, at this point, to speculate about Parsifal or deconstruct his tale in a Derridian fashion. It is possible, once the complex web of medial limitations, generic expectations and historical implications has been loosened and we have been allowed a view into the interconnectedness of the relations between medium, genre and history, to succumb to the temptation of looking instead of listening. In his summary treatment of Heidegger's thought, George Steiner alludes to the philosopher's seeming insensitivity to music:

> Music is almost wholly absent from Heidegger's considerations [...] this is a drawback, for it is music which might best have instanced two of Heidegger's foremost propositions: the fact that meaning can be plain and compelling but intranslateable [*sic*] into any other code [...] (114).

More important, however, than any shortcoming in aesthetic appreciation on Heidegger's part is his privileging of the visual aspect of signification at the expense of the acoustic[14].

Heidegger creates the conditions for such a privileging when, in his "The Way to Language", he offers what, by his own admission, is a makeshift ("Notbehelf") translation of a brief but crucial passage from Aristotle's "On Interpretation". Heidegger claims that in Aristotle's assertion, "what takes place in the making of vocal sounds is a sign of what there is in the soul in the way of passions", the word "sign", *semia* in Greek, should be translated as "that which shows" ("das Zeigende") (114). Following this dubious, seemingly capricious, translation, Heidegger continues:

---

[14] This privileging of showing at the expense of saying is what makes Heidegger's thought so felicitous for Silverman and Wurzer in their discussion of filming, but so problematic for my discussion of listening to these three articulations of the Parsifal story.

> Aristotle's text has the detached and sober diction that exhibits the classical architectonic structure in which language, as speaking, remains secure. The letters show the sounds. The sounds show the passions in the soul, and the passions in the soul show the matters that arouse them. Showing is what forms and upholds the intertwining braces of the architectonic structure. (115)

Once the sign is understood in this manner, it is free to participate in the work of *aletheia* which, again according to Heidegger's own idiosyncratic etymological emphasis, is an activity of uncovering (115).

When signification is (mis)construed and adumbrated in this manner, one can intentionally turn a deaf ear to the tone of voice with which the various versions of Parsifal speak. To do so encourages a reading of Parsifal in which the character exists as a supplement to his own story and the grail is no more than an empty cup, an empty sign, an *aporia* waiting to be filled with critical inscription. Such a speculative reading is too easily seen and seen through. Following such a reading, one can only gaze in impassive and dumbfounded silence – like one of Nietzsche's eternally ruminating herd – at the linguistic design of Parsifal's quest and its traces, his *Nachlass*.

In a general sense such privileging of sight and the neglect of sound poses a danger for criticism and is possibly a symptom of our own decadence. Ong is both more circumspect and more patient than I with Derrida, Deconstruction, and its dangers. He situates the textualist approach as a part of the ongoing exchange between orality and literacy, and along the trajectory of what he characterizes as the technologizing of the word:

> Our complacency in thinking of words as signs is due to the tendency, perhaps incipient in oral cultures, but certainly marked in chirographic cultures and far more marked in typographic and electronic cultures, to reduce all sensation and indeed all human experience to visible analogies [...]. We reduce sound to script and the most radical of scripts, the alphabet [...]. In contending with Jean Jacques Rousseau, Derrida is of course quite right in rejecting the persuasion that writing is no more than incidental to the spoken word. (75-76)

Ong does conclude, however, with the assertion that "it would appear that the textualist critique of textuality, brilliant and to a degree serviceable as it is, is still itself curiously text-bound. In fact, it is the most text-bound of all ideologies." (163-65)

When Nietzsche voices his intention to philosophize with a hammer, he announces the movement of philosophy away from the abstract and ideal domain of being and into the performative domain of becoming. Already in the *Birth of Tragedy*, he stated his intention to be a musical Socrates, but it is not until *The Twilight of the Idols* – whose title announces the beginning of the end of the era idolizing speculative thought – that Nietzsche more fully realizes this performative style of philosophizing. In this, the last of his books the philosopher saw in print, Nietzsche again takes up the case of Socrates. He presents Socrates as an actor, a *poseur*: "Everything about him is exaggerated, *buffo*, caricature." (41) He goes on to describe Socrates as "the first fencing master" who shows "his own form of ferocity in the knife-thrust of the syllogism" (42). These descriptions of Nietzsche's life-long exemplar and antagonist – his own greatest idol and essential sounding board – must be read with the context of the hammer in mind. Whereas Socrates wields a sword that wounds, Nietzsche's hammer elicits resonance. When Nietzsche turns to philosophy's obsession with reason and the philosophical idols who have followed its speculative path, he ironically concludes that these thinkers are a "[...] denial of all that believes in the senses, of all the rest of mankind: of all that is mere people" (45). And in a devastatingly sarcastic call to arms for such would-be philosophers, Nietzsche cries: "Be a philosopher, be a mummy, represent monotono-theism [...]" (45).

Unlike speculative critics, what I hope to have made possible in this essay is a critical clearing where these three articulations of Parsifal are allowed to speak, and in which their various resonances may be clearly heard. When I set out to listen to these voices, my goal was to attune one set of ears to their tone of voice – the way they said what they said – and the other to the semantic content of their speech. After sounding out each story, one way to characterize each of the three articulations of Parsifal examined above is with expressive terms drawn from the domain of musical performance itself. The characteristic tone of Wolfram's premodern romance is *fuocoso* – fiery, ardent, and impetuous. The tale is alive with passion and animated by the potential dangers of both love and battle. The tone of Wagner's modern music drama is *morendo*: his purified Parsifal seems to be dying away, expiring, gradually diminishing in tone and time. The tone of LaGravanese and Gilliam's postmodern film is *strepitoso*: it is loud, noisy and overstated. The microphone of the story stands too near the amplifier of the medium; what we hear is mainly distortion.

Instead of those tone-deaf thinkers who specialize in mummifying themselves and the objects of their study, Nietzsche's performative philosophy echoes the activity of the performing musician – one who deciphers and interprets the marks of the manuscript intellectually and physically translates them into sound. In such a performative philosophy, aesthetic expression and hermeneutic activity are identical activities. With one set of ears attuned to the potential sounds signified by the musical text and another to the qualities of the actual music being made, Nietzsche's performative philosopher sounds out ideas and deems them beautiful or deformed, ordered or confused, based upon their resonance. Such a strategy sounds right to me. It has the ring of truth.

References

Attali, Jacques. *Noise: The Political Economy of Music*. Brian Massumi, trans. Minneapolis: Univ. of Minnesota Press, 1985.

Beckett, Lucy. *Parsifal*. Cambridge: Cambridge Univ. Press, 1995.

Blondel, Eric. "Philosophy and Music in Nietzsche". *International Studies in Philosophy* 18 (Summer 1986): 87-95.

Chrétien de Troyes. *Perceval ou Le Conte du Graal*. Charles Méla, trans. Paris: Livre Poche, 2003.

Dahlhaus, Carl. *The Music Dramas of Richard Wagner*. Arnold Whithall, trans. Cambridge: Cambridge Univ. Press, 1979.

_____. "Wagner, Richard". *The New Grove Dictionary of Music and Musicians*. Stanley Sadie, ed. London: MacMillian, 1980.

Derrida, Jacques. *Of Grammatology*. Gayatri Spivak, trans. Baltimore: Johns Hopkins Univ. Press, 1974.

_____. *Spurs: Nietzsche's Styles*. Barbara Harlow, trans. Chicago: Univ. of Chicago Press, 1978.

Eschenbach, Wolfram von. *Parzival*. Helen M. Mustard and Charles E. Passage, trans. New York: Vintage, 1961.

The Fisher King. Terry Gilliam, dir. Richard LaGravanese, screenplay. Tristar, 1991. Voyager Company, 1992.

Green, D.H. *Medieval Listening and Reading: Primary Reception of German Literature 800-1300*. Cambridge: Cambridge Univ. Press, 1994.

Groos, Arthur. *Romancing the Grail*. Ithaca: Cornell Univ. Press, 1995.

Harty, Kevin J. "Lights! Camelot! Action! – King Arthur on Film." *King Arthur on Film*. Kevin J. Harty, ed. London: McFarland, 1999. 12-15.

Heidegger, Martin. *Nietzsche*. David Krell, trans. San Francisco: Harper, 1979.

_____. *Unterwegs zur Sprache*. Pfullingen: Neske, 1959.

_____. "The Way to Language". *On The Way to Language*. Peter D. Hertz, trans. New York: Harper and Row, 1971. 111-36.
Higgins, Kathleen. "Nietzsche on Music". *Journal of the History of Ideas* 47.4 (October–December 1986): 663-72.
Janz, Curt Paul, ed. *Nietzsches Musikalïsche Nachlass*. Basel: Bärenreiter, 1976.
LaGravanese, Richard. *The Fisher King: The Book of the Film*. New York: Applause Books, 1991.
Latour, Bruno. *We Have Never Been Modern*. Catherine Porter, trans. Cambridge: Harvard Univ. Press, 1993.
MacIntyre, Alasdair. *After Virtue*. 2nd ed. Notre Dame: Univ. of Notre Dame Press, 1984.
McCreless, Patrick. "Motive and Magic: A Referential Dyad in *Parsifal*". *Music Analysis* 9.3 (1990): 227-65.
Mosley, David. "Nietzsche's Petöfi Songs: The Philosopher as Composer". *Yearbook of Interdisciplinary Studies in the Fine Arts* 2 (1990): 683-702.
Nietzsche, Friedrich. *The Birth of Tragedy*. Ronald Speirs, trans. Cambridge: Cambridge Univ. Press, 1999.
_____. *The Case of Wagner*. Walter Kaufmann, trans. New York: Vintage, 1967.
_____. *Werke*. Giorgio Colli and Mazzino Montinari, eds. Berlin: de Gruyter, 1967-.
_____. "On Music and Words". Walter Kaufmann, trans. *Denver Quarterly* 13 (1978): 16-30.
_____. *Twilight of the Idols*. R.J. Hollingdale, trans. New York: Penguin, 1990.
Ong. Walter. *Orality and Literacy: The Technologizing of the Word*. New York: Methuen, 1982.
Page, C. *Voices and Instruments of the Middle Ages*. Berkeley: Univ. of California Press, 1986.
Safranski, Rüdiger. *Nietzsche: A Philosophical Biography*. Shelley Frisch, trans. London: Norton, 2002.
Sivouja-Gunaratnam, Anne. "Kundry as Abject. Unpublished Manuscript.
Steiner, George. *Heidegger*. New York: Penguin, 1980.
Wagner, Richard. *Parsifal: Original Text and English Translation*. Stewart Robb, trans. New York: Schirmer, 1962.
_____. *Richard Wagner's Prose Works*. William Ashton Ellis, trans. London: Kegan Paul, 1892.
_____. *Religion and Art*. William Ashton Ellis, trans. Lincoln: Univ. of Nebraska Press, 1994.
_____. *Selected Letters of Richard Wagner*, Stewart Spencer and Barry Millington, eds. and trans. New York: Norton, 1987.
Weiner, Marc A. *Richard Wagner and the Anti-Semitic Imagination*. Lincoln: Univ. of Nebraska Press, 1995.
Whithall, Arnold. "The Music". *Richard Wagner: Parsifal*. By Lucy Beckett. Cambridge: Cambridge Univ. Press, 1995. 61-86.
Wurzer, Wilhelm, and Hugh Silverman. "Filming: Inscriptions of *Denken*". *Postmodernism, Philosophy and the Arts*. Hugh Silverman, ed. New York: Routledge, 1990. 173-86.
Zumthor, Paul. *Introduction à la poésie orale*. Paris: Seuil, 1983.

'Opera about Opera'
Self-Referentiality in Opera with Particular Reference to Dominick Argento's *The Aspern Papers*

Michael Halliwell, Sydney

Opera is a self-conscious genre, and from its origins in the late sixteenth century has frequently celebrated its own self-referentiality. This culminated in the work of Richard Strauss, particularly his operas, *Ariadne auf Naxos* (1912/16) and *Capriccio* (1942). Dominick Argento's opera, *The Aspern Papers* (1988), based on Henry James's tale, "The Aspern Papers" (1888), further extends these ontological concerns in a work which can be seen as a profound meditation on the nature of contemporary opera. Argento's opera takes its cue from James's tale, itself concerned with the nature of the literary life, and transforms this into an exploration of the continued viability of opera as an art form. Argento's opera embodies aspects of a clearly identifiable trend during the last two decades towards a more accessible musical idiom in operatic practice, and suggests that if opera is to survive it will have to 're-discover' certain fundamental, perhaps even 'conservative', elements which have characterised the genre since its inception.

In one of his travel pieces, "From Chambéry to Milan" of 1872, Henry James describes an excursion he had made to Lake Como where, as he observed, one was aware of "the constant presence of the melodious Italian voice" (96-97). This excursion, James recalls, "lasted long enough to suggest to me that I too was a hero of romance with leisure for a love affair, and not a hurrying tourist with a Bradshaw in his pocket". James's romantic view of Como suggested to him "novels of 'immoral' tendency – being commonly the spot to which inflamed young gentlemen invite the wives of other gentlemen to fly with them and ignore the restrictions of public opinion". He asked himself where he, metaphorically speaking, had seen this all before. His answer?

> Where indeed but at the opera when the manager has been more than usually regardless of expense? Here in the foreground was the palace of the nefarious barytone, with its banqueting-hall opening as freely on the stage as a railway buffet on the platform; beyond, the delightful back scene, with its operatic gamut of colouring; in the middle the scarlet-sashed *barcaiuoli*, grouped like a chorus, hat in hand, awaiting the conductor's signal. It was better than being in a novel – this being, this fairly wallowing, in a libretto.

What then, apart from absorbing some local colour, does the famously unmusical Henry James have to do with opera? Surprisingly, he has been the source for at least eight full-length operas in English[1].

* * *

Opera has always been a self-conscious art form. It is a hybrid with a history of perpetual tension between the demands of the text and those of the music[2]. This fundamental conflict between words and music is as old as opera itself and has been the self-reflexive subject of several operas. Perhaps the first well known example is Antonio Salieri's *Prima la musica e poi le parole* (1786). The opera was commissioned for a performance at Schönbrunn Palace during which members of the Burgtheater's Italian troupe presented it at one end of the Orangery, while at the other end members of the German troupe gave Mozart's *Der Schauspieldirektor*, also commissioned for the occasion. Both operas take an amusing look at the world of opera singers, and there is some light-hearted parody of *opere serie*.

The most intense and critical engagement with the art form itself started in the nineteenth century, and one can see such concerns reflected obliquely in Richard Wagner's *Tannhäuser* (1845) and *Die Meistersinger* (1868), where the role of the artist in society is explored. However, it is really with Richard Strauss that this self-referential concern with opera's status finds its most intense and sustained expression. In Strauss's *Ariadne auf Naxos* (1912/1916), he and Hugo von Hoffmannsthal attempted a modernist

---

[1] Cf. Halliwell 23-34. The major English-language operatic versions of James are: Argento, *The Aspern Papers* (1988); Benjamin Britten, *The Turn of the Screw* (1954) and *Owen Wingrave* (1971); Philip Hageman, *The Aspern Papers* (1988); Donald Hollier, *Washington Square* (1988); Douglas Moore, *The Wings of the Dove* (1961); Thea Musgrave, *The Voice of Ariadne* (1974); and Thomas Pasatieri, *Washington Square* (1976). There is a French version of *Washington Square* by J. H. Damase, *L' Héritière* (1974), and a curious version of "The Aspern Papers" entitled *Singspiel in due atti ... da Henry James, con framenti di Lorenzo Da Ponte,* by Salvato Sciarrino (1978).

[2] The fact that many of the early operatic characters could reasonably be expected to use song as a means of communication hints at the tension between words and music right from the beginnings of opera. The suspension of belief necessary for the appreciation of opera has been a 'problem' right from the outset! (cf. Katz, 1994: 28)

synthesis between *opera seria* and *opera buffa*, with abrupt juxtapositions of these tragic and comic elements. In contrast, Hans Pfitzner's opera, *Palestrina* (1917), is a serious look at the role of the artist in society in the context of conservatism in conflict with modernism. Pfitzner himself regarded it as a reflection upon *Die Meistersinger*, and he looks back to Wagner rather than further forward into the twentieth century. Alban Berg's *Lulu* (three-act version, 1979) is characterised by a similar self-reflexivity when compared with *Ariadne auf Naxos*, and can be seen, in some respects, as an opera about the process of writing an opera.

Strauss's most direct consideration of the nature of opera itself is *Capriccio* (1942), where the debate on the hierarchy between words and music becomes the actual subject of the opera itself. The conflict is not resolved in favour of one or the other, and the opera is characterised by its use of stylistic elements from almost the whole of operatic history. Although in musical idiom a profoundly conservative work, it does point forward to some of the operatic concerns of the 1960s and 1970s. Peter Conrad observes that the operatic works of Strauss and his librettist Hoffmannsthal are:

> engaged in a shame-faced debate on the possibility of their own existence. They have that self-interrogatory anxiety which has increasingly overtaken modern works of art, making them ask whether they can live down their internal divisions or whether they dare claim to be art at all. (*Romantic Opera and Literary Form*, 135)

The Second World War brought about a great change in opera aesthetics, and the radical experimentation of the 1950s and 1960s obviously had its effect on opera as well. Some post-war works stand out. Luciano Berio's first full-length theatrical piece, *Opera* (1970), which interweaves three different types of theatre within the theme of mortality, and Mauricio Kagel's *Staatstheater* (1967-70), which investigates opera as both genre and institution, are fundamental critiques, almost negations, of the art form itself – perhaps reflecting Pierre Boulez's famous call to blow up all the opera houses. John Cage's five works, each called *Europera* (1985-91) are, in fact, a deconstruction of the art form[3]. Indeed, opera was seen by most of the musical *avant garde* of the period as a dying, if not an already dead art form. All these works break completely with the

---

[3] See Lindenberger ("From Opera to Postmodernity" 240-264) for an extended discussion on the performance and 'meaning' of these works.

notion of illusionism in opera and certainly help to redefine and extend the possibilities of the art form.

The radical experimentation of the second half of the twentieth century has, however, not been as fruitful as might have been envisaged, and there has been a strong element of neo-romanticism in operatic creativity during the last twenty years or so. It is within this 'new/old' direction that a work such as Argento's essentially conservative opera, *The Aspern Papers* (1988), can be located. Although it is an opera which examines the very nature of the art form, it does not radically depart from the conventions of late romantic opera[4]. Although more *avant garde* in conception and presentation, John Corigliano's lushly romantic *The Ghosts of Versailles* (1991) is situated in a similar tradition. Like Argento, Corigliano uses the device of the opera-within-an-opera, loosely based on the third Beaumarchais play, although in a much more expanded and integrated form than Argento[5].

* * *

James's tale, "The Aspern Papers", first appeared in *The Atlantic Monthly* from March to May 1888[6]. Although not a meta-fictional work in the contemporary sense of the word, "The Aspern Papers" is self-consciously concerned with the relation of art to life and with the boundaries between worlds. James remembers while on a visit to Florence first becoming aware of the existence of Jane Clairmont, "the half-sister of Mary Godwin, Shelley's second wife, and for a while the intimate friend of Byron and the mother of his daughter Allegra" (*The Aspern Papers* 29). This fascinating link with the

---

[4] Argento's operas are characterised by their 'grateful' and effective writing for the voice, not a characteristic of much of the operatic output during the 1960s and 1970s. In many ways, Argento could be seen as the musical heir to Strauss and Puccini (cf. Kirk 321).

[5] Of course, the use of a play-within-the-play is a long established dramatic device, and the operatic equivalent is similar in its foregrounding of the already prominent aspect of self-referentiality in opera (cf. Lindenberger, *Opera: The Extravagant Art* 141-42).

[6] Its origins are fully documented in James's Preface to the revised version of the tale included in the New York Edition (1908) of his works.

literary past was intensified by James's discovery of an American sea-captain who ingratiated himself with Clairmont in the hope of obtaining material relevant to Shelley's life. On Clairmont's death, the captain approached her niece "on the subject of his desires. Her answer was: 'I will give you all the letters if you marry me'" (*Notebooks of Henry James* 72). "The Aspern Papers" draws heavily on this incident, changing the locale from Florence to Venice and giving the plausible reason that the Clairmont figure would have been able to conceal herself more easily in "a city of exhibition" (*The Aspern Papers* 48) – a typical Jamesean irony.

In the tale, Clairmont becomes Juliana Bordereau, the mistress of a long dead American poet, Jeffrey Aspern. Besides the dramatic possibilities inherent in this situation, James indicates in the Preface another aspect which fascinated him:

> I delight in a palpable imaginable visitable past – in the nearer distances and the clearer mysteries, the marks and signs of a world we may reach over to as by making a long arm we grasp an object at the other end of our own table. The table is the one; the common expanse, and where we lean, so stretching, we find it firm and continuous. That, to my imagination, is the past fragrant of all, or almost all, the poetry of the thing outlived and lost and gone, and yet in which the precious element of closeness, telling so of connections but tasting so of differences, remains appreciable. (1984: 31)[7]

Argento's opera *The Aspern Papers*, based on James's tale, was first performed in Dallas in November 1988 and is, in many ways, paradigmatic of contemporary operatic trends[8]. From one perspective it can be seen as a meditation on the current state of opera and is a work that exploits many of the techniques and facilities of modern music theatre while anchoring itself firmly within traditional operatic convention. Argento has shifted the locale of the tale from Venice to Lake Como, a strategy justified by the

---

[7] J. Hillis Miller (37) observes of this passage that James's definition of such a past connects it with Sigmund Freud's definition of the uncanny and posits this aspect of the tale as a direct link with "The Turn of the Screw".

[8] Of all the operas based on James apart from Britten's *The Turn of the Screw*, (and to a lesser extent, *Owen Wingrave*), this work appears the most likely to gain a permanent place in the current operatic repertoire. It has received subsequent productions in Sweden, Britain, and Germany. Elise K. Kirk maintains that "Stephen Sondheim is to musical comedy what Dominick Argento is the opera." She notes his sympathy for the voice and quotes him as saying that "operas are about people, not events or concepts […]. Through music, the character is no longer a stranger […]. I want my work to have emotional impact, I want it to communicate, not obfuscate. I am always thinking of my audience, how they will hear it, and what it will mean to them […]. The voice is our representation of humanity […] all music begins where speech stops." (321)

transformation of Aspern from poet to composer[9]. Argento has taken the theme of literary composition from James and expanded it to include artistic and musical composition. He responds to James's tale which is so self-consciously about the literary life with an opera itself so conscious of the operatic life: the life of the opera, the life *in* the opera, and the 'operatic' life around or outside the opera.

This opera is, in many ways, paradigmatic of contemporary operatic trends; it offers, in postmodernist terms, a self-reflexive analysis of the nature of the operatic art form itself as well as of its world of performance, and is a work which has absorbed modernist elements such as atonality and narrative disjunction and transformed them into an opera which uses traditional operatic structures self-consciously and with an ever-present hint of parody[10].

Argento has increased the number of characters in James's tale to eight[11]. Aspern features as a major character in the opera, becoming a famous composer. The younger Juliana is a celebrated singer; Signor Barelli is an impresario and former lover of Juliana; Sonia is a singer and present mistress of Barelli, but in love with Aspern. Tina remains essentially the same in the opera (cf. Sutcliffe 14-18). There are two servants as in the tale, and a portrait painter. The narrator becomes "The Lodger, a critic and biographer", an introspective, yet pivotal character, whose operatic realisation illustrates

---

[9] There is naturally a loss in this transferral of the tale from Venice to Lake Como. Many commentators have pointed out the centrality of Venice to the ultimate effect of the tale. Cf. Maves, who notes the pervasive atmosphere of "sensuous decay and neurasthenic languor" (88), while Graham sees Venice as "bringing together past and present, vanished power with present beauty, land and sea, *piazza* and *sala*, grandeur and intimacy, its publicities and its arcana, richness and dilapidation, all in one vision of harmony and light" (66). Apart from the meta-textual resonances that Graham has isolated, Venice, in operatic terms, has a similar evocative power. The weight of operatic tradition is something well captured in Moore's Venetian scenes in his adaptation of *The Wings of the Dove* (cf. Halliwell 23-34). It is fascinating to think of what Argento might have made of this aspect of his source had he kept Venice as his locale!

[10] I would not argue that this opera is postmodernist as such, but it certainly exhibits postmodernist elements. McHale argues that the dominant mode of modernism was "epistemological", while in postmodernism it is "ontological" (9), and certainly the dominant mode in Argento's opera is ontological. Much of the parodic element in the tale is amplified in Argento's opera, particularly in musical terms (cf. Holland 147). *The Aspern Papers* is frequently concerned with the minutiae of operatic life, and it is this interest in the trivial as well as in the idea of 'high art' that could be seen as one of the aspects which might considered postmodernist about *The Aspern Papers*.

[11] James's tale concentrates the focus almost exclusively on the triangle formed by the Narrator, Juliana, and Tina Bordereau. There are other characters, but they remain peripheral to this main drama.

some of the difficulties of translating a self-conscious character such as James's narrator into a viable operatic figure.

Much has been made in the critical response to James's tale about the exaggerated nature of the narrator. It could be argued that this finds a parallel in Argento's concern with the self-referential nature of opera itself. James's tale is narrated by a homodiegetic, first-person narrator, and it is in the accommodation of this narrator that some of the most interesting aspects of this operatic adaptation are to be found. Wayne C. Booth raises the issue of the reliability of James's narrator, and he has identified three distinct registers within the narrative voice in the tale: "the narrator's self-betrayals"; his "efforts at straightforward evocation of the past"; and the "passages of mumbling, as it were, that lie between" (361). He feels that James is unsuccessful in his attempt to integrate these three voices into a single narrator who is "used on the one hand to reveal his own deficiencies with unconscious irony and on the other to praise praiseworthy things" (362). Booth considers that it would have been better if James had "preserved for a reliable voice the right to evoke the true visitable past and used the present narrator only on jobs for which he is qualified" (364). Kenneth Graham, however, has argued that the narrator "is not meant to bear continual judicial scrutiny from outside", but is:

> at once reliable and unreliable, objective and subjective. We can stand outside him with one part of our minds, judging his selfishness and irresponsibility, aided by moments of obviously 'loaded' irony against him and also by moments where the narrator expressly judges himself. This allows us to resist full illusion and to see around the dangerous subjectivity of his narrative. It also helps us to read a meaning into his motives and his experience that goes far beyond his conscious understanding of them [...] what we experience is a perpetually dual and moving thing: we are always moving into the narrator, and moving out of him. (59)

In this sense, the unreliability of the narrator is an essential aspect of the method of the tale. The narrator is presented as perceptive in his understanding of the two women, but, of course, his relationship with them is clouded by his overwhelming desire for possession of the papers. His powers of observation are acute, and his frankness concerning his own intentions lull the reader into an acceptance of his reliability. However, the ending of the tale finally reveals to the reader all the 'gaps' in his narration and achieves James's apparent aim of a more complex reversal in the reception of this focaliser at the closure of the narrative. Although James's mode is realistic, there are striking elements within the tale which work against this surface realism and draw attention to the artifice of the work itself, elements which have surely given some impetus to the self-conscious concern of Argento's opera which, itself, constantly questions its own status as a work of art.

This frequent critical reference to the grotesque and exaggerated nature of the narrator is summed up in Graham's description of him as "too obsessive to be 'natural', too feverish, too mannered in his expression; too literary by half", yet Graham observes that the narrator "draws us straight into his fantasy-realm, where 'reality' unexpectedly seizes us in the form of powerful and almost hallucinatory images, which lose nothing of seriousness for their comicality" (60). Graham describes the distortion which is part of the "exaggeration in artistic creation in general", and further observes that many of James's characters are paradoxically "often not quite human, and yet are utterly full of life" (60), a factor which needs to be seen in relation to the overall melodramatic element in James[12]. Graham's description of the element of exaggeration in James's characters has its counterpart in what could be described as the *Steigerungstendenz* in opera[13].

The change in the title figure from poet to composer facilitates a range of operatic transformations, including the introduction of Sonia as a quintessentially operatic rival to Juliana. Sonia is to sing a role in the new opera, *Medea*, by Aspern, which, in Argento's opera, is seen and heard in the process of composition. The betrayal of Juliana by Aspern, which is implied in James's tale, becomes reality in the opera. The "papers" of the tale now become the lost manuscript of the opera *Medea* – with its relevant echoes of the betrayal of the mythical Medea by Jason which provides a telling

---

[12] Holland observes that the "The Aspern Papers" "is no less a horror story for being a subtle caricature, a deft but fantastic parody of the creative process, the process of confronting the historical past, and the very Gothic conventions it uses." (136)

[13] John Carlos Rowe remarks: "Literature's appeal to its fictionality may be read as the subtlest of all ruses, because it so often transforms its fictionality – its ephemerality – into a claim for unique insight into and understanding of reality." (56) One can perhaps see a similar manoeuvre in opera, particularly in Argento's operatic version of James's tale. Opera's insistence on its own artificiality is one of the most significant distinguishing features of the art form, yet the music in opera is often regarded as offering a unique insight into the noumenal realm. Opera claims for itself the ability through music to probe psychological depth in a way not available to the same extent in other performative genres. In this sense opera strives for psychological realism and 'truth', not naturalistic representation.

subtext in the opera. The Lodger, as critic and biographer, believes the manuscript to be still in existence. The occasional mythical allusions in James's tale are amplified by the introduction and complete integration into the events of the opera of the Medea story, which acts as a continuous commentary on the main events of the opera[14].

Probably the most important structural transposition is the division of the action into two time frames. Half of the action occurs in the summer of 1835 and the other half – the Jamesian story – set in the summer of 1895, which acts as a frame. It is almost as if James's "palpable imaginable visitable" past, which is sought by the narrator in the tale, is actually recovered in the opera.

In the tale we are given hints as to what transpired during the relationship between Aspern and Juliana, but in Argento's opera these events are directly portrayed, with the consequent loss of some of the Jamesean ambiguity. The action in 1895 acts as both a frame and a commentary on the events sixty years before, while the figure of Juliana provides a tangible physical and thematic link between the two periods. She serves, in a sense, as the narrator and interpreter of the earlier events while participating fully in the events in both time frames. The fluidity of movement between the two time periods corresponds roughly to the step-by-step development of the narrative of the tale. In the opera, each 1835 part of the narrative looks forward to, and prepares for the subsequent 1895 scene. This structure roughly parallels the leisurely build-up of tension, stage-by-stage, which characterises the tale.

The emphasis in the opera falls equally on the triangular relationships between the Lodger, Juliana, and Tina in the 1895 part, and that of the young Juliana, Aspern, and

---

[14] Of course, the use of the mythical figure of Medea has strong meta-operatic overtones. There are well over twenty operas based on this figure, but the model for Aspern's opera is probably that of Italian composer, Luigi Cherubini (1760-1842), whose opera *Médée* (1797) is perhaps the best known and most frequently performed. This opera was 'revived' for a series of performances in the 1950s and 1960s for the legendary Greek/American soprano, Maria Callas. Many of Callas's great attributes of a voice of unique timbre and acting of mesmerising dramatic power were embodied in her performances of the title role. In fact, she made a film of the play by Euripides. Although one must not draw fanciful parallels, there are certain similarities in the depiction of Juliana in Argento's opera and Callas. Certainly the greatest 'diva' of her time, Callas was involved with powerful men outside the immediate operatic sphere. Callas's emotional (and vocal) vulnerability has been compared to that of the Spanish mezzo-soprano, Maria Malibran (1808-1836), who exerted a similar fascination on the operatic world of her day. She, of course, could also be seen as a model for Juliana, again not necessarily in terms of her life, but in the aura she exerted.

Sonia in the 1835 scenes - both traditional operatic configurations[15]. While the Aspern of the tale was based somewhat loosely on the figures of Percy Bysshe Shelley and Lord Byron, the composer Aspern resembles the composer Vincenzo Bellini (1801-1835), who had a villa at Lake Como, and who also possessed something of the romantic aura of these poets.

* * *

The structural intricacy of Argento's opera is one of its most impressive features, but I would like to look briefly at several scenes where its self-consciousness is, in my view, most acute. The opera is in two acts, each preceded by a prologue. In the first-act prologue, the two time periods of the opera are juxtaposed which, of course, mirrors the method of the opera as a whole. The 'old' Juliana is seen in a wheelchair attempting to remember the words of a song[16]. Juliana acts as a frame narrator for these two periods, and it is her memory which gives the audience access to the earlier period[17]. As she describes the events of fifty years earlier, it becomes apparent that the opera is not primarily concerned with *what* happened but with *why* it happened. Juliana, as narrator, conjures up the figures of the earlier period, giving 'life' to these characters. In fact, the Lodger, later in the opera, seems to 'live' through the figure of Aspern, the ultimate goal of his quest. One of the major thematic elements is also introduced in this opening scene and is encapsulated in the comments by Juliana concerning typical operatic rivalries and

---

[15] It is appropriate that Aspern is replaced by the Lodger in this triangle: the Lodger is portrayed as 'living' only through Aspern.

[16] Argento explains this device: "I had to have something *by* Aspern that the 1835 people knew and could sing – something that wasn't from *Medea*, as that had never been published." (qtd. in Sutcliffe 16) There is a complex layering of fictionality operating here – an imaginary song by an imaginary composer which gives 'credibility' to the fictionalised events which are framed by the 'real' events of the tale/opera! In musical terms, the song uses the device of the twelve tone row, but only eleven tones occur. The final tone is missing as she cannot complete the song. The reason for this becomes apparent as the opera takes its course.

[17] As with Captain Vere in Benjamin Britten's opera *Billy Budd* (1950/51), the events of 1835 are coloured by our knowledge of Juliana fifty years later.

intrigues. *The Aspern Papers* is full of 'inside' jokes or allusions which are very much part of the over-heated operatic world, probably both that of 1835 and the present! It is this juxtaposing of the trivial with 'high art' that could be seen as a distinctly postmodernist element of *The Aspern Papers*.

The frequent use of literal song in *The Aspern Papers* also contributes to its particular qualities of operatic self-consciousness which, in turn, reflect its postmodernist flavour[18]. This suggests a particular musical genre: the barcarolle (appropriately enough, it is a paraphrased version of Longfellow's poem "Cadenaddia, Lake of Como"), a distinctive musical form in 6/8 time, which highlights the deliberately reflexive intentions of the composer in alerting the audience to its status as song. In a musical discourse which is characterised by what could be called a rhythmically flexible and melodic recitative (characteristic of much post-war opera, and, particularly, main-stream American opera of the last twenty years), the singularity of a strict and insistent rhythm such as this has the effect of drawing attention to itself as a discrete formal element in the musical discourse. There is, of course, an echo of the famous barcarolle from *The Tales of Hoffmann* by Jacques Offenbach, and the evocation of older musical styles in a contemporary work results in an abrupt audience awareness of the artifice of what they are witnessing[19].

The link between the present and the past is made visual when Juliana extends her arms to embrace Aspern. With this 'frame-breaking' device, the audience is immediately made aware of the opera's thematisation of its own artifice[20]. It is as if the memory of Juliana has conjured up the vision of these four characters – which includes

---

[18] The intrusion of literal songs into operatic discourse naturally emphasises the artifice of the art form. Cf. Lindenberger, who has observed that the intrusions of literal song in an opera "generally mark those moments of high intensity" during which "we are made to feel that the opera is briefly revealing its emotional center to us" (*Opera: The Extravagant Art* 85).

[19] Carolyn Abbate remarks that narrative song in opera frequently produces an "exaggerated musical simplicity" which is not a musical failure but "a musical gesture whose meaning must extend beyond the notes of the song itself to the song as performance (heard by the operatic characters) and narration". She cites many examples of songs recomposing "(in an alternative way) the plot of the opera that it inhabits" (138). Of course, operatic history is full of examples of the use of phenomenal song as a form of *mise en abyme*.

[20] Cf. Bell (191) for a discussion of the framing devices in this tale.

her younger 'self' – from the past. She has 're-created' them, and a direct link between the events of 1835 and those of 1895 is established. (In fact, one could imagine a production of the opera in which the whole of the subsequent 'action' of 1835 could be seen as taking place within the mind of Juliana!) The two time frames of the opera occur simultaneously in this opening scene and then separate only to join once more at the end of the opera.

In Juliana's narration, Argento has dramatised both of James's narrative modes of 'picture' and 'scene' (cf. Halliwell 23-34). In narrative terms she is somewhat analogous to a figural narrator where the events of 60 years before are filtered through her consciousness. In musical terms, her narration is both 'noumenal' and 'phenomenal': noumenal in the sense that it provides information for the audience, and phenomenal in that it is a moment of self-reflexivity where the 'performance' is foregrounded (cf. Abbate 17). One is conscious of the role of the four operatic characters (which includes the young 'Juliana') as performers as well as characters.

The actual characters in the 'real' story become intertwined with the roles they play in the opera *Medea*, characters of greater dimension and of heroic and 'god-like' stature – operatic, in fact. Yet the vision of the four characters in the Prologue also seems to be a comment on their own insubstantiality: they are described as "sweet visions" (Argento 9) which will ultimately fade. It can be argued that Argento, echoing James, is introducing the idea of the nature of the artistic impulse, its belief in its own immortality, and the possibility of its own destruction.

* * *

Scene 2 of the opera, *Midsummer of 1835, 'Quartet'*, is remarkable for its fusion of different levels of operatic discourse. Juliana is heard rehearsing an aria from Aspern's new opera. Seated in the garden is Aspern, having his portrait painted with the impresario Barelli looking on. This is the same portrait which features prominently in the 1895 part of the opera and which provides an effective iconic link between both parts[21]. This scene is an example of operatic *mise-en-abŷme*, with the contents of Juliana's 'aria' reflecting the events of the opera as a whole and the larger opera (Argento's *The Aspern Papers*) 'framing' the 'smaller' opera (Aspern's *Medea*) within itself. The smaller opera thematically, in turn, mirrors the larger work. It is a complex scene, with three stylistically different musical discourses occurring simultaneously: the archaic nineteenth century romantic 'high style' of Juliana's aria; a free-flowing conversation between Barelli and Aspern; and the painter's sharply perceptive, recitative-like, interjections.

There is a sense of exaggeration and distortion evoked by the deliberate contrasting of the three different discursive levels. The ultimate reality is – as one later learns – the exaggerated and apparently most 'artificial' one of *Medea*, although the comments of Aspern, Barelli and the painter appear, on the surface, more 'real'. There is also a temporal telescoping in operation here from the 'present' 1895 back to 1835, to the origins of opera, and further back to a mythical prehistory.

The dominant musical discourse established in the previous scene had been characterized by a melodic recitative, and the introduction of the new mode – Juliana's aria, a quasi-Bellinian pastiche – results in an arresting contrast between the new form of discourse and the existing dominating one. The painter's commentary is another, contrasting level of discourse couched in short, *staccato* musical phrases. There is an elaborate layering process occurring here. Life is being captured by art on two levels: through the portrait as well as on the broader thematic level of the opera itself.

Juliana's aria is emotionally charged as it is part of a dramatic scene from *Medea* during which Medea prepares to kill her children, and is appropriate to a conventional view of an operatic 'high style'. The Medea story is used as a constant paradigm of the relationship between Aspern, Juliana, and Sonia. Allied to this is the complex use of parody in this opera, frequently embodied in the excerpts from the fictive opera, *Medea*,

---

[21] The portrait can also be seen as a link with the figure of Orpheus as well, a figure who is omnipresent in this opera. In the legend, the Maenads dismembered him, and his head washed up on the island of Lesbos. All that remains of Aspern, particularly after the papers are destroyed, is his 'head' – the portrait.

with its deployment of an older musical style and convention[22]. Juliana's vocal line as well as the orchestral accompaniment explicitly imitate the early nineteenth-century romantic gestures of Bellini, Gaetano Donizetti, and early Giuseppe Verdi. Yet, at the same time, the harmonic idiom is unmistakably late twentieth century[23].

The myth of Medea is also used as an ironic reflection of the events that take place during the summer of 1835. In the embodiment of both Juliana and Sonia as singers, there is a conscious examination and criticism of operatic 'performance' as such: the myth of the opera *diva* is constantly foregrounded. These parodic elements also play an important part in the representation of the relationships in the opera. There are three different and mutually reflective conflicts being portrayed. Juliana is being betrayed for Sonia; Barelli is being betrayed for Aspern; Medea was betrayed for Creusa. Simultaneously, there is also an examination of the concept of 'authorship' here as Aspern ponders aloud the possibility of expanding Sonia's part (his relationship with Sonia is seen to be a vital influence on the final shape of the work of art), an ironic comment on the realities of operatic production and the brutally pragmatic world in which 'high' art is created. Thus, the final shape and effect of the opera is determined by a variety of factors, not necessarily all of them 'artistic'; Argento's opera deconstructs the idea of the integrity and autonomy of the work of art[24].

In addition to the investigation of the genre of opera itself, there also appears to be a persistently self-conscious debate within *The Aspern Papers* on the nature and function of contemporary opera. The deliberate use, at times, of what might appear to some as a

---

[22] Lindenberger argues that the juxtaposition of diverse forms of operatic discourse enables "the composer to reflect ironically on the particular notions that these forms are meant to embody" (*Opera: The Extravagant Art* 80), and further notes that parody stresses the "continuity of a tradition at the same time that it deflates earlier works within that tradition" (102). Said, writing about late romanticism and modernism in music, remarks that "parody and critique propose themselves as the only true novelty in so ripe and exhausted a period" (46-47).

[23] The piano is used consistently in this opera to depict aspects of operatic performance in a variety of practical manifestations. It is both an aural and a visual symbol, and provides both an aural and visual link between the two stories. In this sense, its function has some similarities with the use of the portrait in the tale.

[24] A precedent for such artistic self-scrutiny is what Conrad sees in the operatic works of Strauss and his librettist Hugo von Hoffmannsthal, which, Conrad argues, continually question their own status as works of art (*Romantic Opera and Literary Form* 135).

strongly anachronistic musical idiom can be viewed as an implied criticism of the esoteric nature and inaccessibility of much contemporary opera (certainly that of the 1960s and 1970s). The evocation of Bellini, among others, illustrates the point that opera has ceased to be the popular art form it was in the nineteenth century. Theodor Adorno, writing in the 1950s, remarks that opera "has been in a precarious situation since the moment when the high bourgeois society which supported it in its fully developed form ceased to exist". He insists that this 'rupture' in the development of opera has to do with the importance and recognition of convention. Opera, he claims, was:

> founded on so many conventions that it resounds into a large emptiness as soon as these conventions are no longer vouchsafed to the audience through tradition. The newcomer – at once barbaric and precocious – one who did not already as a child learn to be bowled over by opera and to respect its outrageous impositions, will feel contempt for it, while the intellectually advanced public is almost no longer capable of responding immediately or spontaneously to a limited store of works, which have long since sunk into the living-room treasure-chest of the petite bourgeoisie. (40)

Argento's opera, on the other hand, seems to suggest that what Adorno argues are outdated conventions are, in fact, fundamental elements which determine and constitute the very nature and existence of the art form. One can perhaps regard this view not necessarily as reactionary, but as a pragmatic recognition of the essential nature of the art form. Luciano Berio offers an eloquently argued evaluation of the role of convention which, of course, is the Janus-face of parody.

> [T]he composer should always be aware that most of the operatic conventions, characters or ingredients on which he is so keen to turn his back are unavoidably present, in more or less explicit form, on stage. Whatever they may do, say or sing, the figures that come and go on the operatic stage, be they never so experimental, will always bear the mark of operatic associations. Those figures, those 'characters' that advance towards us, seem to have already sung arias, duets, cavatinas and ensembles. Even if still and silent or employed in unexpected vocal behaviour, they seem all to be 'singing' because, whatever they may do, they implicitly carry about them the signs of operatic experience. They are inhabited by them and themselves inhabit a space – the opera house – that is never empty because it throngs with memories and ghosts (operatic ones, of course) that impose their presence and their model. Every form of musical theatre played out within an opera house is also, inevitably, a parody. (298)

In Scene 4, *Late Summer: 'Trio'*, a situation similar to the opening of Scene 2 is represented[25]. Sonia and Aspern are rehearsing a duet from the new opera, *Medea*, with vocal lines reminiscent of early nineteenth-century Italian opera with its arpeggio accompaniment and singers in parallel sixths[26]. Juliana interjects in short, sharp phrases, giving critical comments on Sonia's vocal technique. This scene similarly juxtaposes different discursive levels: the operatic excerpt is contrasted with Juliana's more prosaic comments which serve, in turn, to recast in ironic mode the operatic element itself. Her hints on vocal technique parallel the painter's comments on his own artistic efforts in Scene 2, not only emphasizing the art that conceals the art, but the deliberate intrusion of criticism of artistic performance within the 'actual' performance as a meta-operatic critique of the notion of performance itself. The exaggerated world of opera performance, both in its intense and heightened theatricality as well as its banality, is also strongly evoked by the juxtaposition of these two discourses, a postmodernist blurring of distinctions between the theatre and 'reality'.

As well as constituting one discursive level, Juliana's comments on vocal technique contain an undercurrent of ambiguity which colours all that she says to Sonia[27]. For example, her line: "You *have* made excellent progress. I hope I don't live to regret it"

---

[25] The first scene, The Prologue, is entitled 'Quintet' – ironic in the sense that there are only four voices present although the character of Juliana is 'doubled' – her young persona as well as her old. The use of alternate, and similarly ironical 'musical' titles for these scenes only occurs in the 1835 – the 'operatic' – part of the opera.

[26] Argento explicitly acknowledged the origin of the music for the opera, *Medea*, as having its model in the operatic music of the 1830s. Of this duet, he remarks: "It begins with clear 1830s gestures – singers in parallel sixths, arpeggio accompaniment, flutes echoing the singers' phrases. But later there is very little I wouldn't just as well write under other circumstances. I wanted to suggest and establish the period quality, then be free to abandon it. The real love music Aspern sings to Sonia after Juliana leaves the room is essentially the same music as that love duet, and there I'm not at all concerned with period references." (Sutcliffe 18)

[27] One could see in this an oblique reference to Wagner's *Die Meistersinger von Nürnberg* – David's explanation of the different singing methods to Walter (I.2) and Beckmesser's later repudiation of Walter's song. The jealousies between Walter and Beckmesser (as rivals for Eva) are paralleled by those between Juliana and Sonia. Of course the reflection in this opera of similar self-reflexive elements in Strauss's operas *Ariadne auf Naxos* and *Capriccio* are pervasive.

(91-92), is ironic and perhaps indicates that she suspects that a relationship has developed between Aspern and Sonia, a suspicion which is about to be confirmed. It more directly refers to the competition between Juliana and Sonia on a professional level – rivalries between prima donnas are the stuff of operatic legend[28]!

The figure of Aspern functions on several levels in the opera, and particularly in this scene: as James's 'original' character; as a 'character' in Argento's opera; as a 'character' within the 'opera' *Medea* within Argento's opera; as 'performer' in a duet with Sonia; as 'composer' of the music he and Sonia are performing; as 'musician' playing the piano which accompanies their duet, and, of course, as the subject of the search by the Lodger/narrator.

The heightened lyricism of Aspern's vocal line carries within itself a self-conscious hint of parody: the stereotypical tenor lover declaring his passion! Operatic intertextuality is ever-present and, indeed, Aspern's line, "You are the real Eurydice" (96-7), with the evocation of a quintessentially operatic figure, provocatively problematises the distinction between 'reality' and myth. In fact, most of the scenes with what appears to be 'genuine' emotion have an element of parody about them. It is as if art and reality cannot be distinguished[29]. One is also aware here of the traditional nineteenth-century operatic love triangle: tenor, soprano, mezzo[30]. Aspern reveals a rather calculating side to his nature when Sonia, uncomfortable about betraying Juliana in her own home, resists his advances. Aspern's reply is practical, if rather cold-

---

[28] A line such as Juliana's enquiry: "shall we have some coffee before the maestro ferries you home?" (92), encapsulates much of opera's intriguing mixture of the elevated and the banal. After the intensity and power of the *Medea* duet, a line such as this is prosaic in the extreme. (It is reminiscent of the oft-quoted line from Puccini's *Madame Butterfly* – "Milk-punch, or whisky?" – which punctuates the higher discourse [in Italian] of the exchanges between Pinkerton and Sharpless.) This sharpens the effect of this discursive juxtaposition and continually reminds the audience of the artificiality of what they are watching.

[29] This is similar to a strategy frequently found in James. As Peter Brooks remarks, this is a "typically Jamesian procedure of ironizing dramatic conventions all the while suggesting their imaginative appropriateness: a way of having one's melodrama while denying it." (163)

[30] Celebrated examples include Radames, Aida, and Amneris from Verdi's *Aida*; Pollione, Norma, and Adalgisa from Bellini's *Norma*; and Don Carlos, Elisabetta, and Eboli from Verdi's *Don Carlos*. Juliana is sung by a soprano, but her vocal line lies consistently lower than that of Sonia. Understandably, it is particularly the world of early nineteenth-century Italian opera which is evoked most effectively.

blooded: "[...] if she knew, she would never sing *Medea*; Barelli would never produce *Medea*; after the premiere we will tell the whole world the truth" (98), an ironic comment on the sometimes brutal exigencies of operatic production. This calculating side to Aspern's nature also deliberately alerts the audience to the parallels to be drawn between him and the Lodger.

As could be expected, Argento expands on James's reference to Orpheus in the tale. Aspern, like Orpheus, is both composer and singer of his own song, and the figure of Orpheus is operatically significant, particularly in this opera which is so self-consciously concerned with the art form. The Orpheus myth has been a fruitful source for composers; however, unlike the mythical Euridice, Aspern's Eurydice/Sonia is the cause of his own destruction[31]. Perhaps one can also see the death of Aspern/Orpheus in this opera as symbolising the decline, and even death, of opera today[32]. The culture that gave rise to this elaborate and 'irrational' form of entertainment exists in this form no longer; can opera therefore continue to exist as a living art form? Corigliano's *The Ghosts of Versailles* seems to pose a similar question, and, perhaps, suggests that opera can only survive in some kind of protected environment. Adorno, in fact, compared opera performance practice to that of a museum: "even in the sense of the [museum's] positive function, which is to help something threatened with muteness to survive" (41). As Conrad asks about the development of contemporary opera: "What fate remains for a modern Orpheus but, in shame and remorse, to lose his voice?" (*A Song of Love and Death* 26) In a sense, Conrad's comment encapsulates many of the postmodernist self-interrogatory, ontological questions posed in Argento's *The Aspern Papers*.

---

[31] Adorno, amongst many others, emphasises the importance of the Orpheus myth, noting that "Gluckian reform went back to Orpheus as the archetype of opera", and he goes on to claim, with justification, that "all opera is Orpheus" (33).

[32] The mythical Orpheus tried, in Conrad's words, to "wheedle death into releasing Eurydice by employing his musical charms [...] he couldn't attain true felicity because he wouldn't consummate love in death, and he lost his Eurydice all over again" (*A Song of Love and Death* 19-20).

Act II of the opera suggests that 'art' is the ultimate reality: truth, perhaps, can be approached through art. There is a reversion back to myth; opera returns to its Greek roots in *Medea* and the figure of Orpheus[33]. This act also sees the culmination of the relentless self-reflexivity of *The Aspern Papers* in the 'performance' of the opera-within-an-opera, *Medea*, which frames this act, thereby foregrounding the opera's meta-operatic elements. *The Aspern Papers* here further extends the epistemological self-regarding of works such as Strauss's *Ariadne auf Naxos* and *Capriccio* into an ontological investigation of the nature of contemporary opera. These epistemological questions culminate in this final act where 'art' is seen as the ultimate reality: 'truth', perhaps, can only be approached through art.

Reading from a copy of Barelli's memoirs, the Narrator outlines the story of the *Medea* while the figures of Aspern, Juliana, Sonia, and Barelli appear on the terrace as they did in Act I – 'dead' figures effectively brought to life through art[34]. They then don the costumes of Jason, Medea, the Princess, and Creon. The self-reflexivity at the heart of the scene is immediately apparent in the estranging effect of having the theatrical characters actually dress in full view of the audience. Here *The Aspern Papers* again casts a glance backwards at Strauss's *Ariadne auf Naxos*, which similarly fuses myth with the 'everyday' in its exploration of the exigencies of operatic performance, as well as the juxtaposition of the comic and the tragic, the sublime and the banal. The

---

[33] With this opera's relentless reversion back to its origins in Greek mythology, there is a strong sense of what Gary Tomlinson describes as opera's return to "a prehistory of musical ritual, musico-dramatic contact with invisible realms, and sung possession" (114).

[34] The physical 'representation' of this opera is described as follows: "*Abandoned by her husband Jason, who plans to marry the King's daughter, Medea's lamentations turn into dark threats. Ordered into exile, she is granted a single day's delay to bid farewell to her children. The King tells Jason and Creusa that their wedding may now proceed. Medea's docile acquiescence may be merely a mask. Employing her sorcery, Medea devises a scheme to destroy her rival. She prepares gifts for the bride imbued with fatal poison. Thrice at the altar of Hecate she invokes the gods of darkness. When Jason arrives for a final visit, Medea pleads with her husband that she be allowed to take their children into exile with her. Jason refuses. Then pleading their welfare she asks that they be permitted at least to take wedding gifts to the Princess, to ingratiate themselves with the royal household. To this, Jason agrees. Delighted with the gifts, Creusa eagerly dons the bewitched mantle. She is seized by convulsions, falls, dies. Too late Jason recognises Medea's treachery. Rushing to her house, he accuses her of the heinous crime. Medea's only response is to go into the house and return with the bodies of the children she has slain.*" (126-145)

shattering of the theatrical illusion (in Brechtian terms) is emphasised by 'exposing' the backstage and normally hidden aspects of operatic representation[35].

In fact, this is the only 'performance' there will ever be of the opera – indeed, a 'meta-operatic' performance – however, it is an appropriately mute one (the stage direction states: *The characters appear to be singing as the 'opera' is performed but no sounds issue from their mouths* (129). The 'narration' takes place on several levels: the verbal text of the Lodger, the unverbalised choral element, the mimed 'action' of the opera, and the orchestra, all combining to produce a 'dramatic' and vivid, yet paradoxically, 'silent' version of the opera, symbolising not only its actual physical fate but perhaps also the symbolic fate of the Orpheus who has lost his voice – perhaps even, the ultimate fate of opera itself!

* * *

The final confrontation between the Lodger and Tina in the opera closely parallels James's concluding dramatic confrontation between the narrator and Tina. The increasing sense of guilt and the pangs of conscience exhibited by the narrator in the tale are suggested in the opera by the series of rhetorical questions that the Lodger poses:

> So that is the price? To marry a ridiculous, pathetic, provincial old maid ... What a strange revulsion grips me! Like a man suddenly awakened by the thought that he had left the house-door ajar or a candle burning under a shelf. Am I still in time to save my goods? Am I still in time? The manuscript seems now more precious than ever; it is absurd to renounce it so easily. But am I ready to pay the price? (208-213)

The title of this scene, "The Score", has something of a typical Jamesian ambiguity with its connotations of success or victory in games-playing, as well as its more direct meaning denoting the manuscript of Aspern's opera. The Lodger's apparent readiness to pay the "price" reflects the theme of financial reward which is an important thematic

---

[35] Of course the tradition of the backstage musical, in which the performance aspects of the genre is explored, has become almost a cliché in both musical theatre as well as film!

concern of the tale. During these reflections of the Lodger, the voice of Tina is heard as she accompanies herself in the song, "No sounds of wheel or hoof-beat" (210), which, as we have seen, was first heard in the Prologue to Act I. The Lodger now recognises it as having been composed by Aspern. This barcarolle sets up a brief musical conflict between Tina's insistent 6/8 rhythm and the Lodger's rapidly moving vocal line, her more relentless rhythm gradually gaining the ascendancy. In his final meeting with Tina in James's tale, the narrator was struck by a change in her. He had left her in a state of acute embarrassment after the failure of her proposal, but now he perceives "a rare alteration in her" (141) which has a startling effect upon him.

This transformation of the appearance of Tina is a projection onto Tina of the narrator's own intense desire to acquire the papers; it is as if through his dedication to art, Pygmalion-like he has brought her, however briefly, fully to 'life', adding a further element of moral ambiguity to his actions[36]. In theatrical terms this is difficult to render, although the opera is able to portray some of this vision of the narrator's in that while Tina sings her song, the Lodger reveals to the audience the effect her appearance has on him. Although Tina's vocal line merges with those of the other four 'characters' and the backstage chorus, her soaring phrases are more prominent as the choral utterances are wordless. Both her lyricism and the lush orchestral accompaniment are also able to suggest something of her momentary radiance: the powerfully enhancing effect that music possesses can convey this brief moment of transcendence for Tina[37].

The dramatic core of this work, as in many operas, is to be found in the many songs[38]. As they sing, the four figures become visible in the cypress grove, wearing their *Medea* costumes; 'life' is being regenerated through art. This song, which the four watching figures sang in the Prologue to Act I, functions as a frame. The events of sixty

---

[36] Cf. Graham, who describes the complexity of cause and effect in this scene in the tale (77).

[37] However, one of the 'problems' of the operatic adaptation is that the beauty of Tina's music tends to convey the impression of a far more dynamic and alluring character than exists in James's tale, even in this moment of transcendence.

[38] Indeed, the use of the song in opera can be seen to have a broad function. There are particular moments of reflexivity in operatic narration which may constitute an "interlude of reflexivity, during which the narrative performance reflects upon the greater performance in which it is embedded" (Abbate 62).

years before have reached their ultimate culmination in the present scene in the music room, and the words of the song are prophetic of the final event of the opera, which is the burning of the manuscript. The destruction of this last link with the past will conclusively dissolve the connection with that "palpable imaginable visitable past" of which James speaks in his Preface to the tale. The relationship between Juliana and Aspern will become nothing more than the subject of anecdote, a footnote in Barelli's memoirs, of less substance than the myth of Jason and Medea. The love between Jason and Medea has at least been immortalised in myth, but the work that was to have immortalised the love between Juliana and Aspern will be nothing more than ashes, less substantial than the "crumbling pages" they sing of in their song.

Tina's final phrase, "And be as if thou hads't not been. Then fade", signals the end of the ensemble, and her next phrase "Good-bye. I hope you will be very happy" (224) ends the whole ensemble in mid-phrase, with the Lodger showing surprise: "I beg your pardon: what did you say?" (225) The narrator in the tale describes his words, "good-bye – Good-bye?" as being uttered "with an inflexion interrogative and probably foolish" (141), which is well captured in the equivalent vocal line of the Lodger.

A musical motif, this time the rising semitone figure that has become directly and unambiguously linked with Aspern, again accompanies this final conversation which, like the previous exchanges between them, takes the form of a flexible recitative. While Tina tells the Lodger that she has burned the manuscript, a similarly easily identifiable 'Medea' leitmotif is heard in the orchestra. The final moments between the Lodger and Tina before the burning of the score have closely followed the tale, and the narrator's observations in the tale become stage directions in the libretto. The opera differs from the tale in that the Lodger wishes to verify the truth of Tina's statement that she has burnt the papers. He:

(*involuntarily moves towards the secretary; checks himself*)
TINA
Oh, you may look if you don't believe me; it isn't locked. (*He doesn't move but continues to stare at the panels, unable to decide.*) You once told me that I couldn't deceive, but perhaps you've changed your opinion. (*For a moment, neither one moves; then suddenly the transformation is over - Tina is again a plain, dingy, older person.*) (227-8)

This final transformation of Tina is accomplished in musical rather than visual terms. The rising semitone phrase which accompanies all of this exchange suddenly stops, and Tina's line, "I can't stay with you any longer" (228), is sung over complete silence in the orchestra, the sudden aural 'gap' suggesting the visual change in her as well as the 'silence' that now exists between them.

Lawrence Holland describes the narrator in the tale as being left alone in a "strangely twisted version of Orpheus' separation from Euridice", who "turns her back on him, but she pauses to look back once, giving him the 'one look' that marks their separation but grips his memory" (154). The narrator, in the tale, keeps the portrait, commenting: "When I look at it I can scarcely bear my loss – I mean of the precious papers." (143)[39] The narrator surely gains some of our sympathy in the process. He has lost the opportunity to live, to consummate the processes of life offered to him by Tina[40].

Tina's final action in the opera is to retrieve the manuscript from within the secretary. The four figures reappear among the cypresses, and there comes the sound of an "indistinct murmuring" (229) from the off-stage chorus as well as a distinctive 'Medea' theme in the violins which makes the connection explicit. She takes one page of the manuscript and sets fire to it with the candle. As she does so, the voice of Barelli is heard: "Ordered into exile, she is granted a single day's delay to bid farewell to her children." (230-1) As Tina lights the next page, Sonia appears singing a line from *Medea* and Barelli disappears. Then Aspern appears singing "Siren singing to siren", and Sonia disappears. Finally Juliana appears and sings: "A hundred years from now, upon a lighted stage, a troupe of singers will enact the ancient legend of our love." (233-5) As a page of the manuscript is burned one of the figures disappears, and after they have all gone, Tina continues burning the manuscript page by page. As the 'text' in

---

[39] It is interesting to note how James altered his first version which was: "When I look at it my chagrin at the loss of the letters becomes almost intolerable." The ambiguity in the second version is increased in the hint that the loss is greater than merely that of the papers.

[40] Booth, however, maintains that "we are left permanently in doubt as to whether he has any suspicion of suffering a more serious loss", the "schemer has shown himself as the chief victim of his own elaborate scheme" (359).

which each character lives disappears, so each of the characters is erased to the sound of their characteristic 'songs'.

The last of the figures (in the cypress grove) to disappear is Juliana/Medea. The tragic myth has been fulfilled: her 'child' (the score/her love for Aspern) is dead. She sings the lines: "A hundred years from, upon a lighted stage, / A troupe of singers will enact / The ancient legend of our love." (233-235) These are the final words of the opera and perhaps signify the transcendence of time by art. However, the destruction of the manuscript has severed the final link with this past. The story of the young Juliana and Aspern, Sonia, and Barelli had, as it were, been conjured up in the memory of the old Juliana at the beginning of the opera, and now it is Tina who lays the 'ghosts' to rest. The opera ends in silence. The room darkens and then the blazing pages cause the room to grow "brighter and quieter" (236), which is Argento's final meta-operatic statement of the artifice that the audience has experienced on stage[41].

The depiction of the destruction of the score is, of course, a telling theatrical gesture, though it is interesting to note a review of the premiere of the opera in *The New York Times* by Bernard Holland (1988) in which he objects to this obvious theatricality[42]. The review is worth quoting at some length, as it makes some provocative points about the difficulties in adapting fiction (and particularly the work of James) for the musical theatre:

> That James's characters are more interesting than Mr Argento's is hardly the composer's fault. Opera is a reductive medium – a purveyor of strong themes and vivid gestures. In Jamesian style, detail creates weight, characters watch other characters and themselves, drawing minute inferences from the turn of a head, a twitching eyebrow, a twinge of conscience or memory, a stress upon a single word in a conversation.
>
> Opera's powers of inference and allusion are more limited. It thrives on the concrete, the palpable. In the novella, for example, the decisive events are not witnessed by the reader; in James's hands, the unseen becomes that much more ominous [...]. James teases us as to the nature of Aspern's papers. Opera, on the other hand, needs something we can see, so it creates a manuscript and waves it in the audience's face [...]. As the novella ends, the Lodger is chilled to hear that the manuscripts have been destroyed the night before. Mr Argento, however, sends him away and then leaves Tina to burn them

---

[41] An ending with significant similarities is found in Moore's *The Wings of the Dove*.

[42] Lawrence Holland sees the burning of the papers in James's tale as the "only act which is now adequate to the tragic experience which has ensued" (152-153).

before our eyes. It is the bold, striking scene James would have abhorred, but the kind that gives opera its visceral – and quite unliterary – appeal.[43]

This view seems too reductive; the opera remains remarkably faithful to the spirit if not the letter of James's tale, and it is debatable whether James 'abhorred' the bold gesture when necessary! The melodramatic impulse remained constant throughout his fiction even if it was not actually physically 'represented' in his later work[44]. Perhaps one could object to Tina's action by arguing that it is inconsistent with the way she is presented in both the tale and the opera. The narrator remarks on a number of occasions that she is so transparently honest and is incapable of deceit that her lying to him now is perhaps psychologically inconsistent with what has gone before if judged purely in terms of psychological realism. However, she has learned the art of 'performance' and deception from two excellent teachers in both Juliana and the Lodger himself[45]. Theatrical as it is, it is important to bear in mind that the burning of the operatic manuscript at the end of the opera needs to be seen in its larger meta-operatic context. This could be seen as Argento's visual dramatisation of the problem of the 'death' of opera – a theme prominent in his opera.

The operatic version of "The Aspern Papers", paradoxically, constitutes a particularly faithful translation of the tale. While departing radically from the original work, it retains and develops many of its themes and concerns, and is peculiarly true to James, in spite of the considerable structural differences. The opera has responded precisely to those elements of fictional self-reflexivity in James's work – his

---

[43] Argento's apparent reason for Tina burning the manuscript was that "Juliana's motivation for suppressing that masterpiece came from [...] the rumor that Helene Berg had hidden Act III of *Lulu* to get even with Alban [her husband] for having an affair with another woman. Aspern's accidental death [...] gives her the opportunity to withhold the work from the world. Why? Out of jealous vengeance? Or as a final tribute to their love? I took James's route and decided to leave the question ambiguous." (qtd. in Sutcliffe 16)

[44] The success of several James films in recent years, even the cinematic adaptations of such notoriously 'difficult' late works as *The Wings of the Dove* and *The Golden Bowl*, are testimony to the inherent theatricality in James's fiction. I have argued elsewhere that it is the constant melodramatic impulse in all of James's fiction that attracts adaptors. (cf. Halliwell 23-34)

[45] One can find a strong parallel with the situation of Catherine in *Washington Square*, a novel that has served as the source for three operatic adaptations as well as several film and television adaptations.

preoccupation with the 'life in literature' in "The Aspern Papers" – in an opera which is concerned with the art form itself on the meta-discursive level, and which exploits traditional operatic devices in a virtual meta-operatic manner. *The Aspern Papers* further extends the epistemological self-regarding of works such as Strauss's *Ariadne auf Naxos* and *Capriccio* into an ontological investigation of the very nature of contemporary opera[46].

Inevitably, a performance of this opera also raises the issue of the validity of musical and vocal lyricism in our postmodern age. Can the desire, and, indeed, the ability to write in an accessible and vocally gratifying style be accepted at face value, and not unavoidably be seen as some form of parody of earlier and what might appear to be outdated operatic forms? This, of course, is not new. Strauss's *Der Rosenkavalier* was seen as similarly conservative and retrogressive at the time of its premiere early in the twentieth century. In spite of these misgivings, a desire for melody, accessible music, and clearly defined theatrical and dramatic values is being answered by contemporary composers and librettists who frequently turn to the great literary resources at their disposal. Only posterity can judge the success of this 'new' direction.

Yet it would seem that operatic conventions have a fundamental and ongoing authority and, indeed, can be seen to be the essence of the art form and are not to be dismissed lightly. An imaginative and creative engagement with these conventions – embodied in many of the great operatic reforms – is what has characterised opera throughout its history; many of the great operatic composers have worked within these conventions, subtly bringing about profound evolutionary change. The radical operatic experimentation that occurred after the Second World War seems to have led into an operatic *cul-de-sac*, and it is through composers such as Benjamin Britten before, and

---

[46] It is in a work such as Argento's opera, that what might appear as the incompatibility of the world of James's fiction and that of opera is, in my opinion, most successfully resolved. James's subtle, internalised and complex consciousnesses would seem to be the antithesis of the melodramatically exaggerated characters that opera demands. However, it is opera's ability effectively to externalise and present the intense emotional and psychological situations central to James's fiction which appears to resolve this paradox. James's synthesis of melodrama and psychological ambiguity makes his work peculiarly amenable to operatic adaptation. James's concern with the ingredients of his art is evident in his constant foregrounding of the art of fiction itself. It is precisely to this aspect of James's work that Argento has responded, revealing a comparable concern with the conventions of his own art.

now Argento and Corigliano, amongst others, that new, viable, and possibly enduring operatic paths may be forged.

References

Abbate, Carolyn. *Unsung Voices: Opera and Musical Discourse in the Nineteenth Century.* Princeton: Princeton Univ. Press, 1991.
Adorno, Theodor. "Bourgeois Opera". David J. Levin, trans. *Opera Through other Eyes.* David J. Levin, ed. Stanford: Stanford Univ. Press, 1994. 25-43.
Argento, Dominick. *The Aspern Papers.* London: Boosey & Hawkes, 1991.
Bell, Millicent. *Meaning in Henry James.* Cambridge: Harvard Univ. Press, 1991.
Berio, Luciano. "Of sounds and images". David Osmond-Smith, trans. *Cambridge Opera Journal* 9.3 (1997): 295-299.
Booth, Wayne C. *The Rhetoric of Fiction.* Chicago: Univ. of Chicago Press, 1961.
Brooks, Peter. *The Melodramatic Imagination.* New Haven: Yale Univ. Press, 1976.
Conrad, Peter. *Romantic Opera and Literary Form.* Berkeley: Univ. of California Press, 1977.
—. *A Song of Love and Death: The Meaning of Opera.* New York: Poseidon, 1987.
Graham, Kenneth. *Henry James: The Drama of Fulfilment.* Oxford: Clarendon, 1975.
Halliwell, Michael. "'The Master's Voice': Henry James and Opera". John R. Bradley, ed. *Henry James on Stage and Screen.* Basingstoke: Palgrave, 2000. 23-34.
Holland, Lawrence B. *The Expense of Vision: Essays on the Craft of Henry James.* Princeton: Princeton Univ. Press, 1964.
James, Henry. *The Notebooks of Henry James.* F.O. Matthiessen and Kenneth B. Murdock, eds. Chicago: Univ. of Chicago Press, 1947/1974.
—. *The Aspern Papers and The Turn of the Screw.* Harmondsworth: Penguin, 1984.
—. "From Chambéry to Milan". John Auchard, ed. *Italian Hours.* University Park: Pennsylvania State Univ. Press, 1992.
Katz, Ruth. *The Powers of Music: Aesthetic Theory and the Invention of Opera.* New Brunswick/London: Transaction, 1994.
Kirk, Elise K. *American Opera.* Urbana/Chicago: Univ. of Illinois Press, 2001.
Lindenberger, Herbert. *Opera: The Extravagant Art.* Ithaca: Cornell Univ. Press, 1984.
—. "From Opera to Postmodernity: On Genre, Style, Institutions." M Perloff, ed. *Postmodern Genres.* Norman: Univ. of Oklahoma Press, 1989. 28-53.
Maves, Carl. *Sensuous Pessimism: Italy in the Work of Henry James.* Bloomington: Indiana Univ. Press, 1973.
McHale, B. *Postmodernist Fiction.* London: Routledge, 1989.
Miller, J. Hillis. "Speech acts in "The Aspern Papers". *Textual Practice* 9.2 (1995): 243-267.
Rowe, John Carlos. *The Theoretical Dimensions of Henry James.* London: Methuen, 1985.

Said, Edward. *Musical Elaborations*. New York: Columbia Univ. Press, 1991.
Sutcliffe, James Helme. "The Argento Papers". *Opera News* 53.5 (November 1988): 14-18.
Tomlinson, Gary. *Metaphysical Song: An Essay on Opera*. Princeton: Princeton Univ. Press, 1999.

APPENDIX

The Aspern Papers
Libretto and music by
Dominick Argento

World Premiere: Dallas Opera: 19 November, 1988. Music Hall, Dallas, Texas

CHARACTERS

In 1835

Juliana Bordereau, an opera singer	soprano
Aspern, a composer	tenor
Barelli, an impresario	bass-baritone
Sonia, a singer; Barelli's mistress	mezzo-soprano

In 1895

Juliana, now an elderly recluse	soprano
Tina, her niece	mezzo-soprano
The Lodger, a critic and biographer	baritone
Pasquale, his servant and gardener (*also Painter*)	bass
Olimpia, a maid (also off-stage voice of Juliana in Prologue II)	soprano

Act One
Prologue: *Quintet* (1895) (Early summer)
Juliana, a former opera singer, recalls events of sixty years before, particularly her dead friends: the impresario Barelli (a former lover); Sonia, Barelli's mistress; and the composer Aspern, her great love who drowned in the lake.
1. *The Lodger* (1895)
The Lodger arranges with Juliana and her niece, Tina, to rent rooms in the villa. Tina describes Juliana's background and career, and he explains his interest in Aspern.
2. *Quartet* (1835) (midsummer)
Aspern is having his portrait painted, watched by Barelli while Juliana rehearses a scene from Aspern's opera *Medea*. Barelli asks Aspern to look after Sonia while he is away.
3. *The Portrait* (1895)
The Lodger reveals his frustration at not having had much contact with Juliana or Tina while hinting at his true object. When they arrive, Juliana suggests that the Lodger take Tina out. Juliana shows him the portrait of Aspern. The Lodger, afraid that Juliana might destroy Aspern material, requests Tina to get hold of any material there may be.

4. *Trio* (1835) (late summer)
Aspern is rehearsing Sonia while Juliana gives her vocal advice. While Juliana leaves, Aspern and Sonia reveal their dilemma concerning their love for each other as well as their respect for Juliana. They arrange a meeting that night – Sonia is to put a candle in her window so that he can be guided across the lake.

5. *The Music Room* (1895)
The Lodger and Tina return from an excursion into the town. Juliana is ill, and the maid summons Tina to Juliana's bedside. The Lodger, alone, moves towards the secretary in which he believes the papers are kept. He is confronted by Juliana, who collapses.

Act Two
Prologue: *The Lost Medea* (1895)
The Lodger reads from Barelli's memoires and reveals that he believes that the lost manuscript of Aspern's opera, *Medea*, could be at the villa.

1. *Duo* (1835) (the end of summer)
Aspern has finished the opera and presents it to Juliana. She suspects his relationship with Sonia and allows the boat to drift away from its mooring. He swims across the lake and is drowned.

2. *The Proposal* (1895)
The Lodger learns of the death of Juliana. Tina reveals the existence of material which she will give him in exchange for marriage. He refuses.

3. *Solo* (1835) (early fall)
A silent and mourning Juliana indicates to Barelli that she wishes to retire and that the *Medea* manuscript has been burnt.

4. *The Score* (1895)
The Lodger, tempted by his desire for the manuscript to agree to marriage with Tina, returns, but she reveals that she has already burnt it. After he leaves, page by page, she burns the manuscript.

Schubert's Strategies in Setting Free Verse

Jürgen Thym, Rochester

> Schubert found some ingenious strategies to cope with the problem of setting free verse. Sometimes he renders the verses as prose (through recitative), but often he is able, through musical forces, to make the lines of free verse "audible" (i.e., he composes them as poetry), and occasionally he shapes the text, again through musical forces, into audible structures suggesting an interpretation of the text that contradicts or goes beyond the poet's poetry. Several of Schubert's Goethe and Klopstock settings will serve as examples.

Free verse is a contradiction in terms. What makes this kind of poetry verse, and what makes it free? And if it is verse, why is it free? Anglo-American and German critics differ considerably in their handling of this question, defining free verse in different ways, and even within both traditions there is a great deal of disagreement. This is not the place to explore the various approaches to free verse; let me simply say that for the purpose of this study I am working with a definition that might be termed **visual** or **graphic**.

In its most provocative form – and I am borrowing here from John Hollander (*Rhyme's Reason* 1) – the visual definition sees free verse as a narrow strip of print constrained only by the need not to exceed too far to the right-hand margin of the page. This definition plays, of course, into the hands of those who regard free verse as prose chopped pretentiously into lines to make it look like poetry. But despite its flippancy, the definition has some merits. Phrased in a more dignified way, it means that the presence of line boundaries signals to the reader that the lines are to be read with the conventions our particular tradition has developed for reading poetry. Furthermore, the line boundaries offer the reader a basis for such a reading. The end/beginning of one line, for example, can be compared to the end/beginning of another; the beginning of a line can be compared to its end; the relation of syntax to line structure can be observed, with the concomitant presence or absence of enjambments; the syntax can be compared to 'normal' syntax, etc. Hollander explores some of these possibilities in several chapters of *Vision and Resonance* (1985) and Charles Hartman works with a version of this definition when he defines poetry inclusively as "language in lines" and free verse as lines organized by non-metrical patterns (11 and 24-25, respectively)[1]. Despite its virtues, this definition raises the real and important question whether free verse can be set **as** free verse, and whether settings of free verse can be distinguished from settings of prose. Nevertheless, I found this visually based definition of free verse most useful for approaching the question of how poetic form affects musical form in free verse settings.

Figure 1 lists all of Franz Schubert's free verse settings. Not surprisingly, perhaps, they constitute only a small fraction of Schubert's settings, hardly a dozen of a total of around 600 songs; moreover, several attempts at setting free verse did not reach the state of completion. Obviously, free verse presented problems and difficulties for a musical idiom that relied very much on regular phrases and periods. The bulk of Schubert's settings falls between 1815 and 1819; most of the poems are by Johann Wolfgang von Goethe, two by Friedrich Gottlieb Klopstock, and one each by Schubert's friend Johann Mayrhofer, as well as Gotthard Ludwig Kosegarten, Novalis, and Ossian in a German translation.

Even though some of the years during which Schubert set free verse, especially the years 1815 and 1816, show a clear preference for strophic settings in his overall output, it is not surprising that free verse poetry does not lend itself to the strophic variety. Instead, Schubert preferred to set free verse as well as prose in through-composed, sectional, cantata-like settings, often involving recitative. It is difficult and perhaps futile to construct a 'development' of Schubert as a composer of free verse. The reasons are obvious: first of all, the time during which he set free verse is short; second, the settings are too few; and third, the poems vary greatly, making very different demands on the composer. For that reason, I thought it appropriate simply to describe Schubert's main strategies for dealing with the compositional problems that free verse presents for

---

[1] A more detailed account of free verse can be found in Wesling (cf. esp. 145-171), Hobsbawn (cf. esp. 89-120), and Beyers.

Figure 1: Schubert's Settings of Free Verse

The settings listed feature unrhymed verse with irregular line lengths and varied arrangements of stressed and unstressed syllables. The list includes poems that meet these criteria, even if they are not written in stanzas of equal lines. (In parentheses are poems that are not irregular enough to be unequivocally considered free verse.)

Title	Poet	Date of Composition	Deutsch Thematic Catalog Number	Gesamtausgabe Location
Szene aus Faust	Goethe	1811-14	D126	GA I 215/9
(Kolmars Klage)	Ossian	1815	D217	GA II 161
Dem Unendlichen	Klopstock	1815	D291	GA III 85
An Schwager Kronos	Goethe	1816	D369	GA IV 204
Das große Halleluja	Klopstock	1816	D442	GA IV 110
(Aeschylos-Fragment)	Mayrhofer	1816	D450	GA IV 128/31
(An die untergehende Sonne)	Kosegarten	1816	D457	GA IV 134
Ganymed	Goethe	1817	D544	GA V 75
Hymne	Novalis	1819	D659	GA VI 42
Prometheus	Goethe	1819	D674	GA VI 71
(Grenzen der Menschheit)	Goethe	1821	D716	GA VI 185
Fragments:				
(Gesang der Geister)	Goethe	1816	D484	GA X 106
Mahomets Gesang	Goethe	1817	D549	GA 110
Mahomets Gesang	Goethe	1821	D721	GA 125

his idiom. Rather than attempting to describe these in the abstract, I should start by looking at two songs, which I have chosen because of the very different kinds of free verse they present, because of the contrasting means for setting them, and also because I think they are some of the more successful settings of free verse by Schubert. My samples are settings of Klopstock's *Dem Unendlichen* and Goethe's *Ganymed*.

Klopstock's poem *Dem Unendlichen* (fig. 2) consists of five stanzas of exalted speech, a sermon in the tradition of Milton's *Paradise Lost* or Abraham a Santa Clara, singing praises to God's majesty. The abundance of imagery and the exuberance of rhetorical devices are typical of Klopstock's free verse poetry. Each of the stanzas has four lines; the lines vary greatly in length. Particularly noticeable in *Dem Unendlichen* are the many enjambments; in only a very few lines does the end of a thought coincide with the end of the line.

Enjambments in free verse, of course, are *Augenpoesie* or poetry for the eye (in analogy to *Augenmusik*), since rhyme and regular meter – devices that signal to the listener line boundaries – are absent in this type of poetry. We can easily perceive enjambments in free verse when we **see** them on the page, but whether we can **hear** them (and whether the composer can make them audible) is a different matter and a difficult question, and we will return to this point later. This mechanism of perception, of course, has consequences for the musical setting of free verse, and we shall see that Schubert in general disregards the line structure unless it coincides with the syntactical units of the poem.

Klopstock's poem can clearly be divided into two sections: stanzas 1 and 2 address the Infinite, and stanzas 3 through 5 address various manifestations of the Infinite in Nature. The difference is underscored through differences in the rhetorical style the poet uses. In the first two stanzas we find a juxtaposition of contrasts through which the poet creates space and distance between God and Man ("wie erhebt [...] wie sinkt [...]"; "Unendlicher [...] Elend, Nacht, Tod [...]"; "unten am Grab [...] oben am Thron"). The sentence structure is complicated by elisions and parenthetical remarks resulting in syntactical tensions that often go beyond the confines of individual lines (lines 2-4 of stanza 2, for instance, express one lengthy exalted statement); the line structure occasionally is in conflict with the syntax and obscures (or rather, syncopates) the obvious parallelisms of syntactical units (e.g., "wie erhebt" at the beginning of line 1 and "wie sinkt" at the end of line 2 in stanza 1).

We encounter a different rhetorical style in the second section of the poem. By and large, the syntax is less complex than in stanzas 1 and 2. Parallel constructions prevail ("Weht, Bäume des Lebens [...] Rausche mit ihnen, kristallner Strom"; "Donnert, Welten [...] Tönt all ihr Sonnen [...]"); moreover, the parallelism of syntactical units is now enhanced rather than thwarted through the line structure. End-stopped lines rather than enjambments are characteristic of the smoother rhetorical style of the second section; only the last climactic stanza picks up the elated rhetoric and enjambments of the first section.

Figure 2: "Dem Unendlichen" (Translation adapted from Ring of Words *158-59)*

Wie erhebt sich das Herz, wenn es dich,
Unendlicher, denkt! Wie sinkt es,
Wenns auf sich herunterschaut!
Elend schauts wehklagend dann, und Nacht und Tod!

Allein du rufst mich aus meiner Nacht, der in Elend, der im Tod hilft!
Dann denk ich es ganz, daß ewig mich schufst,
Herrlicher! den kein Preis, unten am Grab', oben am Thron,
Herr Herr Gott! den, dankend entflammt, kein Jubel genug besingt.

Weht, Bäume des Lebens, im Harfengetön!
Rausche mit ihnen ins Harfengetön, kristallner Strom!
Ihr lispelt, und rauscht, und, Harfen, ihr tönt
Nie es ganz! Gott ist es, den ihr preist!

Donnert, Welten, in feyerlichem Gang, in der Posaunen Chor!
Du Orion, Wage, du auch!
Tönt all' ihr Sonnen auf der Straße voll Glanz,
In der Posaunen Chor!

Ihr Welten, donnert
Und du, der Posaunen Chor, hallest
Nie es ganz, Gott; nie es ganz, Gott,
Gott, Gott ist es, den ihr preist!

Textual Changes in Schubert's setting: 2/1 "Tode" instead of "Tod"; 2/2 "daß <u>du</u> ewig"; 2/4 "Herr" only once; 4/1 "Welten, donnert in feierlichem Gang, Welten, donnert in der Posaunen Chor"; 4/2 omitted; 5/1 „ihr Welten, <u>ihr</u> donnert"; 5/2 „Und" omitted.

Translation:

How my heart leaps when it thinks
of Thee, O Infinite One! How it sinks
when it looks down upon itself!
Mourning it sees, then, misery and night and death!

But Thou callest me out of my night, Thou who provides support in misery and in death!
Then it comes over me that Thou createst me for eternity,
Noble One! for whom no praise, below in the grave, above in the throne,
Lord, Lord God! glowing with thanks, no rejoicing is sufficient.

Wave, trees of life, with the sound of the harp!
Roar with them in the sound of the harp, o crystal stream!
No matter how it murmurs and throbs, harps, your sound
Is never enough! God is it whom ye praise!

Thunder, worlds, in your solemn course; in the chorus of trumpets,
thou Orion, Libra, thou as well!
Sound forth, all suns in your shining row,
In the chorus of trumpets.

Ye worlds, thunder,
And you, chorus of trumpets, resound,
Never enough, God, never enough, God,
God, God is it whom ye praise!

The first two stanzas addressing the Infinite are composed by Schubert as recitative (ex. 1). The harmonic, rhythmic, and melodic flexibility of the recitative allows Schubert to follow the speech rhythm of the poem. He sets the syntactical units of the stanzas to vocal phrases of varying length, marking each of them with instrumental insertions reminiscent of the majestic slow section of a French overture or improvisatory figures that one might encounter in a C.P.E. Bach or Ludwig van Beethoven Fantasy. In other words, he composes this section of the poem as prose. The recitative style is not arbitrarily superimposed on the stanzas; on the contrary, the musical prose of the recitative corresponds well to the structural and rhetorical qualities of the text.

Stanzas 3 through 5 are composed as song. The smoother rhetorical style of this section as well as the parallel constructions, at least at the beginning of the section, may have suggested the different vocal idiom (ex. 2). With the tetrameter line "Weht, Bäume des Lebens, ins Harfengetön!" Schubert establishes a clear-cut, four-measure phrase (mm. 22-26), which is repeated with some rhythmic adjustments, speeding up the declamation, for the hexameter line "Rausche mit ihnen ins Harfengetön, kristallner Strom!" (mm. 26-30) Having established the four-measure phrase structure as boundary or norm for his setting of stanza 3, he now is even able to bring out the enjambment of lines 3 and 4 (or, to refer to my earlier formulation, to make it "audible") by extending the next phrase to five measures and thereby emphasizing the prominently placed word "nie" at the beginning of line 4 (m. 34). In setting the exalted conclusion of the stanza ("Gott ist es, den ihr preist!"), Schubert briefly returns to a form of recitative style (mm. 35ff).

Stanza 4 is, by and large, a repeat of stanza 3 transposed down a fourth. Here Klopstock's free verse is apparently too free for Schubert's needs, and for that reason he regularizes the poem drastically. In order to maintain the parallelisms that resulted in two four-measure phrases in the setting of stanza 3, Schubert omits "Du Orion, Waage, du auch!" altogether and rewrites the first two lines as pentameters: "Welten, donnert in feierlichem Gang / Welten, donnert in der Posaunen Chor." Lacking the emphatic text that he set to recitative at the end of the third stanza of stanza 3, Schubert here moves directly into stanza 5.

Example 1: "Dem Unendlichen", mm. 1-10

Example 2: "Dem Unendlichen", mm. 22-37

Example 3: "Dem Unendlichen", mm. 54-71

Stanza 5 is a summary statement: all the verbal material presented here has been introduced in earlier stanzas ("Donnert Welten [...] in der Posaunen Chor [...] nie es ganz [...] Gott ist es, den ihr preist"), but the material is rendered here in an ecstatic syntax full of exclamation and almost stammering repetition. (It may be difficult to find another lyric poem in which the same word occurs three times in a row.) Schubert marshals what we may want to consider a most felicitous musical device in order to balance the tension between line structure and syntax caused by the enjambments in this stanza (ex. 3). While the piano continues its accompaniment in triple meter (most clearly seen in the bass), the vocal part performs a hemiola pattern, pitting itself against the triple meter (mm. 57-63); this allows the singer to give declamatory emphasis to the exalted statements "hallest nie es ganz; Gott, nie es ganz, Gott, Gott, Gott ist es". For the setting of "den ihr preist", Schubert returns in the vocal line to the closing formula of stanza 3, but brings it now in augmentation, thereby giving it climactic weight.

Ganymed (fig. 3) has been analyzed so often by literary scholars that we can confine ourselves here to a few remarks concerning the overall structure of Goethe's famous paean[2]. Goethe divides his poem into five stanzas, of which the second and fourth are only couplets. Because of their visual appearance, the couplets function within the poem as punctuation marks, as it were, setting off the three larger sections as well as inviting comparisons between the couplets, on the one hand, and the larger sections, on the other. The couplets, indeed, mark important stages in the basic progression of the poem, beginning with Ganymede's vague stirring to reach out for the Other, a yet undefined "Du" of the poem ("Dass ich dich fassen möcht"), and his decision to reach out to the Other, though still fearful of the direction his longing will take him ("Ich komm", and "Ach, wohin?"). Stanzas 1 and 3 go into detail on the origin of the longing. The first describes the experience in exalted rhetoric and convoluted syntax, identifying the object of desire in lines 3 and 8 as masculine ("Frühling, Geliebter") and as feminine ("Unendliche Schöne"). The third stanza fleshes out the pantheistic feelings in more

---

[2] Goethe/Trunz (485-87) and Lugowski provide a good introduction. The reader also should be alerted to the substantial writings on "Ganymed" (Goethe and the settings by Schubert and Wolf as well as their relation to tropes encoding issues of sexuality and desire) by Lawrence Kramer (cf. "The Schubert Lied" 200-236; *Music as Cultural Practice* 165-175; and *Franz Schubert* 93-128).

Figure 3: "Ganymed" (Translation adapted from Ring of Words *62-65)*

Wie im Morgenglanze	In the bright light of the morning,
Du rings mich anglühst,	How you glow at me,
Frühling, Geliebter!	Spring, beloved!
Mit tausendfacher Liebeswonne	With love's thousand-fold joys
Sich an mein Herz drängt	My heart is filled
Deiner ewigen Wärme	By your eternal warmth's
Heilig Gefühl,	Hallowed emotion,
Unendliche Schöne!	infinite beauty!
Daß ich dich fassen möcht'	O that I might embrace you
In diesen Arm!	In my arms!
Ach, an deinem Busen	Ah, on your bosom
Lieg' ich, schmachte,	I lie, languishing,
Und deine Blumen, dein Gras	And your flowers, your grass,
Drängen sich an mein Herz.	Press against my heart.
Du kühlst den brennenden	You cool the burning
Durst meines Busens,	Thirst of my bosom,
Lieblicher Morgenwind!	delightful morning breeze.
Ruft drein die Nachtigall	The nightingale calls
Liebend nach mir aus dem Nebeltal.	Lovingly to me from the misty valley.
Ich komm', ich komme!	I come, I'm coming!
Wohin? Ach, wohin?	To where? Ah, to where?
Hinauf! Hinauf strebt's,	Upward, upward I strive!
Es schweben die Wolken	The clouds float
Abwärts, die Wolken	Down, the clouds
Neigen sich der sehnenden Liebe.	Bow down with yearning love
Mir! Mir!	To me! To me!
In eurem Schoße	Into their lap,
Aufwärts!	Upwards!
Umfangend umfangen!	Embracing, embraced!
Aufwärts an deinen Busen,	Upwards to Thy bosom,
All-liebender Vater!	All-loving father!

Textual Changes in Schubert's setting: 1/5, "Herze" instead of „Herz"; 3/2, "lieg' ich und schmachte"; 4/2, "Ach, wohin? Wohin?" (change of word order); 5/1, "Hinauf strebt's, hinauf!" (change of word order); textual repetitions of 5/1 and 5/3-10.

concrete images of Nature as "Blumen", "Gras", "Morgenwind", and "Nachtigall", as well as through a more discursive syntax. Stanza 5 brings Ganymede's ascent and final union with the Deity in a rhetorical style full of incomplete sentences and exclamation marks capturing the ultimate ecstasy he finds as his yearnings are fulfilled. As many critics have noted, this union draws androgynously on both male and female images of Nature and the Deity, and it projects the experience as both active and passive: "umfangend umfangen" are perhaps the keywords of the poem.

Schubert's song exemplifies another approach to setting free verse: using musical structures as containers in which the vocal lines are embedded and allowing the lines to be shaped by the correspondences of these musical structures. The setting of the first three lines of *Ganymed* is a case in point (ex. 4). Schubert starts in the piano with an utterly conventional eight-measure prelude that can be broken down into two four-measure phrases establishing antecedent and consequent. This model immediately begins to repeat just before the voice enters; the last measure of the first period (m. 8) is also the first measure of the next. Rather than bringing another antecedent-consequent pair, Schubert now doubles the antecedent phrase to produce identical "containers" for the first two very different lines of the poem. Because the second line has one syllable less than the first, the vocal line can be repeated literally only by giving two pitches to one of the syllables of the second line, and Schubert very felicitously brings the melisma on the word "du, thereby highlighting what must be considered the essence of the poem. (*Ganymed* is a poem about love and yearning for the Other, the "Du" that is addressed in ever changing ways during the course of the poem.) Closure of the double antecedents is reached with an extension of three measures presenting the line "Frühling, Geliebter" over a dominant pedal and cadencing in A-flat major. It is noteworthy that Schubert relates both words that identify the "Du" to each other by means of a sequence, producing a kind of musical 'rhyme'. And it is equally noteworthy that the motive that is sequenced is a diminution of the melisma on the word "du". In other words, developmental procedures borrowed from the tradition of instrumental music are used here as a means of shaping free verse, creating correspondences and underscoring the relations of the words "du", "Frühling", and "Geliebter".

Example 4: "Ganymed", mm. 1-18

The last five lines of the first stanza are a grammatical monster that hardly makes sense at first reading, and only by reversing the order of the lines – by turning them into prose, so to speak – can we comprehend the meaning of the sentence (fig. 4). The unusual word order, the near-incomprehensibility of the lines is, of course, a rhetorical strategy by the poet to bring out the stammering, ecstatic quality of the feelings

Figure 4: "Ganymed": First stanza reorganized as prose

Unendliche Schöne,	Endless beauty,
Das heilig Gefühl	the hallowed emotion
Deiner ewigen Wärme	of your eternal warmth
Drängt sich an meine Herz	presses on my heart
Mit tausendfacher Liebeswonne!	with thousand-fold raptures of love!

conveyed by the poem's persona. No setting would be able to enhance the comprehensibility of the lines, and Schubert does not even attempt this (ex. 5). Instead he groups the highly irregular lines into two pairs (mm. 19-23 and 23-27) and uses the last line to achieve closure in C-flat major, the key of the next section (mm. 27-31). The lines "mit tausendfacher Liebeswonne" and "sich an mein Herz(e) drängt" are set identically, and "deiner ewigen Wärme" and "heilig Gefühl" also receive similar settings. These four lines, that is, produce two similar but contrasting phrases (we may say that they 'rhyme' musically), while "unendliche Schöne!" is set off by a different

Example 5: "Ganymed", mm. 18-31

piano texture and a different vocal style which already foreshadows the conclusion of the song on "all-liebender Vater!" We may quarrel with Schubert about the declamatory problems caused by the way he shapes free verse here into two pairs of corresponding lines. The way he treats "Liebeswonne" is somewhat flippant, and the emphasis on "an" rather than on "Herz" appears to be an oddity, but his setting has the advantage of cutting through the syntactical complexities of the lines as if through a Gordian knot, and on a different level they reinforce, through musical 'rhymes', the meaning of the lines, that is, the synonymity of the imagery. After all, "Liebe", "Herz", "Wärme", "Gefühl", and "Schöne" are metaphors that stand for the same emotional striving, the longing for a "Du".

The overall form of the setting has been commented on by Lawrence Kramer ("The Schubert Lied" 224; *Franz Schubert* 122-127), and in continuation of his lucid comments on the tonal disposition and its interpretive implications, I offer a few additional remarks. *Ganymed* is indeed highly sectional and, except for the climactic last section, without large-scale repetitions. Schubert's division into four sections of varying length, centering around A-flat major, C-flat major, E major, and F major, however, contradicts Goethe's design in quite a number of ways (see brackets in fig. 5).

The two couplets that group Goethe's lines visually into five separate sections and that provide important clues for the interpretation of the poem are appropriated in Schubert's setting by the larger sections that follow them. The music of the second couplet (ex. 6) initiates the perpetual eighth-note motion that becomes the driving force and unifying factor of the finale, even leads into the next section with an accelerando and functions harmonically as a dominant preparation of the final key of F major, which, as Kramer has pointed out, underscores the question-answer relation between the second couplet and the last stanza – indeed the turning point in the poem.

While this is a most felicitous device of musical interpretation, Schubert's other structural junctures come in for some questioning. The first couplet is a case in point (ex. 7). The first couplet ("Dass ich dich fassen möcht / in diesen Arm!") is joined with the first two lines of the next section ("Ach an deinem Busen, / lieg ich, (und) schmachte") by identical settings. Schubert's solution may be questioned on several

Figure 5: "Ganymed" – Musical Structure

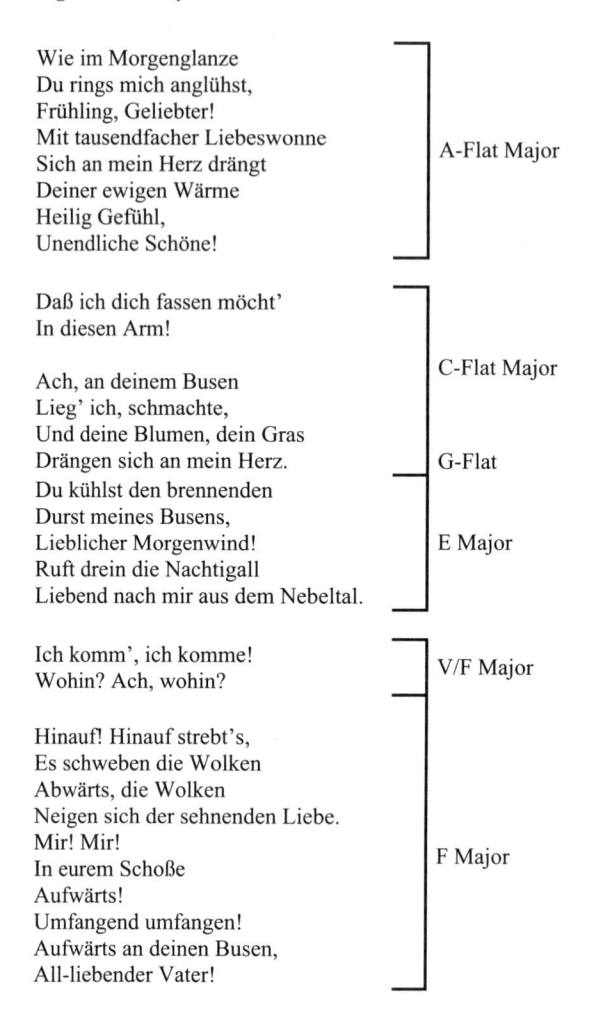

Wie im Morgenglanze Du rings mich anglühst, Frühling, Geliebter! Mit tausendfacher Liebeswonne Sich an mein Herz drängt Deiner ewigen Wärme Heilig Gefühl, Unendliche Schöne!	A-Flat Major
Daß ich dich fassen möcht' In diesen Arm!	C-Flat Major
Ach, an deinem Busen Lieg' ich, schmachte, Und deine Blumen, dein Gras Drängen sich an mein Herz.	G-Flat
Du kühlst den brennenden Durst meines Busens, Lieblicher Morgenwind! Ruft drein die Nachtigall Liebend nach mir aus dem Nebeltal.	E Major
Ich komm', ich komme! Wohin? Ach, wohin?	V/F Major
Hinauf! Hinauf strebt's, Es schweben die Wolken Abwärts, die Wolken Neigen sich der sehnenden Liebe. Mir! Mir! In eurem Schoße Aufwärts! Umfangend umfangen! Aufwärts an deinen Busen, All-liebender Vater!	F Major

Example 6: "Ganymed", mm. 68-75

Example 7: "Ganymed", mm. 32-41

grounds. The "dich" and "deinem" in these lines refer to two different kinds of "Du", because the implicit gestures of the couplet reach out or up, whereas stanza 3 describes the gesture of embrace. Goethe's poem, that is, is constructed as a puzzle that waits until the last stanza – in fact, the last line – to coalesce the contradicting personifications of the "Du", whereas for Schubert, as is evident from his settings of the first three lines of stanza 1, the identity of all the "Du's" is clear from the beginning. Schubert no doubt reduces some of the richness of the poem here.

The beginning of the E major section in Schubert's setting likewise contradicts Goethe's design (ex. 8). Schubert considers the lines "Du kühlst den brennenden Durst / meines Busens, / lieblicher Morgenwind" to be a turning point in the poem and highlights his interpretation, perhaps overemphasizing it, through what appears at first glance to be superficial word-painting. The relation of the trills to the breezes of the morning wind and of the sixteenth-note figure (not shown in ex. 8) to the beckoning calls of the nightingale is a little too obvious. And yet, it is really the very concrete images of Nature that lead Ganymede to merge his pantheistic feeling with the desire for union with his all-loving father. This point of view is underscored by the fact that the perpetual eighth-note motion mentioned earlier as the unifying feature of the final section has its origins in the left hand of the piano exactly on the word "Morgenwind".

Changes in texture contribute very much to the sectionalism of the setting as well as to offsetting key words and key lines in the poem. Schubert begins his song almost as an independent piano piece that becomes the carrier or container for the vocal part (ex. 4), resulting in a peculiarly passive quality with which the persona of the setting introduces himself (cf. Seelig). When Ganymede's stirrings become more active ("Dass ich dich fassen möcht"), the texture changes to the typical voice-plus-accompaniment variety (ex. 7), that is, leaving space for the vocalist to gain prominence. Finally, in the last section, voice and piano join forces in presenting the same melody in the ultimate union of Ganymede with his Father (ex. 9). In other words, the textural changes very much support the emotional development described in the poem from a vague, inarticulate perception of longing to more active and concrete stirrings to the final fulfillment in the "umfangend umfangen" union with the Deity. The final arrival on the words "all-liebender Vater" is marked through extensive melismas and a chordal texture that

Example 8: "Ganymed", mm. 46-56

Example 9: "Ganymed", mm. 105-121

harkens back to the setting of "unendliche Schöne" at the end of the first section (compare exs. 5 and 9), thus underscoring the identical rhythm of both lines, as well as creating musical correspondences between the female and male poles of Ganymede's yearning.

By way of summary and conclusion, I would like to make a few comments on Schubert's choices of vocal styles (of recitative and song) for his setting of free verse. For a composer of the early nineteenth century, though not necessarily for a Lied composer of the nineteenth century, recitative is an obvious strategy for setting free verse, and Schubert uses it fairly frequently. (His setting of Goethe's "Prometheus", for instance, alternates recitative and song-like sections in response to the different rhetorical strategies which the poet uses for his verses of defiance.) To make this choice, I think, is in a way to set free verse as prose. Recitative is formulaic; it offers no obvious ways of translating into music the kinds of boundaries that lines bring to free verse, and it does not encourage listeners to listen for formal and semantic meanings in melodic curves and harmonies. It just gets the text across. It does, however, preserve the syntactic and rhetorical emphases of sentences, much as prose does as well. (By admitting, then, that to choose recitative is in a sense to treat free verse as prose, I am not excluding the possibility that the recitative can heighten, modify, or otherwise contribute to the expressivity of the language set. But recitative signals to the listener a set of game rules very different from those the listener uses to approach other kinds of setting.)

In most cases, however, Schubert sets free verse as song. When he does so, melody, rhythm, and harmony willy-nilly become forces that shape the text. (In addition to the beginning of *Ganymed*, Schubert's setting of Goethe's *An Schwager Kronos*, with the vocal part grafted on a perpetual motion in the piano, pursues a similar strategy.) Extending the metaphor of recitative as prose, and drawing on Hartman's definition of verse as language in lines, I would like to suggest that resources of song thereby create what can be seen as the functional equivalent of rhyme, or meter, or line. Sometimes Schubert uses these formal resources in ways that reinforce the poem, sometimes in ways that go beyond the original, contradict it, or set it aside in favor of purely musical considerations. At other times, Schubert takes a fairly Procrustean approach to free verse by lopping off phrases, adding repetitions and syllables, and ignoring line boundaries in ways that make the texts more regular or establish new formal schemes. Although this technique may make lovers of poetry squirm, it often allows him not only to fulfill formal needs but also to interpret the poem. In other cases, however, Schubert uses his resources in analogy to the formal features that contribute to the meaning of the original poem. In free verse, as laid out initially, line boundaries present a fundamental tool for the poet, making expressive enjambments possible, as well as other parallels and contrasts between syntax rhythms and line structure. Although Schubert ignores many of these line boundaries, he often finds ways of translating those that make prominent contributions to the sense of expressivity of the poems.

The kinds of tensions between syntax, line boundaries, and rhythms that justify the word "verse" in the term "free verse" find their analogy – but not their imitation – in the very different relations Schubert establishes between the words of the poems and the formal resources of music. To refer to my prose/poetry analogy one last time, Schubert's non-recitative settings set his texts as poetry, but not necessarily as the poet's poetry[3].

References

Beyers, Chris. *A History of Free Verse*. Fayetteville: Univ. of Arkansas Press, 2001.
Fehn, Ann Clark, and Jürgen Thym, "Repetition as Structure in the German Lied: The Ghazal and its Musical Settings". *Comparative Literature* 41.1 (Winter 1989): 33-52.
Fehn, Ann Clark, and Rufus Hallmark. "Text and Music in Schubert's Pentameter *Lieder*: A Consideration of Declamation". *Studies in the History of Music I: Music and Language*. New York: Broude Brothers, 1983. 204-246.

---

[3] This essay originated as a lecture co-authored with the late Ann C. Fehn as part of a project, undertaken jointly by Fehn, Rufus Hallmark, and myself, studying the impact of poetic forms on the setting of lieder in the nineteenth century. Several of these studies have been published: Hallmark/Fehn, "Text Declamation in Schubert's Settings of Pentameter Poetry"; Fehn/Hallmark, "Text and Music in Schubert's Pentameter *Lieder*"; Fehn/Thym, "Repetition as Structure in the German Lied"; and Thym/Fehn, "Sonnet Structure and the German Lied".

Goethe, Johann Wolfgang. "Dem Unendlichen". *Franz Schubert: Die Texte seiner einstimmig komponierten Lieder und ihre Dichter*. Vol. I. Maximilian and Lilly Schochow, eds. Hildesheim: Olms, 1974. 219-20.
—. "Ganymed". *Gedichte*. Erich Trunz, ed. and comments. Munich: C.H.Beck, 1993. 46-47.
—. *Gedichte kommentiert von Erich Trunz*. Munich: Beck, 1994.
Hallmark, Rufus, and Ann Clark Fehn, "Text Declamation in Schubert's Settings of Pentameter Poetry". *Zeitschrift für Literaturwissenschaft und Linguistik* 9 (1979): 80-111.
Hartman, Charles. *Free Verse: An Essay in Prosody*. Princeton: Princeton Univ. Press, 1980.
Hobsbawn, Philip. *Metre, Rhythm and Verse Form*. London and New York: Routledge, 1996.
Hollander, John. *Rhyme's Reason*. New Haven and London: Yale Univ. Press, 1989.
—. *Vision and Resonance*. 2nd ed. New Haven and London: Yale Univ. Press, 1985.
Kramer, Lawrence. *Franz Schubert: Sexuality-Subjectivity-Song*. Cambridge: Cambridge Univ. Press, 1998.
—. *Music as Cultural Practice 1800-1900*. Berkeley and Los Angeles: Univ. of California Press, 1990.
—. "The Schubert Lied: Romantic Form and Romantic Consciousness". Walter Frisch, ed. *Schubert: Critical and Analytical Studies*. Lincoln: Univ. of Nebraska Press, 1986.
Lugowski, Clemens. "Goethe: Ganymed". *Interpretationen 1: Deutsche Lyrik von Weckerlin bis Benn*. Jost Schilleweit, ed. Frankfurt/Main and Hamburg: Fischer, 1965. 47-64.
The Ring of Words. Philip L. Miller, ed. New York: Norton Library, 1973.
Schochow, Maximilian and Lilly, eds. *Franz Schubert: Die Texte seiner einstimmig komponierten Lieder und ihre Dichter*. 2 vols. Hildesheim and New York: Olms, 1974.
Seelig, Harry E. "Hugo Wolf's 'Ganymed': An Emancipated Musical Androgyne for Our Time?" Unpublished lecture. German Studies Conference. Albuquerque, New Mexico, 1986.
Thym, Jürgen, and Ann Clark Fehn, "Sonnet Structure and the German Lied: Shackles or Spurs?" *Journal of the American Liszt Society* 32 (1992): 3-15.
Wesling, Donald. *The New Poetries: Poetic Form Since Coleridge and Wordsworth*. London and Toronto: Associate Univ. Presses, 1985.

False Assumptions
Richard Strauss's Lieder and Text/Music Analysis

Suzanne M. Lodato, New York

When I first began work on text-music relations in the songs of Richard Strauss, I proceeded from an assumption typically made by musicologists who conduct art song analysis – namely, that the musical setting in an art song directly engages poetic structure and semantic meaning either by straightforwardly reflecting these elements or working clearly against them. But close examination of the music and text of Strauss's songs revealed that his musical settings often have little to do with poetic style. Instead, his musical language is analogous to that resulting from German naturalistic prose techniques, particularly Arno Holz's *konsequenter Naturalismus* ("consistent naturalism"), which was characterized by such thoroughgoing depiction of minute detail that readers of his prose works were often unable to maintain a coherent perspective. Both the episodic nature and discontinuous textures of Strauss's musical style reflect this "consistent naturalism" more often than they reflect the structure or semantic meanings of the poems; in turn these techniques imbue the song text with new meanings. Using two of Strauss's lieder as examples, I illustrate that in the investigation of song, analytical models must take into account the possibility that the most important text/music relationships will be those outside the immediate scope of direct correspondences between poetry and music.

Although research into the area of music/literature relationships has expanded rapidly over the past fifteen to twenty years, little attempt has been made to place these relationships in a historical context by examining how a particular style of poetry or a literary movement may have influenced the overall musical style of a composer who sets that poetry. My study of Richard Strauss's (1864-1949) middle-period lieder – that is, those written between 1894 and 1906 (Lodato, "Richard Strauss and the Modernists") – has revealed that the techniques of *fin-de-siècle* Germanic naturalist and impressionist literature strongly influenced the development of his musical style, which was distinguished by extensive use of sudden textural changes; prolonged, unprepared, unresolved dissonance; episodic writing; graphic pictorial representation by musical means; and what has been called "rapid, disjunct and often fragmented *parlando* [that] verges at times on melodrama" (Crawford 34). Assessing this repertory from the standpoint of contemporary literary techniques yields valuable insights not merely into musico-poetic relationships, but more importantly into Strauss's style as a product of *fin-de-siècle* European culture. As strong as these relationships are, though, their nature is not immediately evident if one takes the fairly typical approach of seeking direct correspondences between poetic and musical styles, structures, or meanings[1]. Close examination of the music and texts in Strauss's songs reveals that such suppositions often yield little meaningful information, because Strauss's musical settings are often weakly related (or totally unrelated) to the styles of their poetic texts. Rather, Strauss's song settings reflect his interest in the German literary modernist agenda in a larger sense, as well as in reconstituting certain modernist prose and poetry techniques into a new musical language that could suit texts from any era or style.

This essay outlines the intellectual framework for the poetry written by members of the modernist literary circle, discusses two important German modernist literary techniques, and illustrates how they influenced Strauss's musical style in two poetry settings.

* * *

Fin-de-siècle commentators noted a marked change in style in Strauss's lieder beginning with op. 27 in 1894, two years after Strauss's first encounters with the German anarchist and naturalist poet John Henry Mackay (1864-1933) and other Berlin modernist poets. The four songs of op. 27 occasioned Strauss's first settings of verse by contemporary German modernist poets: Mackay, Heinrich Hart (1855-1906), and the socialist poet Karl Henckell (1864-1929), and a spate of lieder settings of modernist

---

[1] In previous work ("Recent Approaches to Text/Music Analysis"), I have discussed the tendency of musicologists who perform melopoetic analyses of song literature to adhere music theorist Kofi Agawu's pyramidal model, in which the analyst assumes that the words at the top provide the basis for the meaning of the song, while the music acts as a reinforcement of that meaning (Agawu 6-7). I began my study of Strauss's middle-period songs making the same set of assumptions. The fact that such an approach proved to be ineffective in analyzing work and music relationships in Strauss's songs does not mean that Agawu's pyramidal model lacks validity. The work for the WMS series by Thym (see this volume), Seelig, and Dougherty illustrates that the pyramidal approach rewards analysts with new insights, whether they are examining metrical relationships (Thym), diverse interpretations of one of Goethe's best-known poems (Dougherty), or relationships among several Hölderlin fragments as constructed by Britten (Seelig).

poetry followed[2]. His opp. 27-44 (1894-99) are distinguished by a preponderance of modernist settings, which comprise 30 out of the 45 songs in these opuses[3]. Opp. 48 and 49 (1900-01) are also dominated by modernist poetry. Several writers noted that Strauss was probably the first lieder composer of the late-nineteenth century to turn to the works of contemporary modernist poets as inspirations for his song composition (Bie 258; Bischoff 95; Bücken 156), and several critics traced a gradual change in his musical style that reflects Strauss's choice of Berlin poetry beginning with op. 27[4]. Only Arnold Schoenberg, who set a large number of poems by Dehmel and Stefan George, among other contemporary poets, and Conrad Ansorge, who also set Dehmel's poetry extensively, placed as much emphasis on the settings of modernist poetry as Strauss. For other contemporaries of Strauss, such as Alexander Zemlinsky, Max Reger, Hans Pfitzner, and Franz Schreker, these poems did not form a major part of their lieder output. These observations and assessments by Strauss's contemporaries and the clear evidence of his interest in modernist poetry seemed to signal that contemporary modernist German poetry caused Strauss to develop musically modernist techniques during the 1890s and early 1900s. But investigations into the agendas and practices of contemporary poets revealed that their work did not meet the expectations generated by their theories.

---

[2] The poetry of the following modernists was set by Strauss in opp. 27-56: Hart, Mackay, Henckell, Detlev von Lilencron (1844-1909), Gustav Falke (1853-1916), Richard Dehmel (1863-1920), Otto Julius Bierbaum (1865-1910), Paul Remer (1887-1943), Carl Busse (1872-1918), Anton Lindner (1874-1929), Conrad Ferdinand Meyer (1825-98), Christian Morgenstern (1871-1914), Emanuel von Bodman (1874-1946) and Oscar Panizza (1853-1921).

[3] Namely, poetry by Henckell, Mackay, Bierbaum, Busse, Dehmel, Liliencron, and Falke.

[4] Gysi looked upon Strauss's contemporaries as having 'provide[d] him the raw materials whereby late Romanticism and realism meet' ["liefert ihm den Rohstoff, wobei Spätromantik und Realismus sich begegnen"] (20). Bücken divided Strauss's lieder output into three phases, the first culminating in op. 22, the second in op. 56, and the last comprising his "late songs". Bücken's "second phase" corresponds to the period that contains all of Strauss's modernist settings and contains several songs in what Bücken terms "impressionistic" style (156-60). Examples are "Traum durch die Dämmerung", Henckell's "Ruhe meine Seele" (op. 27/1, 1894), and Bierbaum's "Freundliche Vision" (op. 48/1, 1900). Bie considered opp. 27 and 29 to be the first high points of Strauss's song output, and Bischoff judged op. 27 to be the most important of Strauss's lieder compositions (Bie 258-259, Bischoff 94). Schuh remarks upon the unusual number of songs Strauss composed from 1894 to 1901 (opp. 27-49) (435-60).

Members of the literary modernist circle, which had formed in Berlin in the 1880s, abnegated what they defined as the empty sentimentality of the highly popular *Münchener Dichterschule*. These Munich School poets, under the patronage of King Maxmillian II of Bavaria (1811-64), wrote poetry characterized by beauty and formal mastery but little substantial content. According to Heinrich and Julius (1859-1930) Hart, two of the earliest *Naturalisten*, the poetry of the Munich writers was divorced from material reality, fleeing into sentimentality, beauty, and dreams (*Kritische Waffengänge*)[5].

In contrast, the naturalist poets found their inspiration in positivism and French naturalism. For them, human behavior was determined entirely by inherited and environmental elements and functioned in accordance with laws of nature rather than the spirit. These *Naturalisten* aimed to depict all facets of day-to-day life, embracing its most mundane or ugliest aspects, endeavoring to portray working class miseries almost clinically, without moral stance or resolution. Many wrote of the experience of the *Großstadt*, portraying their struggles to make sense of the rapid changes in Berlin life as the city mushroomed into a metropolis. The manifestos that served as a preface to their seminal anthology, *Moderne Dichter-Charaktere* (1885), called for socially-informed subject matter and rejected outmoded, time-worn forms and motives. The *Münchener Dichterschule* concentrated on aesthetic and formal values, employing stanzaic structures, classical meters, and rhyme schemes. Aiming to depict the commonplace in contemporary life, the *Naturalisten* proposed to eschew these traditional techniques and features in favor of a freer poetic form and style that allowed for stanzas and line lengths of varying length, more prose-like meters, and darker subject matter that reflected the experiences of the poor and working classes in burgeoning metropolises like Berlin.

However, despite the Berlin circle rhetoric, almost none of the approximately 220 poems in *Moderne Dichter-Charaktere*, nor those of many other early German literary naturalists, conform to the gritty, realistic subject matter or the departure from

---

[5] The Harts were referring to such writers as Felix Dahn (1834-1912), Paul Heyse (1830-1914), Emanuel Geibel (1815-84), and Hermann von Lingg (1820-1905).

traditional form and poetic language called for in the manifestos of the *Naturalisten*. The traditionalist orientation of these self-described modernist poets was the first stumbling block in my own project. The subject matter, language and structures of the poems in Strauss's op. 27 – Hart's "Cäcilie" and Henckell's "Ruhe, meine Seele!" (both published in *Moderne Dichter-Charaktere*), and Mackay's "Heimliche Aufforderung" and "Morgen" – reveal none of the changes in poetic language that these poets so vociferously demanded. Of the four, only "Ruhe, meine Seele", the first of the set, reflects the German literary modernist program of the 1880s in its reference to the protagonist's deep unrest as well as the momentous and distressing times in which he lived. Henckell's language probably refers to the political and social challenges to the primarily urban-based Social Democrats during the *Gründerzeit*. (Henckell was active in socialist politics, an interest that he shared with many naturalist poets, although unlike him, they tended merely to pay lip service to such commitments[6].)

Not only were many of the naturalist poems traditional in form, structure, and use of language; Strauss actually favored such poems. Even when Strauss did set a poem written in the naturalistic (or later, impressionistic) style, his music did not necessarily reflect that style directly in the poetry setting, and conversely, modernist musical techniques are just as likely to turn up in Strauss's settings of romantic or folksong poetry.

A closer examination of "Ruhe, meine Seele" illustrates the conservative approach of Henckell and other early naturalists, as well as the types of poetry techniques that attracted Strauss to a poem for setting (fig. 1)[7]. Henckell's twenty-four line poem is tightly organized by a consistent trochaic dimeter and rhymes at the end of each four-line group. Although the poem consists of one long stanza, punctuational stops occur

---

[6] Throughout the late 1880's and early 1890's, Berlin naturalists affected a political stance, expressing support for the Social Democrat party, whose activities had been outlawed by Bismarck in 1878. Some naturalist poets became actively involved with socialist politics. For example, Henckell studied Marxism and met Social Democrat emigrés during his stay in Zurich. He often wrote *Gelegenheitsgedichte* ("occasional poetry") for Social Democrat meetings and events. The 1893 *Buch der Freiheit*, edited and compiled by Henckell, was commissioned by the Socialists. Also, Arno Holz's (1863-1929) self-designation as a *Tendenzpoet* ("partisan poet") situates him with politically active socialists. See Schutte, 24, referring to Arno Holz's poem "Selbstporträt," which appears on p. 78 of *Lyrik des Naturalismus*.

[7] All translations are mine unless otherwise noted.

Figure 1: "Ruhe, meine Seele!" ("Rest, My soul!")
Karl Henckell, published 1885

Nicht ein Lüftchen,	No small breeze,
Regt sich leise,	Gently stirs,
Sanft entschlummert	Softly asleep
Ruht der Hain;	Rests the grove;
Durch der Blätter	Through the dark covering
Dunkle Hülle	Of the leaves
Stiehlt sich lichter	The luminous sunshine
Sonnenschein.	Steals away.
Ruhe, ruhe,	Rest, rest
Meine Seele,	My soul,
Deine Stürme	Your storms
Gingen wild,	Went wild,
Hast getobt und	You have raged and
Hast gezittert,	You have trembled,
Wie die Brandung,	Like the surf,
Wenn sie schwillt!	When it swells!
Diese Zeiten	These times
Sind gewaltig,	Are violent,
Bringen Herz und	They bring distress
Hirn in Noth –	To heart and mind –
Ruhe, ruhe,	Rest, rest,
Meine Seele,	My soul,
Und vergiß	And forget
Was dich bedroht!	What threatens you!

every four lines, except at line 12, where the absence of an end-line stop creates an eight-line group in the middle of the poem. Not only the tight construction, but also the frequent alliteration and the repeat of the lines "Ruhe, ruhe, / Meine Seele" unify the poem.

The structure of the poem would lead one to expect a closed, tune-like melody, neatly sectioned off into balanced, periodic phrases, perhaps organized into antecedent/consequent relationships, with clear cadences at larger sectional demarcations. One might also expect a fairly consistent rhythmic pattern around which the vocal line is structured, supported by an accompaniment pattern, perhaps with a repeating figure that accents the typical strong beats of the four-beat-per-measure pattern.

Instead, Strauss sets this tightly conceived poem to a highly flexible, almost speech-like melody, in which phrase lengths are asymmetrical, running counter to those of the poem. Some phrases begin 'early' or 'late' in relation to previous phrase patterns. Strauss replaces a number of metrical accents with prosaic speech accents, but then distorts the speech rhythm by means of lengthening or shortening syllables and creating unusual inflections by employing large intervals that are out of place in the context.

Distortion of syllabic length, pitch inflection, and even prosaic syllabic accents were seen in nineteenth-century lieder, but in the songs of such predecessors as Franz Schubert, Robert Schumann, and Johannes Brahms, such treatment of the language served to conform the text to underlying metric and rhythmic patterns that formed the basis for closed melodic structures. The accents and inflections of the poetry were absorbed by symmetrically-based, tuneful melodies whose closed nature reflected the single, dominating *Stimmung* of the lyric poem.

Strauss often violates this tradition of lyric poetry setting by composing melodic lines similar to the endless melodies of Richard Wagner's music dramas (and the songs of Franz Liszt and Hugo Wolf). In Wagner's "endless melody", each pitch is intended to be meaningful and necessary; that is, pitches that simply fill out a symmetrical phrase pattern or fulfill a cadential formula are avoided, a practice that results in an open-ended, flexible melodic line that conforms closely to word accents. But while Strauss's vocal lines are rhythmically and metrically flexible, his technique differs from Wagner's in that his declamation often distorts the inflection and rhythm of the words, even if, as in the case of "Ruhe, meine Seele", he himself often chooses to supplant poetic meter with prosaic speech rhythms. In other words, Strauss chooses highly structured poetry, 'corrects' its rhythms and inflections to bring them more closely to prosaic speech accents, then in turn distorts those 'corrections'. How and why might Strauss have developed this technique of setting poetry, and what could have stimulated him to do so?

The answers lie in the practices of later literary naturalists. These practices are most cogently articulated in the writings of the poet and author Arno Holz (1863-1929).

Before 1885, Holz's works, like those of most other naturalists, were innovative only in terms of subject matter, not form or technique. The formal mastery of the *Münchener Dichterschule* poet Emanuel Geibel (1815-84) had served as Holz's model early in his career. When in 1885 Holz became one of the first naturalists to become disenchanted with socialism as the catalyst for societal revolution, he turned to aesthetic considerations, promoting a revolution in literary style instead. Because, like other poets, he had difficulty reconciling lyric expression with the rendering of day-to-day experience, he focused on prose and drama and returned to poetry later on (Völker 211).

While working on prose, he developed theories of writing based on what he called *konsequenter Naturalismus* ('consistent naturalism'), which he first put into practice in the 1889 short-story collection, *Papa Hamlet*, co-authored with Johannes Schlaf (1862-1941). In *Papa Hamlet*, Holz and Schlaf's consistent naturalism involves the most detailed depiction possible of visual and aural experience, background, and behavior as it changes moment by moment. Adalbert Hanstein dubbed consistent naturalism *Sekundenstil* (that is, a style in which "time and space are portrayed second by second") (157, qtd. in Brands 122), and Heinrich Hart defined *Sekundenstil* somewhat deprecatingly thus:

> A chain of individually executed, minute descriptions of situations, outlined in a prose language that seeks to cling steadfastly to reality by renunciation of every rhythmic or stylistic effect, in true reproduction of every noise, every breath, every pause – that was what the new technique aimed for. And the new technique was at the same time the new art.[8]

> He [Holz] used the example of a leaf falling from a tree to explain his ideas. The old kind of art could only say of the falling leaf that it sinks to the ground in a spiraling motion. The new art describes this process second by second; it describes how the leaf, illuminated on one side, appears red, on the other a shadowy grey, and how, a second later, this is reversed; it describes how the leaf first falls vertically, then is blown to one side, then falls vertically again, it describes – heaven knows what else it has to report.[9]

---

[8] "Eine Kette von einzelnen ausgeführten, minutiösen Zustandsschilderungen, geschildert in einer Prosasprache, die unter Verzicht auf jede rhythmische oder stilistische Wirkung der Wirklichkeit sich fest anzuschmeigen sucht, in treuer Wiedergabe jeden Lauts, jeden Hauchs, jeder Pause – das war es, worauf die neue Technik abzielte. Und die neue Technik war zugleich die neue Kunst." (Hart, "Literarische Erinnerungen" 68, qtd. in Brands 122).

[9] "Er entwickelte seine Ansicht am Beispiel eines vom Baume fallenden Blattes. Die alte Kunst hat von dem fallenden Blatt weiter nichts zu melden gewußt, als daß es im Wirbel sich drehend zu Boden sinkt. Die neue Kunst schildert diesen Vorgang von Sekunde zu Sekunde; sie schildert, wie das Blatt, jetzt auf dieser Seite vom Licht beglänzt, rötlich aufleuchtet, auf der andern schattengrau erscheint, in der nächsten Sekunde ist die Sache umgekehrt, sie schildert, wie das Blatt erst senkrecht fällt, dann zur Seite getrieben

Holz and Schlaf present trivia in a seemingly indiscriminate manner. Neither the narrator nor the reader can distinguish important from unimportant details; the action appears to lack direction. Readers can find the sheer volume of minutiae in these stories particularly strange or disturbing precisely because the authors present so much more detail than can be observed in day-to-day experience (Osborne 44-47). As John Osborne states: "The *Sekundenstil* deprives us of the possibility of a panoramic view; it expresses, though it does not state explicitly, a sense of loss and anxiety in a fragmented world." (47)

An excerpt from "Der erste Schultag", written by Holz in 1887 and published in the *Papa Hamlet* collection, presents an early example of this style (fig. 2)[10]. Violent subject matter, realistic language, wealth of detail, and multiple perspectives characterize this passage. The constantly fluctuating surface detail in the narrative depicts characters' shifting psychological states (Pascal 157).

This passage highlights a particularly effective technique of disorienting the reader – multiple perspectives, which are seen in an early example of *erlebte Rede* (literally, 'experienced speech'). *Erlebte Rede* is basically equivalent to free indirect speech, a narrative technique that temporarily dispenses with the objective narrator who provides the reader with landmarks, such as 'he said', 'they thought', etc., in relaying the story. Instead, the narrator loses authorial distance from the character and tells the story from within the character's perspective. The reader must ascertain such shifts from changes in grammar and content. The excerpt from "Der erste Schultag" contains examples of this technique. Only the phrase the "crazy Jewish dog" ("Wahnsinnigen Judenhund") in line 9 indicates that the point of view is the schoolteacher's rather than the students' or the narrator's, while the "huge, red room" ("die ganze, grosse, rothe Stube") in lines 14-15 shows that point of view has shifted to that of the student Lewin.

---

wird, dann wieder lotrecht sinkt, sie schildert – ja, der Himmel weiß, was sie sonst noch zu berichten hat." (Hart, "Literarische Erinnerungen" 69, qtd. in Osborne 43).

[10] Pascal presents a detailed analysis of this excerpt on p. 157 of "Arno Holz, *Der erste Schultag*". He use the version of the story published in Holz's and Schaf's *Neue Gleise* in 1892 (the entire *Papa Hamlet* collection was published in *Neue Gleise*).

Naturalist poets encountered more difficulties meeting their goals in poetry than in prose, but they persisted in attempting to develop poetic techniques that would produce the same effects as consistent naturalism did in prose. By the late 1890s, Holz had returned to writing poetry and promoting a revolution in poetic style. He and other naturalist poets did not completely break with the conventions of lyric form, but they did make changes in poetic technique during the 1880s and 1890s that featured renunciation of rhyme; attempts to employ a more natural, prose-like syntax and rhythm while continuing to observe some metrical conventions; supplanting strophic form by dissimilar and irregular sections and verses; and the inclusion of a large number of banal, fleeting images as influenced by Holz's use of consistent naturalism in his prose works (Völker 230).

The linguistic and expressive flexibility of these innovations particularly suited the *Großstadtlyrik*, which, like the *Großstadtroman* ("poem" or "novel" "about the metropolis"), stressed the constant, quick and frequent shift of events in urban life (Pascal, *From Naturalism to Expressionism* 143). However, as Völker illustrates using an excerpt from Henckell's poem "Im Café" (1888) as an example, the attempt to mix traditional rhyme with depictions of minute detail and fragmented images often resulted in rhythmic clumsiness:

Gläser klirren,
Plaudereien schwirren,
Übers Billard saust der glatte Ball;
Zigaretten glimmen,
Blaue Wölkchen schwimmen,
Flinke Kellnerschöße überall.[11]

---

[11] Glasses clink,
Small talk hums,
The glossy ball whizzes over the billiard table;
Cigarettes glow,
Small blue clouds float,
Waiters briskly darting everywhere.
Quoted from Schutte 141, in Völker, 229.

Figure 2: "Der erste Schultag" ("The First Day of School")
Arno Holz, (1887)

Der Herr Rektor Borchert hatte sich jetzt aufrecht mitten auf sein Podium gestellt. Seine Lippen waren weiss geworden. Seine kleinen, spitzen Zähne knurrschten, als ob er an etwas kaute.
"Herkommen, Knubbel?!"
Aber der kleine Lewin hörte nichts mehr. Er lachte nur immer und lachte und lachte ...
Jetzt endlich war der Geduldsfaden des Herrn Rektor Borchert mitten entzwei gerissen! Mit einem Satz war er auf den wahnsinnigen Judenhund zugesprungen, hatte ihn an seinem schmierigen Jackenkragen zu packen gekriegt und schleifte ihn nun wuthschnaubend auf sein Katheder.
"So ein Hund !! So ein Hund!!!"
Die "Knubbels", die wieder ganz muckchenstill geworden waren, hatten alle unwillkürlich ihre Augen fest zugemacht. Die ganze, grosse, rothe Stube schwamm jetzt in Blut. In Blut. Oh! ...
Da!!
Plötzlich, mitten durch all das grausenhafte Schnauben und Gurgeln vorn, hatte draussen vom Flur her deutlich ein feines, schrilles Glöckchen angeschlagen.
Kein "Knubbel", der nicht jetzt seine kleinen, rosa Oehrchen spitzte!
Das reine Christglöckchen! Es klingelte jetzt, dass es nur so eine Art hatte.

Headmaster Borchert had now placed himself in the middle of his lectern. His lips had become white. His small, pointed teeth ground together as if he chewed on somethng.
"Come here, blockhead?!"
But little Lewin [Jewish student] heard nothing more. All he did was laugh and laugh and laugh ...
Now Headmaster Borchert's patience was finally torn in half! With a leap he had pounced onto the mad Jewish dog, caught him by his greasy jacket collar and, now foaming with rage, dragged him to his desk.
"Such a dog! Such a dog!!!"
The "blockheads," who had again become completely silent, had all involuntarily shut their eyes tightly. The whole, huge, red room now swam in blood. In blood. Oh! ...
There!!
Suddenly, in the midst of all the gruesome snorting and gurgling in the front of the room, a fine, shrill little clock had struck clearly from the corridor.
There was no "blockhead" who did not now prick up his tiny, pink ears!
The pure little clock with Christ on it! It chimed now; only it had such a sound.

The most radical solution to this problem was offered by Holz himself, who turned to experiments with blank verse and what he called *notwendiger Rhythmus* ('necessary rhythm') (Holz, *Revolution* 29, 62-63). Holz aimed to rid modern poetry of rhythm for its own sake, but because he viewed rhythm as the fundamental poetic element, he sought in each poem the 'necessary rhythm', which 'grows newly from the content each time, as if nothing else before it had ever been written' (Holz, *Revolution* 44-45)[12]. The difference between necessary rhythm and prose lies in the poet's concern for effects of sound that prose lacks. Holz gives as an example the prose sentence, "Der Mond steigt hinter blühenden Apfelbaumzweigen auf" ('The moon rises behind blooming apple tree branches'), which is transformed into the poetic lines:

Hinter blühenden Apfelbaumzweigen

steigt der Mond auf.

In the latter version of the sentence, writes Holz, the sound and the content are one: 'The first sentence only reports, the second represents' (Holz, *Revolution* 44-45)[13]. This poetic line, which employs necessary rhythm, brings into relief the shadows of the branches against the moonlight, while at the same time strengthening the force of the moon's image by creating a caesura at the end of the first line and a stronger accent on "steigt" than was present in the prose sentence. Dividing the sentence after "Apfelbaumzweigen" creates a four-syllable phrase that contains three strong accents. In addition, the strengthened accent on "steigt", as well as its closer proximity to its prefix, "auf", shifts the reader's focus to the sense of the moon's ascent. In this way, Holz uses rhythm to express content rather than rhythm for its own sake[14].

---

[12] "...wächst, als wäre vor ihm irgend etwas anderes noch nie geschrieben worden, jedes mal neu aus dem Inhalt".

[13] "Der erste referiert nur, der zweite stellt dar".

[14] Note also that Holz has centered the two lines in the latter version of the sentence. This realignment exemplifies Holz's *Mittelachsenverse* or *Mittelachsenlyrik* ('middle axis verse' or 'middle axis poetry'), that is, verse or poetry in which words are centered instead of lined up along the left margin (*Revolution der Lyrik* 29, 62-63). Holz's *Mittelachsenverse*, particularly as seen in his poetry collection, *Phantasus* (1899), enabled him to convey content by illustrating "tone pictures" (*Lautbilder*) typographically (*Revolution der Lyrik* 29). Aligning verses along an imaginary middle axis rather than along the left margin also allowed Holz to juxtapose lines of radically different lengths while facilitating ease of reading (*Revolution der Lyrik* 62).

When I reconsidered these literary practices in light of Strauss's musical style, the rationale behind the composition of "Ruhe, meine Seele" and similar songs in Strauss's output became clear. It is this combination of consistent naturalism and necessary rhythm found in the literary experiments of the later German naturalists that characterizes the musical style of Strauss's middle-period lieder, even when the poetry that he set did not contain these characteristics. In Strauss's lieder, 'truth' of expression by means of non-periodic phrasing, partial resistance to set forms, and frequent and fleeting textural changes takes precedence over the 'beauty' of form, periodic phrasing and consonant harmonies. The first set of musical features correlate with the characteristics of consistent naturalism and necessary rhythm, in which the rhythms of poetic language are generated by content rather than metrical formulae, and attention to mundane detail can blur the poem's affective focus.

I return to "Ruhe, meine Seele" to show how Strauss applied these techniques to musical poetry settings. In this reading of the poem, Strauss imparts a conversational flow to the metrical poetic language by enjambing groups of two lines, creating phrases that are longer than those in the poem. In the song setting, the first four lines comprise a pair of two-measure phrases, yet the sense of balance between the two phrases is undermined by their non-parallel rhythmic profiles (mm. 4-7) (ex. 1). Then, after setting up an expectation of two-measure units, Strauss immediately defeats it beginning in line 5 by shortening the setting of lines 5-6 to a measure-and-a-half (mm. 8-9). Syllabic accents are also altered: the phrases "Nicht ein Lüftchen" and "durch der Blätter" drift in on the weak beats of their respective measures, "nicht" and "durch" deprived of their strong poetic stresses in favor of more realistic speech accentual patterns. "Leise", "sanft", and "stiehlt" are lengthened out of proportion to their lengths in the poem, but in keeping with their importance in establishing the mood of these first lines. Measures 4-5 (lines 1-2: "Nicht ein / **Lüft**-chen regt sich / **lei**-se") and 8-9 (lines 5-6: "**durch** der Blät-ter dunk-le / **Hül**-le") almost sound as if they are triple meter, further strengthening the impression of a flexible metric and rhythmic setting of the text[15]. The next line

---

[15] I thank David Francis Urrows for pointing out the triple-meter setting of these lines.

Example 1: "Ruhe, meine Seele!"

Richard Strauss, op. 27/1, 1894, mm. 1-13

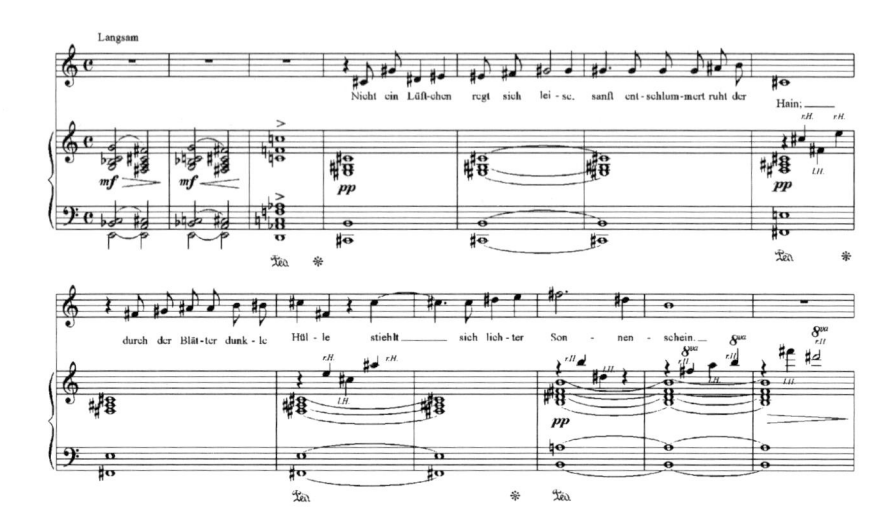

(line 7) begins 'early' (m. 8) on "stiehlt", which is disproportionately long (two-and-a-half beats), and the length of "Sonnenschein" (mm. 9-12) is extended so that lines 7-8 now span three-and-a-half measures. Line 7 not only begins 'early,' but each note of the entire phrase is lengthened as the pitch ascends to a climactic and extended F-sharp, the highest pitch in the song so far, on "Sonnenschein". Overall, accentuation is carefully placed to conform not to the poetic meter, but to speech accents. But the speech accents that Strauss highlights become undermined themselves by distortions in the lengths and inflections of individual syllables or words, as well as odd, disjunct leaps in pitch that seem out of place in the surrounding melodic profile. The rest of the poetic lines are set similarly. However, by no means has Strauss undermined the overall structure of the poem. For example, by employing this "triple meter" in mm. 4-5 and 8-9, he reinforces the poetic structure by creating a parallel between the poem's beginning line, which is the first of a four-line section ending in a semicolon, and the fifth line, which begins another four-line section ending in a period. Furthermore, the extended F-sharp on "Sonnenschein" demarcates clearly the end of the first eight-line section of the poem. In keeping with Holz's aims, Strauss altered and freed textual rhythms without transforming Henckell's poem into prose.

Subtle examples of Strauss's musical consistent naturalism can also be seen in this song, in which Strauss assigns brief, unprepared mimetic or color effects to a few words. The large descending minor-seventh leap on "Hain" reveals the peaceful, protective, tomb-like nature of the grove, while pointillistic, high-pitched single notes in the piano part that anticipate the sun's rays recur in seemingly random fashion under "Hülle", "stiehlt", and "Sonnenschein". Later, on "wild", ripping grace note figures in the bass line of the accompaniment suddenly color the word. They will reappear, growing in intensity during the middle section of the song. As is the case with Holz's consistent naturalism, effects are fleeting and unprepared. The listener's focus is suddenly drawn to moments within the larger picture. Strauss differs from Holz in his sparse use of such techniques, but his judicious employment of pinpoint musical mimesis or coloration within the short form of the song distracts the listener from the overall *Stimmung* of the poem quite effectively.

Another setting of Henckell's poetry – "Das Lied des Steinklopfers" – exemplifies Strauss's application of both of these techniques in a slightly different way (fig. 3). As is the case with "Ruhe, meine Seele", "Steinklopfers" consists of a traditionally strict metric pattern (iambic dimeter), rhyme scheme and verse structure, although the subject matter is contemporary, reflecting Henckell's interests in socialist politics. This *Arbeitsgedicht* (worker poem) or *Soziallyrik* (socialist poem) actually benefits from its strict, confining, rhythms that depict the monotonous and hopeless existence of the stonecutter. The *moto perpetuo* staccato accompaniment in Strauss's setting directly reflects the onomatopoetic effects brought about by Henckell's use of alliteration, hard consonants, words of one or two syllables, and the strict iambic dimeter of Henckell's lines.

Although it is aurally provocative, this correspondence between musical style and words offers less of interest than the means by which Strauss combines these mimetic

Figure 3: "*Das Lied des Steinklopfers*" ("*Song of the Stonecutter*")
Karl Henckell, published 1899

Ich bin kein Minister,	I'm no minister,
Ich bin kein König,	I'm no king,
Ich bin kein Priester,	I'm no priest,
Ich bin kein Held;	I'm no hero;
Mir ist kein Orden,	To me no orders,
Mir ist kein Titel	To me no title
Verliehen worden	Has been granted
Und auch kein Geld.	And no money either.
Dich will ich kriegen,	I will fight you,
Du harter Plocken,	You hard block,
Die Splitter fliegen,	The splinters fly,
Der Sand stäubt auf –	The sand dust rises –
"Du armer Flegel,"	"You poor brat,"
Mein Vater brummte,	My father growled,
"Nimm meinen Schlägel;"	"Take my mallet,"
Und starb darauf.	And died.
Heut' hab' ich Armer	Today I, poor man,
Noch nichts gegessen,	Have yet had nothing to eat,
Der Allerbarmer	The All-merciful
Hat nichts gesandt;	Has sent nothing;
Von gold'nem Weine	Of golden wine
Hab' ich geträumet	I've dreamt
Und klopfe Steine	And hammer stones
für's Vaterland.	For the Fatherland.

techniques with both consistent naturalism and necessary rhythm to yield the kinds of effects that contemporary poets strove to obtain.

Strauss applies the principles of consistent naturalism here by reducing sentences and phrases to small fragments, undermining the listener's ability to perceive the larger structure or meaning of the music or the text (ex. 2). The vocal line of the first verse, which is embedded in and completely dependent upon the chord tones of the hammering accompaniment to illustrate the stonecutter's entrapment, is chromaticized enough so that no clear tonal center is evident, despite the cadence on E-flat on the word "Held" in

Example 2: "Das Lied des Steinklopfers"
Richard Strauss, op. 49/4, 1901, mm. 1-9

m. 6[16]. The short phrases that cover four words each (equal to one poetic line) quickly follow one upon the other but lack direction or an overarching shape. Brief *glissandi*, seeming to appear from nowhere, intrude upon the *moto perpetuo* piano figures as the stonecutter dreams of wine (e.g., mm. 36 and 38; ex. 3). The listener becomes focused on the moments created by these phrases and figures, rather than the arc of the song.

Strauss's own brand of necessary rhythm is seen in distorted textual inflections that create disjunctures in the vocal line, pulling individual words away from their semantic contexts. Words such as "kein" and "mir", both unaccented words in the poem, consistently fall on high pitches in the vocal line and initiate large downward leaps onto strongly accented words, an inflectional pattern that distorts that of normal speech. Later in the song, Strauss adds to these inflectional irregularities distortions of the rhythmic pattern that he established at the beginning of the song (three eighth notes followed by two quarter notes), altering the rhythmic pattern flexibly to reflect his interpretation of the text. Although phrases are still restricted to four words each, note values increase, and the distance between phrases widens as the stonecutter remembers the incident that sealed his fate: the passing of the hammer from his father to him as his father died (mm. 17-25; ex. 4). In the song's extraordinary reprise, Strauss's techniques of necessary rhythm morph into consistent naturalism, as Strauss further fragments the text so that the listener viscerally experiences the stonecutter's mental and emotional deterioration. Strauss truncates phrases of the first eight lines to two words each and completely cuts lines 3 ("ich bin kein Priester") and 7 ("verliehen worden"), leaving long gaps in the vocal line (mm. 44-51; ex. 5). As the song continues its reprise, more lines disappear as the stonecutter loses his ability (in Strauss's interpretation) to fully articulate his thoughts. The listener is left with the stonecutter's muttered repeat of "für's Vaterland" (ex. 6).

In terms of both the highly flexible rhythms of the vocal lines and the depiction of the smallest details, Strauss here fulfills the aims of literary naturalist poets more effectively than they themselves did. Moving beyond assumptions that I had made

---

[16] In fact, the vocal setting of the first and second halves of the stanza each contain eleven out of the twelve semi-tones contained within the octave (the first phrase is missing F-sharp; the second is missing A-sharp).

Example 3: "Das Lied des Steinklopfers", mm. 35-39

Example 4: "Das Lied des Steinklopfers", mm. 17-25

Example 5: "Das Lied des Steinklopfers", mm. 44-51

Example 6: "Das Lied des Steinklopfers", mm. 72-79

regarding music as directly reflective of textual structure and meaning enabled me to see Strauss not merely as composer, but as poet. His poetic experiments in musical show elegantly that in the investigation of song, analytical models must take into account the possibility that the most important text/music relationships will be those outside the immediate scope of direct correspondences between poetry and music.

References

Agawu, Kofi. "Theory and Practice in the Analysis of the Nineteenth-Century *Lied*". *Music Analysis* 11.1 (1992): 3-36.
Bie, Oscar. *Das deutsche Lied*. Berlin: Fischer, 1926.
Bischoff, Hermann. *Das deutsche Lied*. Die Musik 16-17. Berlin: Bard, Marquardt, [1905].
Brands, Heinz-Georg. *Theorie und Stil des sogenannten "Konsequenten Naturalismus" von Arno Holz und Johannes Schlaf: Kritische Analyse der Forschungsergebnisse und Versuch einer Neubestimmung*. Bonn: Bouvier, 1978.
Bücken, Ernst. *Das deutsche Lied: Probleme und Gestaltung*. Hamburg: Hanseatische-Verlagsanstalt, 1939.
Crawford, John C. and Dorothy L. *Expressionism in Twentieth-Century Music*. Bloomington: Indiana Univ. Press, 1993.
Dougherty, William P. "Mignon in Nineteenth-Century Song: Text, Context, and Intertext". Lodato/Aspden/Bernhart, eds. 123-141.
Gysi, Fritz. *Richard Strauss*. Potsdam: Athenaion, 1934.
Hanstein, Adelbert. *Das jüngste Deutschland: Zwei Jahrzehnte miterlebter Litteraturgeschichte*. 2d ed. Leipzig: Voigtlander, 1901.
Hart, Heinrich. "Cäcilie". *Moderne Dichter-Charaktere*. 188-189.
—. "Literarische Erinnerungen". *Gesammelte Werke*. Julius Hart, ed. Vol. 3. Berlin: Fleischel, 1907.
Henckell, Karl, ed. *Buch der Freiheit*. Berlin: Buchnandlung des "Vorwärts", 1893.
Henckell, Karl. "Ruhe, meine Seele!" *Moderne Dichter-Charaktere*. 288-289.
Holz, Arno. *Phantasus*. Berlin: Sassenbach, 1898/99. Reprint ed. Gerhard Schulz. Stuttgart: Reclam, 1978.
—. *Revolution der Lyrik*. Berlin: Sassenbach, 1899.
Holz, Arno, and Johannes Schlaf. *Neue Gleise*. Berlin: Fontane, 1892.
Kritische Waffengänge. Heinrich and Julius Hart, eds. New York and London: Johnson Reprint Corp., 1969.
Lodato, Suzanne Marie. "Recent Approaches to Text/Music Analysis in the Lied. A Musicological Perspective". Walter Bernhart, Steven Paul Scher, and Werner Wolf, eds. *Word and Music Studies: Defining the Field. Proceedings of the First*

International Conference on Word and Music Studies at Graz, 1997. Word and Music Studies 1. Amsterdam: Rodopi, 1999. 95-112.

Lodato, Suzanne Marie. "Richard Strauss and the Modernists: A Contextual Study of Strauss's *Fin-de-Siècle* Song Style". PhD diss. Columbia Univ., 1999.

Lodato, Suzanne Marie, Suzanne Aspden, and Walter Bernhart, eds. *Word and Music Studies: Essays in Honor of Steven Paul Scher and on Cultural Identity and the Musical Stage.* Word and Music Studies 4. Amsterdam: Rodopi, 2002.

Mackay, John Henry. "Heimliche Aufforderung". *Das starke Jahr.* Zürich, 1890. 27-28.

—."Morgen". *Das starke Jahr.* 110.

Moderne Dichter-Charaktere. Wilhelm Arent, Hermann Conradi, Karl Henckell, eds. Leipzig: Friedrich, 1885.

Osborne, John. *The Naturalist Drama in Germany.* Manchester: Manchester Univ. Press, 1971.

Pascal, Roy. "Arno Holz, *Der erste Schultag.* The Prose-Style of Naturalism". Hinrich Siefken, Alan Robinson, eds. *Erfahrung und Überlieferung: Festschrift für C.P. Magill.* Cardiff: Univ. of Wales for St. David's Univ. College, 1974. 151-165.

—. *From Naturalism to Expressionism: German Literature and Society 1880-1918.* London: Weidenfeld and Nicolson, 1973.

Schuh, Willi. *Richard Strauss: A Chronicle of the Early Years, 1864-1898.* Mary Whittall, trans. Cambridge: Cambridge Univ. Press, 1982.

Schutte, Jürgen, ed. *Lyrik des Naturalismus.* Stuttgart: Reclam, 1982.

Seelig, Harry E. "'Wozu [Lieder] in dürftiger Zeit' [1958]? Britten's *Sechs Hölderlin-Fragmente* as 'Literary Song Cycle'". Lodato/Aspden/Bernhart, eds. 101-122.

Völker, Ludwig. "'Alle Erneuerung geht von irgendiener "Prosa" aus'. Die lyrische Moderne und der Naturalismus". Robert Leroy, Eckart Pastor, eds. *Deutsche Dichtung um 1890: Beiträge zu einer Literatur im Umbruch.* Bern: Lang, 1991. 203-235.

Music and the Spoken Word

Speaking Melody, Melodic Speech

Lawrence Kramer, New York

This essay seeks to conceptualize a familiar but little-studied phenomenon, the intermediate form of expression between song and speech that arises when a melody associated with words is sounded without the words being sung. This 'singing melody' is interpreted in its historical context and illustrated with reference to works in three disparate genres drawn from the past two centuries: instrumental works by Schubert, Britten's opera *Billy Budd*, and the film *Casablanca*.

In memoriam Steven Paul Scher

The relationship between music and the spoken word is usually conceived in terms of actual sound: a segment of music supports, enhances, subverts, or obscures a speech act. But one of the most common types of relationship is more virtual than actual. It happens when music itself 'speaks': that is, when a musical phrase associated with certain words is used motivically, but without the words being either uttered or sung. Such 'speaking melody' is songlike but not song, not speech but still speechlike; there is nothing else quite like it. The melody, precisely, does not sing; it speaks, and what it says is definite and understood, as if a virtual voice had uttered the substance of the words without their sound. Speaking melody is a device basic to accompanied song, to musical theater, and even to instrumental music, but there has been virtually no theorizing about it. This paper proposes to start some.

One basis for this initiative is a recent effort by Slavoj Zizek to theorize the relationship of words and pictures to what he, following Jacques Lacan, calls the Real, the unsymbolizable substrate of reality in the usual sense of the term. Voice figures importantly in this model but music does not, a defect I hope to rectify. A second basis is the anatomy of speaking melody itself, a kind of triple counterpoint involving the melody per se, the words virtually enunciated by it, and the "melody" of intonation – the palette of timbres, breath sounds, pitch contours, vibrations, inflections, and so on – available to speech as material support and to music as an object of imitation. Starting from the last, these elements form a continuum running from inarticulate vocal substance to full articulation to the 'spiritualized' form in which melody absorbs articulate speech, only to rejoin, at this upper limit, the sheer materiality of the intonational matrix. This encounter at the limit entails the recognition of a material or musical excess, sometimes slight, sometimes more. My theorization will accordingly dwell on the concept of excess, surplus, or remainder, and this in two distinct, partially opposed senses. But before we arrive at that point the stage of theory will need some historical setting, for this is a theory that will try to keep firmly within a historical horizon.

Music is constantly singing songs without words. Singing that way is how music speaks. Once words have been joined to a melody, the words seem to saturate the music so that the music can voice them afterwards even in their absence. Their absence even seems preordained by the thoroughness with which their presence is assimilated; the music is saturated, but the words have been absorbed. This process, to be sure, occurs within certain limitations. The words involved tend to be simple – just a phrase or two, sometimes memorable, sometimes not – and when sung they tend to come at the beginnings of melodies or in refrains, the segments of music most likely to be recalled or repeated with the words unvocalized. The remarkable thing is how articulate those unvocalized segments are.

Such musicalized speech in the absence of words – speaking melody – conveys the verbal utterance as an intentional object rather than as an object of perception. We know the words but do not hear them; they bypass the senses that the music addresses. The language is distilled to a kind of essence, a term meant here in the double sense of a core of spirit or meaning and of a volatile liquid known by the penetrating aroma it leaves behind when it has seemed to vanish. Speaking melody channels the semantic flux of music into a definite but transient form, something not just nameable but named. In so doing, it both reveals and protects against a dread of meaninglessness that lurks at the fringes of much musical experience. Speaking melody highlights both the charismatic value of the musical aphorism – the mystique of the Proustian "little phrase" – and the vacuity potentially created by its repetition.

From one point of view, widely held in the eighteenth century, speaking melody is best understood as an explicit or reflexive form of the basic condition of melody itself. For Jean-Jacques Rousseau, melody is precisely an imitation of speech; its expressive contour mimics the intonational flow of expressive verbal utterance.

> By imitating the inflections of the voice, melody expresses plaints, cries of suffering or joy, threats, moans; all the vocal signs of the passions fall within its province. It imitates the accents of [various] languages as well as the idiomatic expressions commonly associated in each one of them with given movements of the soul. [...] This is where musical imitation acquires its power, and song its hold on sensitive hearts. (282)

At best, of course, this claim takes a historically limited repertoire of melodies as a universal norm, but its obsolescence as a proposition does not exhaust its force. The underlying notion that melody distills expressive speech to its essence has great durability. And it is not always tilted in favor of speech: rather the reverse. Even for so unmusical a thinker as Sigmund Freud, it is the musical element of speaking melody that makes it compelling.

In his reconstruction of the experiences behind his famous "Revolutionary Dream", the analysis of which takes up several discrete sections of *The Interpretation of Dreams*, Freud recalls humming Figaro's defiant aria "Si vuol' ballare, signor Contino" from Wolfgang Amadeus Mozart's *The Marriage of Figaro* after witnessing some imperious behavior at the railway station by the reactionary minister Count Thun (226). The words not uttered establish a frame of reference. But it is the music, into which the words have been absorbed, that carries the force of impudence, resentment, and rebelliousness. Freud's text quotes the words, but the reader who eyes them without hearing the music in the mind's ear will miss more than half the point. The hearing even has to go beyond the melody per se to the way it was performed. Freud is a little dubious that anyone else at the station would have recognized the familiar tune, implying that he may have been humming it off-key or with some other changes that would indicate his resentment. In other words, he was in all likelihood distorting the tune under the pressure of his feelings. The distortion forms a surplus of expression, a remainder, that marks the rage of a liberal against political reaction and a Jew against anti-Semitism. Meanwhile, the melody per se identifies Freud with Mozart's Figaro as a figure of triumphant impudence, and perhaps also with Mozart himself as a figure of resistance by genius to aristocratic privilege.

The same balance of force and signification occurs every time a vocal phrase is picked up by an instrument or ensemble, whether in an abstract composition or in musical theater, on a movie soundtrack or in everyday life: Freud was hardly alone in humming, singing, or whistling an accompaniment to events in the process of living them. Film especially, or video more broadly, makes constant use of speaking melody, so much so that it seems basic to video forms not only as an auditory supplement, but also as an element of visuality. One can, it seems, see more, see better, in both the visual and conceptual senses, when speaking melody is somewhere in the picture.

But speaking melody is not a neutral form. Whether because it involves the absence of word and voice, or because its historical development connects that absence with the imagery of disembodiment and the uncanny, of distance in time and remoteness in space, speaking melody above all exists in a modality of pathos. It is nostalgic; it suggests mourning and memory; it hangs on to bits of the past that need to be let go. In so doing it acts like a material-aesthetic form of "melancholia" in the classic psychoanalytic sense of clinging to the past by internalizing lost objects and reproaching them inwardly for the loss they represent. Of course this is only a tendency, not a law. It is not hard to find exceptions. But the tendency is strong: no law, but perhaps a rule, a model with a long shadow.

Freud's dream analysis is a case in point because it does seem like an exception: "Si vuol' ballare" is defiant, not mournful. But in Freud's account it is really both, its aggressiveness a scant disguise for political and personal nostalgia. The melody harbors a longing for the hopefulness of Freud's happy childhood in the time of the liberal "Bürger" ("Bourgeois") Ministry of which he writes elsewhere in the dream book. "It began to dawn on me", he says there, "that [another, thematically related] dream had carried me back from the dreary present to the cheerful hopes of the days of the 'Bürger Ministry', and that the wish that it had done its best to fulfill was one dating back to those times". Symbolized by the pleasure ground of the Prater, the famous park on the city's outskirts, the Vienna of the "Bürger" Ministry conjoined the love of Freud's parents for their son, a fortuneteller's prophecy of a great future for him, and the hope of full assimilation for Austria's Jews (226)[1]. Without the loss of that fair early world the music in the "Revolutionary" dream is pointless. Figaro's defiance at the train station is the hopeless defiance of an exile in his own land.

What gives speaking melody such power? Freud's narrative suggests that one answer lies in the gap between the expressiveness of the melody and the meaning of the words. The words tell us, or would if we could hear them, what the melody says, but the message thus delivered is always incomplete. We know that the tune in the slow movement of Gustav Mahler's First Symphony is saying "Frere Jacques" or "Brüder Martin", but what we are to do with this information the melody does not say. If one subtracts what the words say from what the melody expresses there is always an expressive remainder, a surplus or excess to deal with. And that remainder is the heart of the matter. With sung melody, the remainder tends to be veiled by the fullness of voice; speaking melody takes the veil away. How does this remainder act, and to what end?

The short answer is that it acts by distorting the texture of ordinary reality – the lifeworld governed by the norms of law and language, Lacan's symbolic order. It does so either to create an incitement to new acts of symbolization or to insist on the presence of something unsymbolizable. To continue with the Lacanian vocabulary, the remainder is either an enhancement of the symbolic or an eruption of the Real.

Zizek's model concerns the latter. His essay "Grimaces of the Real" focuses on the human face as a primary locus of symbolic reality and examines how the Real – the terrible enjoyment of living substance devoid of rule or reason – makes its appearance

---

[1] The other dream involved here is goes by the sobriquet "Uncle with the Yellow Beard"; its latent content overlaps that of the "Revolutionary" dream in an extensive network of associations. Freud traces his wishes all the way back to his mother's pride, shortly after his birth, at a fortuneteller's statement that she had brought a great man into the world; to childhood revisitations of the scene of the prophecy in the Prater, where another prognostic said that Freud would become a cabinet minister – the image on which the whole pattern converges; and to the hopes for full assimilation of the Jews that the Bürger Ministry inspired: "My father had brought home portraits of these middle-class professional men [of the Ministry] – Herbst, Giskra, Unger, Berger and the rest – and we had illuminated the house in their honor. There had even beeen some Jews among them. So henceforth every industrious Jewish schoolboy carried a Cabinet Minister's portfolio in his satchel." (225-26)

by agonized facial distortion. Many of Zizek's examples also involve the voice, which produces a grimace when it cannot come to utterance. The voice in such cases is an object that gets stuck in the throat; it is "what cannot burst out, unchain itself, and thus enter the dimension of subjectivity", which is also the dimension of symbolic reality. "The first association here", writes Zizek,

> is Munch's Scream [...] [where] it pertains to the very essence of the depicted content that the scream we perceive is mute, since the anxiety is too stringent to find an outlet in vocalization. [...] [This] structural muteness is indexed within the painting itself by the absence of ears from the homunculus's head: as if these ears, foreclosed from the (symbolic) reality of the face, return in the Real of the anamorphotic stain the form of which recalls a gigantic ear." (117)

Ana/morphosis: form as de-formation, deformity. The remainder of mingled desire and repulsion left over by any act of symbolization here returns by indelibly disfiguring the act of symbolization itself[2].

But not all remainders are anamorphotic stains. An alternative type is one of the topics canvassed by my book *Musical Meaning*. One of the commonest notions about music is that one cannot express what it means in words; something, and that the most important thing, is always left over. Yet these musical remainders have nothing monstrous about them; quite the contrary. And Edvard Munch's "Scream" looks like the very antithesis of music. So what would happen, I wondered, if instead of treating the musical remainder as either an ineffable *je ne sais quoi* or as a negative principle, an abstract curb on articulate meaning, we tried to regard it as a positive phenomenon, a concrete involvement with the problem of meaning? The remainder in that case would not be what disqualifies me from speaking about music or from finding new contexts in which the music becomes meaningful. On the contrary, it would be the rationale and the motive for me to keep on speaking and contextualizing. The remainder would deny a

---

[2] Zizek's initiative can be understood as an effort to extract the kernel of truth from the truism that no act of symbolization is ever complete. Lacan defines the Real, to the extent that he defines it at all, as that which resists (evades, escapes) symbolization. Taking this resistance psychoanalytically rather than metaphysically, he understands the Real as pertaining to (being "of") the subject's unspeakable desire. Zizek regards the Real as a kind of agency, and a powerful one at that. Rather than forming a negative, indiscernible limit on the power of the symbol, it intervenes continually in symbolic processes, marking its presence obtrusively with its signature stain or deformity. And because these extrusions of the Real are indeed linked to desire, they can never be escaped. For Zizek, reality (the symbolically constructed world) is pockmarked by them.

portion of meaning in the present only in order to promise it, though never all of it at once, in the future. The anamorphotic remainder that impedes the hermeneutic would be joined to a metamorphic counterpart that promotes the hermeneutic. And these two different remainders would actually be one and the same.

Of course texts and pictures have such remainders, too; the grimaces of the Real have opposites in every medium. What makes the musical remainder special? And what, more particularly, is special about it in the case of speaking melody?

Where the Real appears, there is probably no point in making distinctions; all the remainders are breaks in the skin of perception, whether they are blots, garbles, or noises. But where meaning hovers just out of reach, distinctions are possible. The hermeneutic remainders of texts and images are relatively abstract and immaterial, the faint traces of the unsaid or unseen. Our everyday confidence in the force of meaning rests to some degree on this faintness. In music, however, the remainder is material and sensuous. Grasping it is fundamental to both musical pleasure and musical power. Music does more than 'have' a remainder; it embodies its remainder. Indeed, one way to define music is as the material-sensuous remainder of interpretation.

Speaking melody is a hybrid of the musical and verbal instances; it combines the material consistency of music with the symbolic value of words, but without merging them together as sung melody tends to do. In the sphere of utterance, the remainder tends to appear as a reduction of articulation to pure phonic substance, intonation denuded of speech. This reduction, like the remainder itself, is subject to a duality whose tensions determine its precise effect in any given instance. On one hand, the reduction may occur when words are choked back, garbled, smeared together; at its outer limit, this verbal implosion would be the equivalent to the sickening distortions of face and voice described by Zizek. On the other hand, intonation may simply replace all or part of a speech act as an overflow of some immediacy or nuance; its distortion would be hermeneutic, at worst enigmatic, and at the extreme a token of intimate, virtually unmediated communication. There is, of course, an endless variety of mixed instances between the two extremes.

Speaking melody belongs to this intermediate domain. Or perhaps one ought to say that the intermediate domain belongs to it. When a melody gives us to apprehend the words we do not hear, it acts as like a detached form of the intonational substrate of speech. The process is like an unveiling of the living substance of the words, the rich materiality that the articulateness of speech regularly obscures. Like the words themselves, this substance is purely virtual. When the unuttered speech is incorporated in the sensory richness of the music, the music tends to assume the status of the terrible but fascinating Real, the unsymbolizable kernel of forbidden/ecstatic pleasure/repulsion at the core of subjective life. Beneath any specific distortion that may mark this effect lies the innate distortion produced by the simultaneous occurrence of verbal understanding and verbal absence, which renders the music palpably but imperceptibly different from what it would otherwise be. The notes aren't different; the melody is. Each of these distortions magnifies the other. This mutual resonance helps explain the emotional force of speaking melody.

But the Real thus made manifest is not the standard Real. Rather it is a Real partly recuperated for the symbolic order, a Real allowed to enter the symbolic as something other than a blot or grimace, something that does not repel meaning but, by assuming an aphoristic, enigmatic, oracular character, attracts it. Speaking melody undoes the grimace of the Real. Its anamorphotic remainder fuses with its hermeneutic remainder. It gives the Real a haven in reality.

Zizek's descriptive terms blot, stain, smear, grimace, let alone phallic anamorphosis, are too extreme in this context. Speaking melody typically trades in slighter distortions, shimmers, or flickers of misperception; if the distortion is too great, the speaking melody turns into travesty – for which, of course, there any many uses – and becomes a device of alienation, as, once again, in Mahler's "Frere Jacques". We need a term for the distortion characteristic of speaking melody, so I will speak here not of blot but a blur, something at the edges of perception rather than "in your face": the smudge of the real.

Thus far, however, both this smudge and the element of pathos in speaking melody describe only general effects; they are points of theory. But such general effects are never, or let us say rarely, realized in their generality. They respond, rather, to particular circumstances; they mark their materiality, their distortion, and their nostalgia in highly particular ways. Speaking melody is a historical form, even a form that insists on rather than insinuates its own historical character.

A useful profile of speaking melody must therefore be historically resonant. To meet that requirement, I propose to examine a series of examples spanning several media across two centuries: an opera and a movie from the 1940s, and a pair of instrumental compositions from the 1820s.

The opera is Benjamin Britten's *Billy Budd* (1951). In this adaptation of Herman Melville's novel, Billy, the innocent "Beauty" or "Baby" aboard a British man-o-war, is falsely accused of mutiny by Claggert, the master of arms. The accusation may be a distorted form of Claggert's desire for Billy, which must not be symbolized; Billy, who stutters under stress, replies in distorted form as well, striking and inadvertantly killing Claggert in lieu of speech. Remainders are thus at the heart of this story, which ends as the ship's captain, Vere, orders Billy's execution despite his obvious innocence. Britten and his librettists, E.M. Forster and Eric Crozier, were primarily interested in Vere, whose dilemma is exposed early in the opera by means of speaking melody.

Talking with his officers about the danger of mutiny, Vere draws attention to a chantey being sung below decks as the crew retires for the night. He takes the chantey as a sign of contentment; it is exactly the opposite. The words express a deep longing to be elsewhere, anywhere but here: "Blow her away, / Blow her to Hilo, Hilo, Hilo […] ." At the end of the scene, Vere, now alone, is distracted by the chantey as he tries to read. The song is already halfway to becoming voiceless, smudged by the distance of its off-stage, below-decks source. Part of it is submerged in the darkness of the low voices singing together. Part of it fades into the distance with the repetitions of "Hilo", which turn the exotic place-name into pure vocalization, more smudge than utterance: a becoming-inarticulate of speech under the pressure of desire[3].

The metamorphosis completes itself a moment later as the orchestra picks up the chantey and makes it the basis of an extended fantasy. What is truly at stake becomes fully apparent when the fantasy takes up the speaking melody of a second chantey, introduced on solo flute. The words will not come until later. Britten wrote this tune

---

[3] Hilo is a port in the Sandwich (i.e., Hawaiian) Islands, as remote as possible from the Atlantic setting of the opera. On another reading, the nonsense that "Hilo" becomes through repetition makes another kind of sense. In the opera's Anglicized pronunciation, it forms a synoptic statement, unrecognized by the singers, of the social (and would-be metaphysical) difference mapped onto the ship's decks: high/low.

before he had words for it – words, he told their author, that should be "as gloomy, homesick, and nostalgic as you like"[4]. The words he received convey a deep longing for release, even for the peace of death: "Over the ocean, over the water, into the harbour, carry me home." Taken together, the two speaking melodies universalize the feelings of which they speak. The men's longing ceases to arise from the circumstances of the narrative and becomes the circumstance from which the narrative arises. The longing becomes manifest as the unfathomable substrate that the opera, at best, can symbolize only in part.

Just a few years before "Billy Budd", Hollywood produced a legendary instance of speaking melody in *Casablanca* (1942). The story has become legendary, too: separated when the Nazis occupy Paris, the lovers Rick and Ilse (Humphrey Bogart and Ingrid Bergman) meet again in Casablanca; Ilse is now married to a resistance leader, and Rick must renounce her so that she, in turn, can support her husband in his struggle. The song "As Time Goes By", as sung at the piano by Rick's employee and emotional minder, Sam (Dooley Wilson), embodies the lost romance.

On separate occasions, first Ilse and then Rick insist on hearing the song, but with a subtle difference. Ilse starts by asking for the music (with the famous "Play it, Sam") but she also wants the words ("Sing it, Sam"). Rick reencounters Ilse for the first time when he interrupts Sam's singing – an interruption that cannot hold up. Alone with Sam later, Rick, too, asks for the song ("Play it!" he says, turning Ilse's plea into an anguished command), even though he cannot bear to hear it; we can see as much in the grimace on Bogart's face. But what Rick asks for is speaking melody, not song, and the film complies. As Sam plays, the orchestra backs up the melody before shifting to the underscore for what follows, a flashback to the lovers' life in Paris[5]. Most of this interpolated narrative is fragmentary; music holds it together, especially "As Time Goes By". Fragments of the melody recur as underscore at all the key romantic moments, each more haunted by impending loss than the last. But it is precisely these moments

---

[4] Cooke and Reed, 65.

[5] Berthold Hoeckner has drawn attention to the song's transitional role here and to its eventual embedding in the flashback it introduces. His reading sees lost time less fatefully than mine, but there is no need to choose between them; they deal with different modes of memory.

that the song, as speaking melody, is bringing most vividly back to life. When Sam actually plays and sings the song for the lovers in Paris, no one suspects its power to do that.

The flashback ends with a return to Rick, still listening as Sam plays. (The playing breaks off at the musical phrase for "and still say", leaving the music for "I love you" to hover somewhere between something still to be said and something no longer sayable.) Far from just invoking a lost time, the song is what refuses to let the time be lost. That, after all, is what the melody says when it speaks: "The fundamental things apply / As time goes by." The fundamental things are those that remain as time goes by, and in this case the most fundamental thing of all is the song itself. If Rick, if Ilse, could forget the song, they could let the past be past. But they cannot forget. The song will not let them; it smudges their every thought with the Real of their love.

The close of the film is haunted by the logic of the song, which it can neither accept nor escape. In the penultimate scene, Rick has firmly resolved to let Ilse go; he will send her away himself. To end the story he will end **their** story. He explains his renunciation with one famous line after another: "We'll always have Paris," "The troubles of three little people don't amount to a hill of beans in this crazy world," "Here's looking at **you**, kid." As he speaks, the orchestra on the soundtrack weaves together phrases from "As Time Goes By"; when he finishes, the strings fill the ensuing silence with a melting rendition of the song's refrain as the camera lingers on a closeup of Ilse's face. The effect is to contradict the narrative ending. It puts the audience in the position of the old Rick, the Rick who refuses to let go of Ilse and Paris – a refusal measured precisely by the original version of the song. The quivering strings of the closing version impart the smudge of the Real and create a complex pattern whereby Rick says one thing and the speaking melody that supports him says something else: the very thing he would like to say, but cannot. The pattern culminates with an epiphany at the level of speech genre: melodrama (that is, music joined to the spoken word, but with a play on the sense of highly wrought narrative) resolves itself in lyric.

Perhaps this outcome is why some people go back to *Casablanca* over and over, as if hoping to meet – just once – with the ending announced by the music, not by the plot. The song, of course, has been heard on the soundtrack before, even heard too often, but it becomes decisive here because Rick is repeating the separation from Ilse that gave the song its power in the first place. In this context the absence of the words becomes the presence of the unspeakable desire that will not permit itself to be renounced. The speaking melody clearly says that the problems of three little people – especially two of them – amount to far more than a hill of beans even in this crazy world.

A lesser world, if not a crazy one, is Franz Schubert's topic in portions of two major instrumental works, his Octet in F Major (D. 803) and String Quartet in A Minor (D. 804), composed during the same two-month period in 1824. Both works quote a song he had composed five years earlier, "Schöne Welt, wo bist du, Fragment aus Schillers Die Götter Griechenlands". The short text bears full quotation:

Schöne Welt, wo bist du? Kehre wieder,	Fair world, where are you? Turn back again,
Holdes Blütenalter der Natur!	Sweet blossom-age of nature!
Ach, nur in dem Feenland der Lieder	Ah, in the fairyland of songs alone
Lebt noch deine fabelhafte Spur.	Still lives your legendary trace.
Ausgestorben trauert das Gefilde,	The died-out meadow mourns,
Keine Gottheit zeigt sich meinem Blick.	No godhead comes before my eyes.
Ach, von jenem lebenwarmen Bilde	Ah, of that life-warm image
Blieb der Schatten nur zurück.☐	Only the shade remains behind.[6]

In both octet and quartet, the only phrase reproduced as speaking melody involves the two words "schöne Welt" ('fair world'). But the two works invoke this phrase to markedly different effect. We need to go back to the song to see how and why.

The passage quoted is less 'in' the song than appended to it by the piano alone. Repetitions of a single three-note figure, static and forlorn, frame the song proper; they also intrude on it about two-thirds of the way through. (Examples 1a and 1b show the framing statements, mm. 1-5 and 50-55.) At each occurrence, this refrain sounds over unchanging 6-4 harmony in A-minor – afloat, as it were, in the no-world of the present. Between the framing statements, we hear a disrupted A-B-A pattern: two A-major sections enclose an A-minor middle section that ends with the intrusion of the refrain. The first A-major section carries the verse to the point where the gods are said to live on only in song; the A-minor section begins with the transition to the fraught word "ausgestorben" ('died-out') and goes on to the end, marking the dismal consequences

---

[6] German text from Schubert's score; my translation.

for latter-day reality. The second A-major section recapitulates the first section's first half, consisting of a double statement of "Kehre wieder, / Holdes Blümenalter der Nature" ('Turn back again / Sweet blossom-age of Nature'). This recapitulation is ironic at best, both in its major key and in the incompleteness of its utterance; its structural inevitability only darkens its implications. The invocation is one that can never be answered, as the closing return of the refrain declares. Deprived of the gods, Nature cannot even say "No." The static futility of the refrain figure expands to envelop the form of the song as a whole.

Example 1a. Schubert, "Die Götter Griechenlands", opening, mm. 1-5

Example 1b. Schubert, "Die Götter Griechenlands", close, mm. 50-55

The dotted rhythm of this figure anticipates that of "Schöne Welt" in the voice, which is, however, sung to different pitches. The speaking melody provides an alternative intonation that is never realized vocally because it is too despairing; its minor mode and harmonic instability too fully confirm the loss that the voice, hoping against hope, still questions with its "kehre wieder". As the song proper begins (ex. 1a), the voice cuts across the piano's oscillating E-D-E with the rising figure C-D-E. The voice and piano do coincide on E, though, at the word "Welt", and again on A at "du" as the harmony finally shifts – though one cannot really say it resolves – from the second inversion to root position. At the end of the song, this alignment, the balance of hope and despair, is lost. The voice reaches its A with the 6-4 harmony still in effect, then falls silent. The piano is left to conclude by repeating its own more melancholy version of the refrain figure. Only after this does the harmony shift again – again not really resolving, and with the voice no longer involved (ex. 1b). The effect is similar to that of the more famous frame structure in the later "Am Meer", another song of loss, where the 6-4 harmony does not even bother to shift. In "Schöne Welt", therefore, it is the forlorn alternative voice that has the last word, and the true word, in a speaking melody rather than the sung one of which it is the shadow, the shade that remains behind[7].

The instrumental quotations in the Octet and Quartet revive this alternative voice, in which the question 'where' cannot really be asked because it has already been answered by 'nowhere'. The third movement of the quartet counteracts this answer precisely by catching the little phrase up in its genre, the minuet, an antique form that fulfils the subsequent statement in Schiller's poem that the fair world survives in fable, though only there. The tight, static shape of the phrase acts as a smudge on the richly wrought minuet theme, but the theme has little trouble coping with it. Or rather, just a little; there is nothing glib about the process. The solo cello begins the movement with a deep, groaning statement of the "Schöne Welt" phrase, the last note of which refuses to let go and draws the other instruments to it in somber-hued imitations. But the overriding lyrical impulse is already at work even as these echoes chime in, and the graceful lilt of

---

[7] It is worth noting that the original version of the song has no shift to root position at the voice's first "du". By adding the shift, Schubert converts its subsequent absence at the last "du" from the restatement of a settled condition to the enactment of a loss.

the minuet emerges from them seamlessly and irrefutably (ex. 2). If the fair world survives only here, we can still be assured that it survives well enough.

Example 2. Schubert, Minuet from Quartet in A Minor, D.804, opening

Example 3. Schubert, Finale from Octet in F Major, D.803, opening

This is an assurance that the octet will not allow. Here the smudge becomes a smear in the guise of wrenching string tremolos that envelop the little phrase (ex. 3). The feverish quivering of the ensemble forms an extended slow introduction to the finale, which it defines precisely as an attempt to seek in original composition the consolation that the minuet claims to have found in genre. The movement is superbly equipped to succeed in this. Its indefatigable first theme frames a sonata exposition unusually rich in melodic variety, and itself varies prolifically and irrepressibly during a development section that it wholly engrosses. But the attempt to recall a vanished world by these means is compromised by its very definition, and the movement nearly founders on it when the introduction returns, briefer but more feverish than before, just prior to the coda. The coda itself seems oblivious, but the listener can hardly be that in good faith. Where the quartet stresses the consolations of fable, the octet dwells on the emptiness of the shades – the ghosts and figments – that the fair world has left behind. Both pieces repeat the little phrase like a forlorn cry, but the quartet follows the text by ritualizing and therefore rationalizing that cry, substituting the generic conventions of the minuet for the rhetorical figure of apostrophe. The octet lets the cry erupt and fade without the intervention of ritual or rationale. Its little phrase is a noisy remainder that the effervescence of the finale cannot assimilate.

The little phrase, then, has larger implications, and not in this one piece alone. What are the larger implications of speaking melody itself? What might its role be in a broader auditory culture?

On the evidence of our examples, the phenomenon of speaking melody would seem to mark the limit of an important hermeneutic principle, as formulated by Hans-Georg Gadamer: "Language is not just one of man's possessions in the world; rather, on it depends the fact that man has a world at all. The world as world exists for man as for no other creature that is in the world. But this world is verbal in nature." (441) Against this, as an exception to it, is the fact that there are many moments in life when language is silent, suspended, but world is not. What we experience at such moments cannot be the verbal nature of the world. Rather we must come into contact with something prior to the world as word, cosmos as logos, and yet something consistent with it. We must experience the imprintability, so to speak, of phenomena by language.

Listening to instrumental music often falls into this category. Such listening can suspend language without at all suspending world; rather the reverse, for the music 'worlds' us very powerfully. When that happens, we can hear the world's latent imprintability as a positive form, but still prior to the realization of any actual imprint. And this is a condition that shows us the world in a special light, perhaps one less susceptible than usual to rationalization and distanced perception. The world thus disclosed is pleasurably smudged by the Real. In this context we can speculate that what speaking melody does is capture the otherwise imperceptible movement between symbolic imprintability and the imprint: the lapse of meaning by which meaning is replenished, a moment inflected by both reason and magic, both surplus and loss.

References

Cooke, Mervyn and Philip Reed. *Benjamin Britten: Billy Budd.* Cambridge: Cambridge Univ. Press, 1993.
Freud, Sigmund. *The Interpretation of Dreams.* James Strachey, trans. New York: Avon, 1965.
Gadamer, Hans-Georg. *Truth and Method.* 5th German ed., 1986. Joel Weisheimer and Donald G. Marshall, trans. Rev. 2nd ed. New York: Continuum, 1989.
Gras, Vernon W., ed. *European Literary Theory and Practice.* New York: Dell, 1973.
Hoeckner, Berthold. "Audiovisual Memory: Transport and Transportation". Paper presented at the conference *Beyond the Soundtrack: Representing Music in Cinema.* Univ. of Minnesota, April 2004.
Kramer, Lawrence. *Musical Meaning: Toward a Critical History.* Berkeley: Univ. of California Press, 2002.
Rousseau, Jean-Jacques. *The First and Second Discourses and Essay on the Origin of Languages.* Victor Gourevitch, trans. New York: Harper and Row, 1990.
Zizek, Slavoj. *Enjoy Your Symptom! Jacques Lacan in Hollywood and Out.* 2nd ed. New York: Routledge, 2001.

Language and/or Music as Man's 'Comfort'?
Beckett's Metamedial Allegory *Words and Music*

Werner Wolf, Graz

In Beckett's oeuvre, music plays an important role, which is underlined in some of his works by the fact that music and language here form plurimedial combinations. Among these works, *Words and Music* (1962) is unique in being the first radio play to stage music – together with words – as an audible dramatic character in its own right. This allegorical play has repeatedly been interpreted, notably with an emphasis on its intertextual and biographical references or with the aim of elucidating individual obscurities. This essay concentrates on some more general issues, in particular on the forms and functions of the interrelation between words and music as well as on the metamedial implications of their representation, as seen against the background of both traditional views of these media and Beckett's aesthetics. Surprisingly, in *Words and Music* the negativity which otherwise pervades Beckett's oeuvre seems, at least temporarily, to be suspended. This happens when Words joins Music in song and when they thus appear to become what their master, an everyman figure, wants them to be: his "comforts". The essay includes a brief discussion of a production of the play with music by Morton Feldman and explores to what extent the apparently successful cooperation of the two media under the direction of music – as well as the tendency to musicalize verbal language observable in *Words and Music* as in many of Beckett's works – can really be regarded as forming one of the rare positive elements in the bleak landscape of the Beckett universe.

1. Introduction: Beckett's *Words and Music* as a realization of several possibilities of combining the spoken word and music

'The spoken word and music': this title of one of the sections of the present volume is open to several interpretations. I shall read it here as designating intermedial relations which can be documented within a given work or performance that involves both media[1]. Moreover, I will restrict the 'spoken word' to publicly performed discourse. Even so, the phrase 'the spoken word and music' still covers various possibilities of how these two media can appear in a work. There is, first, the plurimedial **combination**

---

[1] I hereby refer to 'intracompositional' intermediality as opposed to 'extracompositional intermediality' (for these two basic forms, see Wolf, "Intermediality Revisited" ch. 2).

of both media as in the opera; second, the reference to **oral language in music**, for instance when an agitated *recitativo* melody or a *Lied ohne Worte* (song without words) evokes a verbal discourse[2]; and there is, third, the reference to **music in oral**, in particular dramatic **texts**[3]. This reference can in turn occur in several variants, notably in the mode of a verbal imitation or in a thematization of music. In the case of thematization, intermedial references can also include explicit metamedial reflections on these two media and their relationship with each other.

Usually, we would expect to encounter these three main forms of treating our subject in separate works. Yet, there is at least one instance where all of them can be observed in one and the same work – plus a curious combination of plurimediality and (explicit) intermedial reference in the form of an **allegorical dramatization of words and music**: this work is Samuel Beckett's *Words and Music*, a radio play, which, as the title shows, almost seems to have been written for being discussed under the heading of 'the spoken word and music'.

This enigmatic play has variously been interpreted[4], mostly with the ambition of squeezing all its details into a "coherent reading" (thus Clas Zilliacus in his path-breaking 1976 interpretation [111]) or even into an "entirely consistent" interpretation (as was apparently James Acheson's aim [59]). While I do not intend to go to the opposite extreme and strive after a pointedly **in**consistent reading, I would, however, like to acknowledge also the ambiguities and the tensions that underly this play, especially if read against the background of Beckett's other works. As opposed to some scholars, my emphasis will be on the metamedial dimension[5] of this play. In particular, I

---

[2] For further details, cf. Lawrence Kramer's contribution to this volume.

[3] In addition, there are two other forms, which, however, are of minor interest here: the evocation of music (e.g. in 'imaginary content analogies', through which a text evokes a musical composition); and 'partial reproduction' (e.g. of a song through the 'associative quotation' of the song text; see Wolf, *The Musicalization of Fiction* chs. 4.4 and 4.5).

[4] Cf., in chronological order, Zilliacus; Worth; Esslin; Frost, "Fundamental Sounds"; Acheson; Becker; Guralnick; Albright; Richardson/Hale; and Ruch.

[5] In spite of its shortness, this radio play has also other centres of interest, which have been highlighted by various scholars. It has been read as an exploration of the human consciousness (cf. Esslin, Acheson), but also as a play centred on the recuperation of the main character's identity (cf. Becker). However,

propose to investigate the way in which the spoken word and music as well as their interrelations are represented, and also the consequences which this representation has for the implied worldview: in contrast to the absurdist, pervading negativity which, according to received opinion, informs Beckett's works, *Words and Music* seems to gesture towards some remnants of positivity. This happens when words join music at the end in song and when both media thus appear to become, as a character in the play hopes, "comforts" to the listener (274). It has been claimed that in this joint effort music appears as the superior medium[6]. We will see to what extent this is true and, moreover, if Beckett here indulges in what Daniel Albright has attributed to some of his works, namely a "sentimentalization of music" (36).

2. *Words and Music*: contexts, genesis, and content

As *Words and Music* belongs to Beckett's less known works, some information on the context, genesis[7], general features and content of the play shall be given before concentrating on the treatment of language and music in it.

The most important context of *Words and Music* is no doubt Beckett's "lifetime passion[...]" for music (Abbott 7) and the prominence of this art in his works. The importance of music for Beckett, who was married to the pianist Suzanne Deschevaux-Dumesnil, played the piano himself and was a great lover of music, is well known[8], so that it may suffice here to recall some general facts: Beckett's affinity to music as a non-mimetic art can be traced in his aesthetics, notably in his aversion to mimesis and

---

some critics also deal with the metamedial or meta-aesthetic dimension of the play (cf. Zilliacus, esp. 112; Schlichting, esp. 233ff.; and Guralnick, esp. 92).

[6] For the superiority of music, cf. Zilliacus 112; this privileging of music is corroborated by an oral statement made by Beckett himself (cf. Schlichting 232 and below, note 22), but has also been relativized (cf. Schlichting ibid.).

[7] For more details cf. Zilliacus 99ff. and Frost, "The Note Man on the Word Man" 47-49.

[8] Cf. Grindea; Knowlson, esp. 186; Abbott 7ff.; Debrock 69ff.; Krance 51; Wolf, *The Musicalization of Fiction* 185-188.

narrativity as well as in his tendency to foreground the acoustic nature of language; it can also be traced in the numerous instances of thematizing music in his texts but also in the occurrence of structural analogies to music in them, which have repeatedly been observed, e.g. in experimental works such as "Lessness" and "Ping"[9]. In addition, in spite of Beckett's hostility towards opera[10], some of his plays even overtly join the spoken word and music, in particular *Cascando* (1963), *Ghost Trio* (1977), *Nacht und Träume* (1983), and *Neither* (1977), a composition by Morton Feldman based on a Beckett text that has been addressed as a "one-hour long opera" (Debrock 70)[11]. Among these plurimedial works, *Words and Music* (1962) is unique in being the first radio play to stage music – together with words – as audible dramatic characters in their own right[12].

Words and Music was originally the result of a collaboration between Beckett and his cousin, the composer John Beckett. The play was first broadcast in the context of the jubilee of the BBC's 40th anniversary in November 1962. However, the audience response was poor (cf. Zilliacus 115 and Acheson 50), and the original version of John Beckett's setting was withdrawn (it is today "unavailable" [Frost, "The Note Man on the Word Man" 47]). Subsequently, there were various alternative attempts at filling in the musical blanks left in the text[13], of which Feldman's composition is the most famous. Feldman's music was created, after Beckett himself, who seems to have had a "special fondness" for the play (Frost, "Fundamental Sounds" 371), had suggested this American composer and later friend of his as capable of completing his text[14]. Feldman's music is

---

[9] Cf. for "Lessness", Catanzaro; for "Ping", Wolf *The Musicalization of Fiction,* ch. 11; and for Beckett's general tendency to use permutation and variation as quasi musical structures, cf. Krance 55.

[10] Cf. Zilliacus 103; Debrock 69 on Beckett's predictable "dislike[...] [of] musical works in which music was made subordinate to storytelling or picturing emotions".

[11] In addition, music is present in the radio plays *All that Fall* (1957), *Embers* (1959), and *Cascando* (1963/64) (for a list of Beckett's radio plays, cf. Worth 192).

[12] A similar procedure was later adopted by Beckett in *Cascando* (cf. Abbott 8).

[13] Worth (208) mentions a composition by Humphrey Searle; Schlichting (236) the composers Aric Dzierlatka and Michael Winrich Schlicht.

[14] For details cf. Frost, "Fundamental Sounds", and Frost, "The Note Man on the Word Man" (which also includes an interview with Feldman).

also the only one available on CD: it exists in two versions[15], one of which will be referred to at the end of this paper.

As the radio only permits the transmission of sound, this implies a substantial reduction in the transmission of drama as both a multimedial and a visual performance. The medium of radio, however, meets a pervading tendency of Beckett's which, in the evolution of his oeuvre, became more and more accentuated, namely an almost lyric tendency to create fictional worlds by ever more reductive, minimal means. As a consequence, less and less mimetic, let alone realistic or illusionist elements detract from the stark impact of his increasingly stylized allegorical portrayals of an absurdist human condition, as mirrored in human consciousness[16]. At the same time, the reductionism operating in Beckett's worlds also leaves more and more space for another typical tendency of Beckett's: the self-reflexive exploration of the artistic medium itself.

As for the play's content, this reductionism can also be observed here: On the level of the *sensus litteralis*, the play consists of the interaction of no more than three characters. There is, first, an old man tellingly called Croak. As the connotations of his name indicate ('to croak' as an informal word for 'to die'), he is one of those decrepit, suffering figures near death with which Beckett's worlds abound. Croak seems to be the master of two reluctant servants, Joe and Bob, with whom he communicates by way of sparing orders, thumps of a club, and groans.

The single setting is never made explicit, but most scholars agree that it points to some feudal context, perhaps a medieval castle[17], in which the two unhappy servants are frequently "pent up [...] in the dark" (272) and where their master repeatedly calls on them in order to be 'comforted' by them.

The action is confined to just one scene. It is in all probability one out of a whole series of similar scenes. Thus, it appears to be in line with the repetitiveness which is

---

[15] For a review of both, cf. Ruch.

[16] For this tendency to reduce fictional plays to a '"theatre in a skull"', cf. Richardson/Hale 285ff. (quotation on p. 286); also, cf. Kesting.

[17] This view was initiated by Zilliacus (cf. 105ff.) and has found various followers, e.g., Esslin 174, 187 or Acheson 50.

one of the devices frequently employed by Beckett in order to reduce the narrative eventfulness of his stories. The play starts in the absence of Croak with Joe and Bob warming up to their tasks as 'minstrels': while Bob alias 'Music' tunes his instruments, Joe alias 'Words' gives out a "Theme" (272), namely "sloth". Meanwhile, Croak approaches, somewhat late, it seems, beseeches the two of them to "[b]e friends" (274), and gives out other themes, first "love" (274) and then "[a]ge" (278). These themes are subsequently developed by both Joe and Bob. The last development triggers in Croak the memory of a face, which was already mentioned at his entrance. This face appears to become the final theme and is linked by Croak with the female name "Lily" (286). When Bob and Joe evoke what Zilliacus has called a "postcoital recuperation as reflected in the face of the woman" (109), Croak falls silent. We do not know what really happens, but it must be something shocking to Joe, as the 'stage direction' of his reaction indicates (cf. 290): Croak lets his club fall and shuffles away, so that the end accentuates the repetitive, cyclic nature of the play with Joe and Bob remaining once again alone as at the opening.

3. *Words and Music* as a metamedial allegory

Like many of Beckett's works, *Words and Music* invites an allegorical reading. Owing to the title and the names "Words" and "Music" given to the two servants, the suggested reading is in this case an interpretation as a metamedial allegory.

In this allegory the meaning of Bob and Joe is relatively clear: they represent two creative faculties[18]: music connoting, according to a received notion, the wordless, emotional side of human consciousness, and words in the sense of conscious language or even of poetry as a metonymy of literature[19].

---

[18] Cf. Esslin 181, who identifies 'aspects of artistic creation' as a major theme of *Words and Music* as well as of other radio plays by Beckett.

[19] Cf. Esslin 186, Acheson 51 and Richardson/Hale 291.

Less self-explanatory are the *sensus allegoricus* of Croak and the allegorical meaning of the setting, which does not seem to have interested the critics. As for Croak, it is problematic to reduce him to a mere 'listener', as Martin Esslin has done (see 174), since a listener would hardly be able to interfere with a performance. Nor is it quite unproblematical to regard him, like Zilliacus, as "the **owner** of the mind in which the play takes place" (112, emphasis mine), since this would not explain how word and music can make utterances in Croak's absence. In contrast to this, I propose to consider Croak a representative of the waking consciousness and the will of a larger, unspecified, to a certain extent perhaps creative mind. This allows me to account for the existence of words and music in Croak's absence, that is, when his will and waking consciousness are inactive. Both language and music, after all, can exist in the human mind independently of the will. In the case of music, one may only think of melodies involuntarily haunting one's consciousness, and as for language, it is present in equally involuntary states such as dreams. Yet, for all his relations to words and music, Croak should not be regarded as an exceptional artist-genius, but rather as a variant of those rather ordinary everyman-figures whom we often meet in Beckett's allegorical works.

What remains is the question of the castle. In accordance with what happens in the reception process of the play as a radio programme, where everything takes place in the listener's mind, I would propose to read the castle as a skull: it is in fact in this space that both the waking consciousness and mental faculties such as language, musical memory, etc., are located. Moreover, such an allegorization would not be unique in Beckett's oeuvre, since in *Endgame* (1958), some years previous to the conception of *Words and Music,* he had already presented his public with a dramatic setting that has aptly been called a "Schädelprojektion" ('the projection of a skull' [see Kesting 50 and passim]).

What is most interesting in our context is the relationship between Words, Music, and Croak and the metamedial meaning of the action. Generally, *Words and Music* as a metamedial allegory treats the following issues: first, the question of the interrelation and the hierarchical position of music and words (or literature); and second, the question of their respective functional potentials and limits. As a part of this second issue, mimesis and the reference to reality are addressed, moreover the problems of expression, creating meaning, evoking the past and consoling man.

As for the relation between Croak, Words, and Music, Croak's attitude towards his servants varies between *"imploring"* them (278) and giving them harsh orders or even calling them "dogs!" (278, cf. also 280). Yet in any case he has one profound wish: he wants them to be his "balms" (278) or his "comforts" (274, 276, 284), as he repeatedly calls them. This indicates some wound in his soul, presumably inflicted by an unhappy love affair with the woman called Lily. Allegorically, this unhappy affair is probably a metonymy of human suffering in general, a crucial element in Beckett's fictional worlds.

Interestingly, in Beckett's play the means of both evoking the past and coming to terms with it through some alleviation of suffering is **art**. The reference to an evocative and at the same time consolatory function of art seems to be reminiscent of Romanticism. Although remnants of Romanticism do play a role in *Words and Music*, one must, however, be cautious with such correspondences. For throughout most of the play, the impression prevails that this yearning for art as a means of recollection, of stabilizing identity and of comforting man is in vain, as Croak's reactions to the individual performances of Words and Music show. His brief responses frequently appear to be tinged by some kind of persisting unhappiness. For instance, his reactions to Word's discourse on love range from a *"Rending sigh"* (274) and a sad "Alas!" (276) to an *"anguished* [...] Oh!" (274) and several *"Groans"* (276, 284, 286). As for his responses to some of Music's contributions, these seem hardly more positive[20]. There are, however, others that betray less dissatisfaction, for Music tends to be more considerate of him than Words: once Music responds in a *"warmly sentimental"* way after an obviously intensely emotional recollection triggered in Croak's mind (282), whereas Words only shows coldness (cf. 284). Thus, there appears a certain hierarchy in the evaluation of the arts with Music as the leading figure. Nevertheless, this must be seen in perspective: when Music repeats his 'love music' *"as before", yet*, this time

---

[20] Cf., e.g., his *"anguished*: Oh!" pp. 276 and 278 (although this could also refer to Words's interruptions) and his groan on p. 282.

"*fortissimo*", this appears to be a particularly persuasive proof of Music's superiority. Yet, in this *fortissimo* repetition, "*all expression* [is] *gone*" (276), and hence the expressive relation of music to love has been lost. This ironic relativization of positivity dovetails with the fact that Croak's reaction to some measures of 'love music' is as "*anguished*" (276, 278) as to Words's discourse on love. Thus, in spite of a certain gradation, the impression remains that neither Words nor Music are real "comforts" to Croak's sufferings.

One can only guess at the reasons why this is so. At least as for Words, a certain incompetence of his may play a role. For the discourse produced by Words is rhetorically stylized, but sounds curiously hollow, repetitive and tautological, witness his rhapsody on love:

> *Words orotund*: Love is of all the passions the most powerful passion and indeed no passion is more powerful than the passion of love. *Clears throat*. This is the mode in which the mind is most strongly affected and indeed in no mode is the mind more strongly affected than in this.
> *Pause* (274)

The impression of meaninglessness, which arises from this and similar passages, also derives from the fact that we are here confronted with a variation of the initial discourse on "sloth" (272). The discourse thus appears to be constructed according to internal, self-referential principles rather than being an attempt at transmitting referential meaning. In view of this denial of the referential function of language it is ironic that these words nevertheless manage to fulfil an expressive function and elicit a "*Rending sigh*" in Croak (274), apparently the beginning of his musings about the mysterious female face. The meaningfulness of what Words says is undermined in yet another respect: when this allegorical character, in the same manner, later on attempts to describe the female face and the 'postcoital scene', there is even a suspicion that this is not a mimetic rendering of some past event in Croak's biography, as all critics have assumed, but rather the creation of a fiction. All this appears to dramatize an almost deconstructionist conception of an autonomous and non-referential language, which six years after *Words and Music* Roland Barthes will describe with the classic phrase: "[...] c'est le langage qui parle, ce n'est pas l'auteur" ('[...] it is language that speaks and not the author') (13). The autonomy of language and the concomitant loss of the author's authority as diagnosed by Barthes also harmonize with the fact that Words, but also Music, do not always obey Croak, the 'authorial' consciousness, but display some remarkable independence of him. What is more, they are also shown to interact without his bidding.

In addition, this interaction, throughout most of the play, is contrary to Croak's repeated wish "[b]e friends" (274, 284). Words and Music are manifestly hostile to each other and interrupt each other's performances, with Words behaving in a particularly aggressive way. The reason for this is easy to see and resides in Beckett's antagonistic and fairly traditional conception of both media: As a pointed opposition between a *"cold"* utterance by Words and a *"[w]arm suggestion"* (284) for the same utterance by Music indicates, Words does not only represent the spoken word, but also 'cold reason', as opposed to the 'warm feelings' associated with music. The emotional expressivity with which Music, in good old Romantic fashion, is repeatedly combined by the 'stage directions' (e.g. *"great expression"* [276]; *"warmly sentimental"* [282]) clashes curiously with Beckett's otherwise notoriously negativistic and anti-expressive aesthetics. Thus, in a dialogue with Georges Duthuit, Beckett vehemently rejected "an art [...] pretending to be able [...] of doing a little better the same old thing" and preferred instead: "The expression that there is nothing to express, nothing with which to express, nothing from which to express, no power to express, no desire to express, together with the obligation to express." (Beckett, *Three Dialogues* 103)[21]

If we are to believe some critics and a remark by Beckett himself, the latent Romanticism in the emotional appreciation of music is reinforced by the conception of the relationship between Words and Music in which the latter appears to be the winning party[22]. In fact, it is owing to the suggestions and invitations of Music that the two media finally cooperate in a song, and after its performance Words 'implores' Music to continue (cf. 290), thus acknowledging Music's superiority.

---

[21] This hostility towards an expressive art is presumably also at the root of Beckett's dislike of opera, in particular of the Wagnerian type.

[22] As Worth writes, "'Music always wins', Beckett said to me, a propos of this play" (210); also, cf. above, note 6.

4. Remnants of positivity in the 'Age-song' as deducible from Beckett's words?

The antagonism between Words and Music and the superiority of Music should, however, not be exaggerated. For the construction of an absolute opposition would disregard the eventual cooperation of Words and Music in two songs – or two parts of one song[23]. The verbal component of this song reads as follows:

```
     Age is when to a man
     Huddled o'er the ingle
     Shivering for the hag
     To put the pan in the bed
 5   And bring the toddy
     She comes in the ashes
     Who loved could not be won
     Or won not loved
     Or some other trouble
10   Comes in the ashes
     Like in that old light
     The face in the ashes
     That old starlight
     On the earth again.
     ....................
15   Then down a little way
     Through the trash
     Towards where
     All dark no begging
     No giving no words
20   No sense no need
     Through the scum
     Down a little way
     To whence one glimpse
     Of that wellhead.
     (282, 288-290)
```

This joint effort of Words and Music, which is accomplished under the leadership of Music, following an order by Croak ("Together!" [278]), constitutes the centre and culminating phase of the play. It structurally combines the three major themes of the play – age, love and the face – and is endowed with a poetical quality which made Everett Frost enthusiastically call it "some of the most exquisite lyric lines [Beckett]

---

[23] This is the view of Frost, who speaks of "**the** poem" ("Fundamental Sounds" 372, emphasis mine).

had ever written" ("Fundamental Sounds" 272). Does this mean then that, in this play, the plurimedial cooperation of the spoken word and music in song is surprisingly meant to belie Beckett's negativist aesthetics, that it points the way to a realm where after all there **is** something to express and something with which to express, that in spite of everything the true meaning of this metamedial allegory is to underline the expressive function of art and in particular of music, and that ultimately the possibility of beauty and a remnant of positivity are revealed?

A number of elements seem indeed to confirm the impression that a joint effort of Words and of Music as the leading force, that a cooperation of both media[24] and not their antagonism, is at the centre of the implied norms. Apart from the poeticalness of the song and its structural importance as a summary of the play's themes, the cooperation of Words and Music is also emphasized by the fact that in this play each medium is shown to engage in some intermedial imitation of features of the other medium. On the one hand, music is attributed a noteworthy rhetoricity. According to Beckett's directions, it receives qualifications such as "*Love and soul music*" (278), it is said to "*Triumph*" (286) or to be "*confident*" (288), to make suggestions, invitations or to utter a "*brief rude retort*" (290). In short, through the referential content and the emotional shading given to its utterances, music is here treated like a language which sometimes even seems to be directly translatable into words, for instance when music is made to 'say' "*adsum*" (274, 278).

If music is thus verbalized (a feature which seems to have escaped the critics' attention), words appear reciprocally to be musicalized (in contrast to the reverse case, this trait has variously been commented on [cf. Zilliacus 108ff.; Guralnick 89; and Debrock 68 and 79]). One manifestation of this musicalization can be noticed in the macro-scale emphasis on form. Musical formalism is present in the structuring device of framing an extended central piece, in which three 'voices' are present, by an 'introduction' and a 'coda' that are given only to two voices and create a cyclical symmetry between beginning and ending. An attempt at approaching musical formalism

---

[24] Cf. Worth 210: "At last [...] they are completely together [...]".

can also be recognized in the obtruding centering of the verbal discourse on several, musically developed themes[25].

The musicalization of the spoken word is even more obvious on the micro-scale, as Zilliacus already noticed. Thus, the tautology mentioned above with reference to Word's 'rhapsody on love', "Love is of all the passions [...]", is not only a negativist device, emptying language of its meaning, but a consequence of the musically inspired principles of repetition, variation and permutation that operate as early as in the first two sentences of the play:

(A) Sloth is of all the (B) passions the most (C) powerful (B) passion and indeed no (B) passion is more (C) powerful than the (B) passion of (A) sloth, this is the (1) mode in which the (2) mind is (3) most affected and indeed in no (1) mode is the (2) mind (3) more affected than in this [...] (272).

"The pattern is ABCBBCBA", as Zilliacus notes for the first sentence of the above quotation (108). It is a beautiful symmetrical arrangement, followed by another symmetry: the repetition of the sequence of elements 1-2-3 in the second sentence. It is true that semantically, the use of the same rhetorical superlatives in 'defining' different "passions", such as love and sloth, creates a contradiction and thus empties language of meaning indeed. Yet this desemanticized text is here functionally justified by the attempt to approach the condition of music in the medium of language.

The fact that Beckett's work thus engages in several forms of combining words and music certainly underlines the relevance of intermediality in it. Yet, in spite of some indications to the contrary, the positive effect of the individual medium as well as the joint efforts of words and music are questionable or at least ambivalent. This becomes clear if one takes into account the cyclical nature of the play, in which at the end nothing really seems to have changed: so the amount of Beckettian entropy has not been reduced. This also becomes clear if one takes a closer look at the song text: it is the evocation of a situation of real or imagined loss, not of fulfillment, and it overtly thematizes meaninglessness in the phrase "no sense" (line 20).

---

[25] Their nature as 'themes' is indeed for once not merely a critical metaphor habitually used by literary scholars but is identified as such expressly in the text. This might even be viewed as a clue planted by Beckett to highlight the musicality of the language used here.

On the other hand, the text also mentions a curious "wellhead" (line 24): it is 'glimpse[d]' at the end of a 'down[ward]' movement (lines 23 and 24), which in this context refers to a woman's eye. This is possibly a metaphor for the essence of the 'soul' hidden in the depths of this eye. Although no lasting contemplation of this essence is mentioned, there seems to be at least a fleeting epiphanic moment. In this promise of a view and its ephemeral status lies a particularly remarkable ambivalence.

A similar ambivalence reigns in what must above all be considered as a key evidence for the implied norms, namely Croak's reaction to the 'Age-song': he remains silent in a "*Long pause*" after the first lines of the song (282), a period in which he struggles with an inspiration which leads him to evoke "[t]he face" (ibid.). After the conclusion of the song he is again silent and is then heard to let his club fall and shuffle away. The meaning of this reaction is deeply ambivalent[26]. It could be utter despair, yet it could also be a positive reaction. The positive view can be supported by the fact that the performance of the song triggers the longest period of silence in Croak: a period during which he is in all probability intensely listening. So Words and Music have at least managed to impress him in some way: some deep experience has been elicited, and the 'shock' which the text mentions as Words's reaction to Croak's silent leaving may mirror an emotion of Croak's that is perhaps so overwhelming that the old man can only weep. Yet, it remains to be asked if this is an altogether positive experience, a "comfort" (274 and passim), as hoped for by Croak: For the last intelligible word uttered by him is an "*anguished* [...] No"! (286) which comes in the interval between the two parts of the 'Age-song'. At the end, Croak's letting fall his club could also indicate a loss of power and of energy: together with his ensuing retreat, this may be viewed as a suggestion that art does not have any invigorating effect, and so it is highly doubtful if it can console.

---

[26] Scholarly interpretations of this ending are in fact deeply divided: they reach from the optimistic view that Words and Music have eventually reached a "genuine expression of feeling" (Worth 195), which overwhelms Croak so that he leaves (Zilliacus harps also on the "rich[ness]" of the artistic "fare", yet, owing to the "elusive[ness]" of the "wellhead" views it less positively [111]) to the pessimistic claim that the fleetingness of the reminiscence leaves Croak 'in utter despair' ("in völliger Verzweiflung" [Esslin 175]). Acheson also sides with the pessimistic view: according to him, Croak fails to find in art the solace of his suffering he hoped for and is not even entertained by the performance of Words and Music (cf. 54), so that Croak's departure is for him "an expression of profound regret over lost opportunities and his inability to compose [...] a song that will ameliorate his sorrow" (60).

Ambivalence persists up to the very end of the play: when Croak has left and Words implores Music to continue, this on the one hand could point to Music embodying, after all, something positive. On the other hand Music, in its answer, is no longer productive but **re**productive: it varies what has already been stated, as if it had lost its inspiration. The last sound one hears, namely Words's sigh, contains a last ambiguity, if we consider only Beckett's written text: it could be a sigh of dissatisfaction or of satisfaction and relief.

Summing up the metamedial issues with which the play's text is concerned, the following can be stated:

1. as for the interrelation and the hierarchical position of words and music, there seems to be a tendency
   a) to emphasize the cooperation of, rather than an antagonism between, the two media and
   b) to underline a certain superiority of music;
2. as for the functions words and music appear to fulfil, there is considerably less certainty:
   a) what appears to be least questionable is the expressive function, in particular of music (it is, however, not to be excluded that this expressivity is undermined by irony, at least with respect to the so-called 'love music' this seems indeed to be the case);
   b) the referential function of creating or affirming meaning is much more problematic; the ephemeral nature of glimpsing the "wellhead" and the tautological definitions of sloth and love argue against Words's ability to fulfil this function in any positive way; yet this result is possibly counterbalanced by the beautiful musicality with which verbal discourse is endowed in some places;
   c) the referential function of words is also debatable, because it seems as if the evocations of Croak's past are mere constructs;

d) in connection with this, the memory function of words is similarly rendered doubtful, and with it the effect of memory as conducive to establishing or corroborating identity;

e) as a consequence of all this, the consolotary function of both words and music is remarkably uncertain, as the ambiguity of the ending shows.

5. Remnants of positivity in the 'Age-song' as deducible from the Feldman/Frost production of *Words and Music*?

As we can see, the text alone is in many respects inconclusive and open. What can be said with some assurance is at best that the Romantic allusions of the play turn out to be thoroughly relative. One must, however, not forget that *Words and Music* is not just a printed text but a plurimedial radio play. One consequently should also take the music into account which Beckett expressly included in the play. Music – in this case Morton Feldman's composition – here becomes part of a performance which, like all performances, necessarily reduces the range of openness which the script leaves. Feldman's rendering of the 'Age-song' and the production of the play's ending are cases in point.

A couple of things are remarkable in the conclusion of the Feldman/Frost production (cf. Beckett/Feldman *Words and Music*): as for the final song, it certainly cannot be called 'harmonious' according to the premises of traditional, tonal music (in the instrumental part the dominant interval, a seventh, precludes this). With the utterly reductive and repetitive melody, which most of the time harps on two recurrent notes only, it may even be called monotonous and thus could be said to point to entropy as a pervading tendency of Beckett's works. Yet this would certainly be too negative a characterization of the effect of Feldman's music: its overall impression is one of amazing quiet in both parts, in Words's song line as well as in Music's accompaniment, and what is more, both parts imitate each other to some extent.

The end is even clearer with reference to our question as to whether music and its relation to words create a note of positivity or not: Music, so to speak, is so kind as to follow Words's "*[i]mploring*" wish twice. This elicits the last sigh uttered by Words: in the Feldman/Frost production, it is not a sigh of pain, but clearly a sigh of relief. So, at least in this interpretation, the balance leans at the end towards the side of positivity – and it does so under the leadership of music. Of course, this positivity is predominantly an effect of a particular interpretive rendering. Yet it should be emphasized that this positive interpretation does **not** go against the grain of Beckett's work, which **does** attribute a conspicuous place to music without altogether sentimentalizing it. Thus, *Words and Music* appears as one of the rare works of Beckett's which possess an openness that at least leaves **some** space for a view of the world and of art that is less negativist as one would expect it from Beckett. What is more, it even **permits** a relatively positive ending.

It should, however, not be forgotten that the consolation at the very end is not felt by the human figure Croak, but by Words. This could be read as a last affirmation of the superiority of music in comparison to words and thus to emphasize an interesting metamedial scepticism, in Beckett's text, towards his own verbal medium[27]. Yet, it is a humanly useless superiority and consolation, since it operates in the absence of the allegorical representative of man. Thus, at the end, negativity seems to prevail in spite of everything. However, the allegorical level is not the only one relevant in this play. If Croak as the internal recipient of Words's and Music's production has left the stage, we, the audience still remain – and are able to appreciate their final cooperation. And we, too, may sigh with relief at the end, even if this is only one possible way of interpreting Beckett's final stage direction "*Deep sigh*" (290).

---

[27] This sceptical evaluation harmonizes with the general scepticism towards language which so frequently can be encountered in Beckett's works.

References

Abbott, H. Porter. "Samuel Beckett and the Arts of Time: Painting, Music, Narrative". Oppenheim, ed. 7-24.
Acheson, James. "Beckett Re-Joycing: *Words and Music*". Phyllis Carey and Ed Jewinski, eds. *Re: Joyce'n Beckett*. New York: Fordham Univ. Press, 1992. 50-60.
Albright, Daniel. "Beckett as Marsyas". Oppenheim, ed. 25-49.
Barthes, Roland. "La Mort de l'auteur". *Mantéia* 5 (1968): 12-17.
Becker, Joachim. "Klangkörper und Mentalchöre: Becketts Hörspiele und das dramatische Werk". *Forum Modernes Theater* 11.2 (1996): 170-184.
Beckett, Samuel. *Words and Music*. Samuel Beckett. *Dramatische Dichtungen in drei Sprachen*. Vol. 2. Elmar Tophoven, German trans. Frankfurt/M.: Suhrkamp, 1981. 270-291.
—. *Three Dialogues*. 1949. *Proust. Three Dialogues*. Samuel Beckett. London: Calder & Boyars, 1965. 97-126.
Beckett, Samuel, and Morton Feldman. *Words and Music*. The Beckett Festival of Radio Plays. Project director Everett C. Frost. CD. Voices International Production, presented by Evergreen Review, n.d.
Bryden, Mary, ed. *Samuel Beckett and Music*. Oxford: Clarendon, 1998.
Catanzaro, Mary. "Song and Improvisation in *Lessness*". Marius Buning, Lois Oppenheim, eds. *Beckett in the 1990s: Selected papers from the Second International Beckett Symposium, held in The Hague, 8-12 April, 1992*. Amsterdam: Rodopi, 1993. 213-218.
Debrock, Guy. "The Word Man and the Note Man: Morton Feldman and Beckett's Virtual Music". Oppenheim, ed. 67-82.
Esslin, Martin. "Samuel Beckett und die Kunst des Rundfunks". Hartmut Engelhardt, ed. *Samuel Beckett*. Frankfurt/M.: Suhrkamp, 1984. 163-196.
Frost, Everett C. "Fundamental Sounds: Recording Samuel Beckett's Radio Plays". *Theatre Journal* 43.3 (1991): 361-376.
—. "The Note Man on the Word Man: Morton Feldman on Composing the Music for Samuel Beckett's *Words and Music* in The Beckett Festival of Radio Plays". Bryden, ed. 47-55.
Grindea, Miron. "Beckett's Involvement With Music". Bryden, ed. 183-185.
Guralnick, Elissa S. *Sight Unseen: Beckett, Pinter, Stoppard, and Other Contemporary Dramatists on Radio*. Athens: Ohio Univ. Press, 1996.
Kesting, Marianne. "Samuel Beckett: Endgame. Endzeit und Schädelprojektion". Heinrich F. Plett, ed. *Englisches Drama von Beckett bis Bond*. Munich: Fink, 1982. 50-75.
Knowlson, James. *Damned to Fame: The Life of Samuel Beckett*. London: Bloomsbury, 1996.
Krance, Charles. "Beckett Music". Oppenheim, ed. 51-65.
Oppenheim, Lois, ed. *Samuel Beckett and the Arts: Music, Visual Arts, and Non-Print Media*. Border Crossings 2. New York: Garland, 1999.

Richardson, Stanley, Jane Alison Hale. "Working Wireless: Beckett's Radio Writing". Oppenheim, ed. 269-294.
Ruch, A. "Morton Feldman's *Words and Music*". http://www.the modernword.com/beckett_feldman_wam.html. Accessed August 22, 2002.
Schlichting, Hans Burkhard. "Hörspiel: Zur Hermeneutik akustischer Spielformen". Helmut Brackert, Jörn Stückrath, eds. *Literaturwissenschaft: Ein Grundkurs*. Rowohlts Enzyklopädie. Reinbek b. Hamburg: Rowohlt, 1992. 225-237.
Wolf, Werner. *The Musicalization of Fiction: A Study in the Theory and History of Intermediality*. Internationale Forschungen zur Allgemeinen und Vergleichenden Literaturwissenschaft 35. Amsterdam: Rodopi, 1999.
—. "Intermediality Revisited: Reflections on Word and Music Relations in the Context of a General Typology of Intermediality". Suzanne M. Lodato, Suzanne Aspden, Walter Bernhart, eds. *Word and Music Studies: Essays in Honor of Steven Paul Scher and on Cultural Identity and the Musical Stage*. Word and Music Studies 4. Amsterdam: Rodopi, 2002. 13-34.
Worth, Katharine. "Beckett and the Radio Medium". John Drakakis, ed. *British Radio Drama*. Cambridge: Cambridge Univ. Press, 1981. 191-217.
Zilliacus, Clas. *Beckett and Broadcasting: A Study of the Works of Samuel Beckett for and in Radio and Television*. Acta Academiae Aboensis 51:2. Abo: Abo Akademi, 1976.

Beckett, Feldman, Joe and Bob:

Speaking of Music in *Words and Music*

Stephen Benson, London

The Morton Feldman realization of Samuel Beckett's radio play, *Words and Music*, offers a palimpsest of the history of the relationship of music and the spoken word. Within the peculiarly disembodied space of the airwaves, Joe (Words) and Bob (Music) are represented in the archetypal situation of striving to express the passions, as nominated by their overseer and reluctant aesthetician, Croak. The piece runs the gamut of vocal expression, from silence and sigh, via murmur and speech, to the twin collaborative peaks of the play's two 'songs'. While *Words and Music* suggests an embarrassment of interpretative riches, I concentrate here on its staging of the variously conflicting and acquiescent sounds of speech and music. As realized by Feldman, a composer who was deeply antithetical to the idea of music with a dramatic or literary underpinning, the piece becomes an allegory of the manner in which music and speech frame one another, not least according to the conventions of both opera and music radio. While we may tend to grant precedence to music – Beckett himself said of *Words and Music* that "music always wins" – the manner in which Joe and Bob speak to and for one another during the course of their memory-haunted dialogue suggests a more complicated interdependence. The Beckett/Feldman *Words and Music* is thus an example of contrapuntal radio (to adapt a phrase from Glenn Gould), in which the voices in counterpoint are the voices of radio itself: words, music, and the sounds and silences between.

There has been a renaissance of interest recently in the practice of counterfactual history, based on the 'what would have happened if?' scenario. While not quite on the level of a triumphant Napoleon at Waterloo, I would like to begin by proposing a counterfactual for Samuel Beckett's 1962 "piece for radio", *Words and Music*. The piece is full of gaps – not just pauses, silences or ellipses, but virtual blank spaces waiting to be acoustically filled in by composed music. This presents a dilemma for the interpreter. Where those engaged in performance studies often chastise bookish types for idealizing play scripts – for ignoring the spoken word in the interests of a safely static and silent text – here the dangers are doubled. To what extent can this particular multimedia text be read without the music? Many critics, no doubt for practical reasons, seem relatively happy to textualize, largely ignoring not only the designated medium, but also half of the sound of the play. To cite just one example, Katherine Worth says of the 'character' of Music in *Words and Music* that is has been imbued with "a remarkably vivid dramatic presence, even without the aid of sound" (10). This is an innocuous view, perhaps, but one which enables and justifies an unproblematized silent reading, placing music-as-sound in the bizarre and paradoxical position of supplement to music-as-character[1].

Yet imagine for a moment a different scenario. Following the letter, rather than just the spirit, of verbal reductionism, Beckett leaves a series of spaces to be filled in by the words of another. It is true that Beckett came close to writing just such a work, in the shape of what is best known in English as *Rough for Radio I* (first written in French in 1961). Here the parts designated for both Music and Voice are left blank, given only the briefest of authorial directions. The piece is only a sketch, however, a very rough unfinished draft of *Words and Music*'s companion piece, *Cascando* (first broadcast in French in 1963), one that Beckett did not want performed[2]. As with all counterfactuals, my alternative *Words and Music* requires a degree of imaginative juggling. Beckett's compositional skills would perhaps have made a rather weak part for Bob (the name given to the 'character' of Music), to say nothing of the dramatist's well-known desire for close adherence to the letter of his own works. Who would dare to impose? I would suggest that it would be relatively difficult to interpret a piece for words and music in which the words were left unspecified, without prior knowledge of the details of an individual realization. What does it say about the relation of music and the spoken word, then, that critics are content to interpret a play explicitly concerned with this relation without hearing a note of music and to interpret not only its conceptual framework, but also its content? The reason we are able to do so is that Beckett makes relatively clear the conceptual underpinning of Music, and so allows the part to be read without being heard. But is it not precisely the acoustic reality of music (however much always

---

[1] A Derridean reading of this supplemental position would, on the contrary, serve to corroborate my argument against silencing the radio play. The self-sufficiency of textual music is reliant upon the 'aid' of what it is supposed to represent: musical sound.

[2] On the subject of what are now known in English as *Rough for Radio I* and *Rough for Radio II*, cf. Esslin ("Beckett's *Rough for Radio*"). For details of Beckett's engagement with the medium of radio, cf. Esslin ("Samuel Becket and the Art of Broadcasting" and "Telling it How it Is"), Frost ("Fundamental Sounds"), and Wilcher.

already conceptualized) that generates the dramatic debate in the first place? The author himself said of the piece that "Music always wins" (qtd. in Worth 16), implying that it is a radio play in which music and language vie for position in an aesthetic hierarchy. To sing its praises without listening to its song thus seems doubly remiss.

In order to engage with some of these questions, I offer a reading of *Words and Music* which foregrounds sound: the sound of music and the sound of words and music as broadcast over the radio. A common way of reading this and other related texts is to use Beckett's various fictional and non-fictional pronouncements on the subject of music[3]. In the interests of a sound-oriented reading, and in an attempt to open up a different view of the work, I have transferred the author-function to the composer (to be introduced forthwith). If this involves some generalizations about dramatic content, it is an interpretative neglect no different in kind from those textual readings that silence the music. And if such a strategy involves deferring to composerly intention, it is at least overt in its bias, as opposed to positing an implicit accordance with an unspoken idea of what music is and does. While a composer-centred reading is, in methodological terms, embarrassingly conventional, it serves a counter-intuitive purpose in this context that I hope makes it worth the blushes.

To return to my counterfactual, the incompleteness required of an unspecified verbal or instrumental part was a relatively common feature of experimental music in the 1950s. An aesthetic of indeterminacy, formulated most expansively by John Cage, was one strand of a wholesale re-evaluation of the theory and practice of music undertaken by what is commonly called the New York School: a re-evaluation of what constitutes music, of the poetics of performance and customs of listening. One of Cage's closest allies was Morton Feldman, and it is Feldman's 1987 realization of Beckett's Music that I will be considering[4]. Beckett himself suggested Feldman as a suitable candidate for the

---

[3] For an exemplary account of *Words and Music* within the interpretative framework of Beckett's lifelong concern for music and musicality, cf. Prieto (218-28).

[4] The Beckett/Feldman *Words and Music* is one of only three realizations to date. Music for the first was provided by the author's cousin, John Beckett, but subsequently withdrawn by the composer himself. A second attempt was made in 1973 by producer Katherine Worth and, at the suggestion of Beckett, composer Humphrey Searle. This was a non-commercial undertaking, however, made primarily for teaching purposes (cf. Worth).

job, and on a superficial level, the two would seem to have much in common: a close engagement with verbal and musical materials as subjects in their own right; an interest in the reduction of the artistic event to a dramatic minimum, concomitant with a concern for repetition, stasis and duration; and a respect for the silence out of and against which the sounds of a performance resonate. Indeed, the first example of the manner in which composed music can be demoted in the process of reading *Words and Music* comes via the generally agreed aesthetic proximity of Beckett and Feldman. If the composer is so close in spirit to the author, the argument goes, we can take the author's word on the music. Feldman intermittently cites Beckett in the course of his essays, and he certainly singled him out as one of the very few writers for whom he would have undertaken such a project[5]. Yet in terms of published work, we can cite just as many examples of constitutive differences in their respective aesthetics – constitutive because they involve elements such as speed, duration and volume, which were central concerns for both. Feldman's music got progressively longer over the course of his career, while Beckett's texts increasingly aspired to fizzle out. Feldman's career-long interest in indeterminacy is markedly at odds with Beckett's stringent attitude toward performance, which is another reason why *Words and Music* might be regarded as atypical: where Beckett had to programme his own withdrawal in the face of someone else's music, Feldman had to keep his music on a tight rein, not to say speed it up a good deal and, for practical reasons, make it a little louder. In fact, despite the aforementioned superficial alliances, Feldman spent much of his composing life working against precisely that concept of music that underpins Beckett's text, a concept founded on an umbilical link between music and the spoken word. To this extent, there are at least two musics in Bob: Beckett's, available in a silent reading of the text and as implied in the relationship of Bob to the two other protagonists (Joe, the word man, and Croak), and Feldman's, available only in a broadcast (or recorded) performance.

---

[5] Beckett and Feldman collaborated (a word we should use cautiously in this content) on a monodrama, *Neither* (1977), and Feldman's last work was an hour-long orchestral composition titled simply, *For Samuel Beckett* (1987). Laws offers a detailed and musicologically informed account of *Neither*, although it is one predicated on the aforementioned aesthetic proximity of dramatist and composer.

The drama of *Words and Music*, however residual, is archetypal. The basic situation concerns the efforts of the twin protagonists to express selected human passions, conditions and experiences, in the interests of affecting Croak, whose listening responses serve to grade the efficacy of the expression. The conceptual music of *Words and Music* is a music that speaks, formally representing the passions and affecting the listener (the same is of course true of the words, but they perform several other functions). As an archetype of music, such a conception has a long heritage but is perhaps most familiar to us as lying at the heart of late Renaissance and Baroque music theory[6]. The birth of modern music out of the spirit of the classics proposes a doctrine of musical affect founded on two interrelated propositions: the power of music to represent the human passions and the extensive basis of that power in the imitation of emotion in speech (including the stimulation and assuaging of emotion according to the rules of oration). There seems to be a degree of latitude in the dating of the shift from the ancient and medieval doctrine of the affections – an objective, representational practice – to the more recognisably modern aesthetics of emotion – a subjective, expressive practice. It could be argued that Beckett sought to include both modes: where Croak is the individual subject idiosyncratically moved by the music, Music is itself represented as an objectifying art, called upon to enact abstract categories of human feeling. As Carl Dahlhaus says of the subject of the two discourses, however, "there is no sharp separation of the various aspects. Often they flow into each other imperceptibly." (*Esthetics of Music* 18) Beckett's Bob represents a conception of music as above all else human. It is "a music of the **subject**" (Lacoue-Labarthe xvii), both the individual subject moved by sound (Croak and, at times, Joe) and the objectified subject who lies behind the genres of passion invoked in the first half of the piece. At those two points in the Beckett/Feldman text at which words and music come together in song, it is the word man who tentatively suggests the first note and basic rhythm and pace of the melody to come. Certainly, Bob answers and melodically elaborates, with Joe singing a largely syllabic setting of the text which is doubled by the instruments. Yet the song

---

[6] Might we read *Words and Music* as a distant, abstracted relative of Claudio Monteverdi's *Orfeo*, in which the prologue figure of La Musica takes centre stage, but is similarly called upon to illuminate a drama of the sight of "the face" of a lost beloved?

conceit at the formally designated heart of the drama tethers music to the spoken word. Music is literally the sound of emotive speech, with Croak's own arousal serving as testament. We thus read Beckett's *stile rappresentativo*, with concern above all for the proper rhetorical setting of the words of the text according to their emotive meaning.

Beckett's Bob thus offers a music of the speaking and feeling subject. The question is whether Feldman's Bob really does what he is tacitly told. To begin to answer this question we need to take into account Feldman's overriding composerly preoccupation, one which crops up periodically throughout his published writings and which links him with a number of the composers of his generation: a preoccupation with "a music that concentrates on sound" (Feldman 56), with "a sound **as a sound**" (60). In a gnomic doodle included in his collected essays, the composer writes a sort of musicological graffito: "Polyphony Sucks." (158) At first glance, it seems improbable that Feldman would believe such a proposition[7]. It was, after all, the sheer contrapuntal exuberance of Renaissance polyphony – its musical sound – that led to serious doubts about the nature of its relations with the all-important Christian Word. Leaving to one side the ecclesiastical context, we might imagine that Feldman would approve of this overpowering sonic experience. Yet polyphony is predicated on a musical argument of part and whole that can be read as essentially rhetorical in nature, based on what Feldman elsewhere terms "differentiation" (12)[8]. One reason why high polyphonic music can, to modern ears, seem unrelated to the text being sung is because the voices are frequently juxtaposed according to preordained compositional devices. Heard through the ears of Feldman, such music is closely allied in methodological terms to the sonata or serial composition: in each case, sound is subordinate to structure or system: "It appears to me that the subject of music, from Machaut to Boulez, has always been its construction. [...]. To demonstrate any formal idea in music, whether structure or stricture, is a matter of construction, in which the methodology is the controlling

---

[7] On the subject of polyphony, it is interesting to note that Beckett's aversion to Bach was a result of what he felt to be the mechanical aspect of contrapuntally-oriented music (cf. Knowlson 192-93).

[8] Dahlhaus identifies differentiation (and its correlate: integration) as a pervasive criterion of aesthetic judgment in the Western tradition. He distinguishes three types: "material", "functional" and "relational" (*Analysis and Value Judgment* 41-45).

metaphor of the composition." (83) Where Feldman made a Cageian distinction between structure or system and concept, his working method (to the extent that we can identify such a method across a varied set of works) was above all else dictated by what he conceived to be the intrinsic qualities and tendencies of sound itself – events on the "aural plane", the surface, of music – prior to their organization according to pre-sonic systems (183). These systems represent our attempts to fix the sounds of music, thereby making them our own. Feldman strove not for an **inhuman**, but an **ahuman** music, stripped of the comforts of both conventional and modernist methods of organization, and so, from that perspective, dehumanized. His music did not seek to imitate in sound some other thing; nor did it seek a relation with the human sounds of speech. Human speech could not have been further from his goal[9]. The question of whether Feldman was concerned with the humanizing of music at the other end of the musical continuum – by the listener – is another matter, although he did remark in passing that it would be his "dream" to witness the demise of the concert hall performance: "I never fully understand the need for a 'live' audience. My music, because of its extreme quietude, would be happiest with a dead one." (57) Perhaps this was a step too far, although one which would serve to explain the name of Croak, the sole audience member in *Words and Music*.

In a withering review of a rather ambitious programme of twentieth-century music conducted by Gunther Schuller in 1962 (the year of the first broadcast of the original *Words and Music*), Feldman writes with barely concealed scorn: "Everything on the program had one thing in common: drama." (10) A similar attitude, albeit minus the youthful polemics, seems to have underpinned his approach to the vestigial drama of *Words and Music*. In a revealing interview about the compositional process, he admitted to not having read the piece from start to finish: "I hardly read it. Oh, of course, I read it. But I started at the end; I started in different places. That was my way to get to know Beckett. Because I couldn't read it without the music, and there was no music." (Qtd. in Frost, "The Note Man" 51) Extrapolating a little, we could say that in contrast to those

---

[9] In the course of a brief meeting that was to result in the short text for *Neither*, Feldman informed Beckett: "it's very seldom that I've used words. I've written a lot of pieces with voice, and they're wordless." (Qtd. in Knowlson 631)

textually-oriented critics mentioned above, there was, for Feldman, no music in the text precisely because there was no musical sound. Unlike other composers and artists of his generation, Feldman tacitly defines music as requiring sound (**musical** sound, to the extent that he disagreed with the Cageian notion that "everything is music") and so declines to acknowledge the conceptual music of the verbal text. What's more, in ignoring the pull of the relatively explicit narrative, Feldman acts as a resisting reader. What he resists is the anthropic pre-sonic system of story, yet another object to be imitated in sound. Feldman's is an anti-dramatic, and certainly anti-narrative, aesthetic, "free", to quote his own words, "from [a] compositional rhetoric" (5-6). We can trace such a stance in Feldman's intermittent disruption of Beckett's directions for Bob. To give one example: in the introductory exchange of the three protagonists, the text prescribes a brief moment of Beckettian mock formality, in which Croak addresses his two comforts in turn. Each is directed to reply "As before", which for Joe, means a repeated "My Lord". Feldman's Bob diverges from the text to the extent that, while each of his four responses oscillates around the interval of a seventh, the soundings differ considerably from one another (ex. 1; the score does not contain the text). The prescribed semantic neutrality of the introductory music is then further undermined when the figure of the interval is clearly sounded again in the course of both the "age music" heard later in the piece and during what is supposed to be "warmly sentimental" music evocative of a female face[10].

It is all too easy to hear Feldman's Bob through Beckett's, both because the dramatist's music is far more familiar to us than the composer's, and because of the hermeneutic privilege the listener will tend to grant to the verbal text. In this instance, a textualist reading would either ignore such overtly introductory material, or, listening to Feldman, simply generalize each of the four individual musical events according to the shared motif: where Joe, in whatever tone of voice, says "My Lord", Bob, in whatever orchestration or rhythmic configuration, says 'seventh' (to the musicological listener, at

---

[10] I am not suggesting that Feldman simply disregarded Beckett's directions or the text itself. Rather, his response is respectful of both the words and the impossibility, and futility, of music that would simply do what the words say (however we might measure such accord). It is this paradoxical position out of which the Beckett/Feldman *Words and Music* arises.

least). What then of Feldman's dedication to the sound of music? To read *Words and Music* through this aesthetic is to feel duty bound to listen closely to, rather than simply to read, the music. In so doing, we face the sheer variety of these small moments: different pitches, different time signatures, different instrumentation, and so on. Feldman's score is organized into thirty-three short sections, or cells, a large majority of which are marked *da capo*. (The published score includes none of Beckett's text and so no part for Joe, even at those points when Joe and Bob come together. It thus stands as the representation of a purely acoustic, as opposed to verbal, text.) One of the means by which music becomes musically meaningful is via repetition and the act of memory required by it, yet Feldman's cells seem calculated to frustrate the rhetoric by which

Example 1: Morton Feldman, "Samuel Beckett, Words and Music,*" mm. 1-9.*

Reproduced by permission of the publisher from Feldman, "Samuel Beckett, Words and Music".

repetition serves to uncover or predicate a pre-sonic pattern: development, foreshadowing, retrospection, motivic and thematic interrelation, and so on. Each of these techniques strives to organize time in the interests of memory, which, for Feldman, is another instance of a "fixing" of musical sounds as a means of making them human (Feldman 137). Conversely, Feldman is concerned with "getting to Time in its unstructured existence [...] in how Time exists before we put our paws on it – our minds, our imaginations, into it" (87). One means of achieving this (note the Feldmanian paradox) is via a deliberate sabotaging of conventional rhetoric: "'formalizing' a disorientation of memory", whereby "there is a **suggestion** that what we hear is functional and directional, but we soon realize that this is an illusion; a bit like walking the streets of Berlin – where all the buildings look alike, **even if they're not**" (138). It is thus the functional nature of repetition against which Feldman writes, a culturally and historically specific function that plays across as well as within works. To return to my small example, at that point at which the text suggests neutral and exact repetition, along the lines of Bob's verbalist sparring partner, Feldman's music gestures towards a congruent musical mode of repetition only to undermine it. Again, "there is a **suggestion** that what we hear is functional" – that is, motivic repetition – but widespread, seemingly arbitrary shifts in register, rhythm, pulse and pitch lead us away from the heuristic linkages of rhetoric towards the singularity of sound. To this extent, Feldman's music strives to hinder precisely those semantic generalizations, such as I made earlier, required to identify the sounding of this alleged figure later in the piece.

The undermining of the rhetoric of repetition is further pursued within individual cells by the use of "very close, but never precisely synchronized, notation" (Feldman 139), what fellow composer Brian Ferneyhough terms "slight phrase decoupling" (445). We hear this at various points in *Words and Music*, not least in the course of the halting melody for the first 'song', the vocal and instrumental parts for which are subtly but pervasively out of synch. For Feldman, such "nonpatterned syncopations" (141) serve again to forestall the imputation of rhetorical intent, in that there is no discernable pattern, no identifiable stylistic underpinning to which the music could be said to refer (beyond this anti-style, of course). In the absence of a rhetorical or symbolic programme, our ears are drawn to the sounds themselves, in particular the sounds of the individual instruments, for instance, two flutes and an unmotored vibraphone, both instruments favoured by Feldman. It was during his Berlin phase that the composer came to conceive of orchestration as one means of circumventing the anthropic fixing of music. At that time, he wrote that "orchestration is the life of music without 'taking thought'" (205), a counter to the short-score scenario whereby music can be boiled down to a pre- or semi-orchestrated essence (as elsewhere, Feldman seems to take to an extreme an element in the music of his own and the preceding generation). Again, against generalizing or reductive tendencies, Feldman proposes an aesthetic of the singular musical sound event.

With so much undermining going on, we might wonder why Feldman agreed to work on such a text. Beyond the simple fact that Beckett was perhaps his favourite author, I suggest that the answer lies with the medium in question. *Words and Music* is designated "A piece for radio", and it is in the form of a radio broadcast that we need to conceive the status of the two key protagonists (yet another reason for attending to sound). Indeed, we could say that the piece is a dramatization of the two dominant sounds of radio, or rather, of what is now the dominant radio format: "talk and music radio" (Crisell 64). *Words and Music* was commissioned by the BBC and broadcast on the Third Programme on 13 November 1962 (the Beckett/Feldman version was first recorded in 1987 and broadcast in 1989). To write a piece for radio in the early 1960s was to be unavoidably aware of the creeping dominance of television, which began in earnest in the 1950s. Yet the early 1960s also saw the advent of transistor radios – the genuinely portable wireless. The inexpensive transistor radio helped radio as a medium to survive by the paradoxical means of letting it blend into the background: it became what is sometimes termed a "secondary medium", that is, a medium that not only allows one to do something else while listening, but that can be switched on without being attended to in any way (Crisell 13). This adaptability has in part led to the dominance of music on radio today. Not only does music not require adaptation in order to meet the requirements of radio (unlike each of the various genres of spoken-word broadcasting); we also do not need to listen to it actively.

Thus, it may seem odd to propose radio as a Feldmanesque medium. Certainly, he showed little interest in radio as used compositionally by Cage and other experimentalists. Rather, radio is attractive as an exclusively acoustic medium: a "**blind medium**" (taken literally, that is; Crisell 3). Radio strips music of the accoutrements of place and objecthood. We are denied access to its source, to its performers, and its performance. Radio may be deeply implicated in the commodification of music, but it does not allow us to hold or to hoard its symbolic embodiment; and compared to recorded music, it refuses manipulation of its linearity (until recently, at least, with the advent of on-demand radio available over the internet). Music is ostensibly the most natural of radio outputs – "perhaps the only kind of output we can enjoy on the medium without feeling in some degree handicapped by a lack of vision" (Crisell 64) – and certainly eminently suitable for a composer seeking to de-objectify music, one striving for a sourceless music devoid of visual or aural origin. From a phenomemological perspective, music on the radio is in fact pure to the point of disquiet. In a passage in which he quotes Beckett, Feldman suggests that the motivic working out – the juxtaposition and differentiation – that is so much a part of the practice and evaluation of art music, is in the interests of keeping anxiety at bay. As he asks, "What if Beethoven went on and on without any element of differentiation?" (87)[11] Thinking this through in terms of radio, we might wonder what the response would be if the music simply went on and on, without explanation, identification, cessation or, perhaps crucially, location. Feldman is right to suggest that music stripped of the various conventions of differentiation might provoke anxiety or boredom (like Beckett, he thought of boredom as a not uninteresting condition). What radio uses to counter this possibility is, of course, speech: hence talk and music radio. This type of programming offers not only one of the prime instances in contemporary culture of the interrelation of music and the spoken word. It is perhaps **the** means by which we can trace the regulation of music by speech. The spoken presentation of music on radio serves above all else to humanize musical sound in two ways. Firstly, in terms of the content of the discourse, speech frames music in order to explain and identify what we have heard or

---

[11] Again, Dahlhaus's discussion of differentiation and integration is pertinent here, particularly in relation to the reception of Feldman's – and, in the literary sphere, Beckett's – work: "The spontaneous suspicion arises that the postulate of the complementation of differentiation and integration – like other aesthetic conceptions based on an organic model – hides a classicistic tendency which leads to injustice toward stylistically archaic or mannered works." (*Analysis and Value Judgment* 42)

will hear, according to one of several presentational genres (*Words and Music* was written for the BBC Third Programme, a public station devoted at the time to high art and its cultures). It locates it in terms of history, genre, tradition and culture, and value. Secondly, the sound of the human voice serves almost literally to personify the music. It is an index of continuity across time, of authority and knowledge. It extends a humanizing presence that situates the musical sound in relation to us, providing foundations for what is in fact a deeply impersonal medium. The speaking voice signifies and regulates the human source of the not-necessarily-human sounds it frames. Where Feldman's project represents an attempt, however paradoxical and fatally flawed, to leave sound alone (and it is of course flawed, for the simple reason that musical sound is itself an intentional object), radio simply refuses to do so.

This brings us close to full circle. In terms of verbal concept and presentational genre, the texted music of *Words and Music* is variously tied to speech. It is a music that is always spoken for, in however celebratory a manner. Conversely, Feldman's intervention is predicated on ahuman musical sounds such as might best be heard over the airwaves, coming from nowhere and no one. What I have sought to achieve in privileging Feldman's Bob is an uncoupling of words and music in the interests of a less wordy music, borrowing as metaphor the composer's own practice of repeated "slight phrase decoupling" (Ferneyhough 445). Perhaps such a strategy says more about the anxiety I myself feel, as a barely literate musicologist, when faced with mixed-media works such as this, in which music resolutely refuses to stay put on the page. While the vocabulary of musicology may seem out of place here, not least in terms of its close involvement with precisely those conceptions of music rejected by Feldman, it at least seems to respect music as sound. In so doing, it acknowledges Feldman's own ethics of music, an ethics manifest in his refusal to conform to a silent, but imperialistic, music of the text.

We could of course go to the other extreme and suggest an alternative coupling, that is, make sound rather than sense our conceptual paradigm. This would be to read the radio play first and foremost as acoustic art, a *Hörspiel*. The Beckett/Feldman *Words and Music* was conceived as a co-production with Klaus Schöning at the *Hörspiel* Studio at West German Radio in Cologne (the only other commercially available production subsequent to the premiere was also made by WDR). As such, it is heir to a tradition of experimental sound art – the New *Hörspiel* – many examples of which had their origins in Schöning's work at the famous studios at WDR (including several of Cage's late radio-related pieces, such as *Roaratorio* of 1979)[12]. Placing *Words and Music* in this admittedly loose generic context would result in a downgrading of the sense of human speech and a promotion of the sound of the voices **as voices**, their "sonorous aspect" (Nancy 234): the various non-verbal human sounds, the sighs and groans, that precede and interlace speech, together with the absent sounds of silence which we might imagine to be shadowed on a radio broadcast by unlocated, and unlocatable, white noise. To read *Words and Music* as a New *Hörspiel* would be to demote music in the interests of sound, in much the same way as more conventional readings demote sound in the interests of sense, and to view music along the lines of the inveterate *Hörspielmacher*, Mauricio Kagel, as always and everywhere a *Hörspiel*, surrounded and infiltrated by the sounds we strive to exclude in order more safely to define the object of our listening pleasure[13]. Rather than idealize the sound of the vibraphone as of an irreducibly different order to any of the words we might put with it (the Cageian line), this would be to conceive of all the sounds and silences in the piece as variously open, or resistant, to musicalization, depending on how we wish to hear them, and to what end.

Yet this interpretative strategy doesn't quite convince. Unless heard as a slightly detuned AM broadcast, *Words and Music* simply isn't noisy enough to qualify as a New *Hörspiel*, to say nothing of that fact that, however vestigial, its narrative is too clearly meaningful. Conversely, as realized by Feldman, it is acoustically too eventful to allow sense wholly to colonize sound. (Beckett and Feldman were, in musical terms, relatively conventional artists. Compared to contemporaneous works – experimental music of the late 1950s and 1960s, or acoustic art of the 1980s – *Words and Music* is squarely 'in the

---

[12] For a wide-ranging history of German radio art, a fertile context for *Words and Music*, cf. Cory. On Cage's radio work, cf. Kostelanetz. Douglas Kahn and Gregory Whitehead's collection, in which Cory's essay appears, is indicative of a renaissance of interest in the theory and practice of audio art.

[13] The topic chosen by Kagel for the 1970 Cologne Seminar for New Music was "Music as *Hörspiel*" (Cory 365).

tradition'.) While the talk of the text undoubtedly dictates our response, however, the sound of the music bothers it more than the text would suggest, and certainly more than is normal for talk and music radio. On the face of it, the Beckett/Feldman piece is the product of a gesture of compromise: Beckett's constitutive silence in the interests of music, Feldman's capitulation to a verbal context for his music. Yet this gesture merely masks what is in fact a non-collaboration. Beckett played absolutely no part in the genesis of the performance, beyond agreeing to allow Feldman to be commissioned; and as we heard, Feldman admitted to subverting the text quite blatantly in the course of preparing to work with it. The pair never discussed the piece, a fact seemingly characteristic of Beckett's attitude to composers, as opposed to directors (Worth 12-13). Feldman once wrote that he was concerned with "writing music, where you thought one way and yet it sounded another" (155). What we have in this *Words and Music* is an unsighted staging of the mismatch: a discreet refusal on the part of realized music to be regulated by speaking subjects, or by the idea that music, however it sounds, will always conventionally mirror the words we put with it. As such, it provides an object lesson in the difference between speaking **of**, and speaking **for**, music.

References

Beckett, Samuel. *Words and Music. Collected Shorter Plays*. London: Faber, 1984. 125-34.
Bryden, Mary, ed. *Samuel Beckett and Music*. Oxford: Clarendon Press, 1999.
Cory, Mark. E. "Soundplay: The Polyphonous Tradition of German Radio Art". Douglas Kahn and Gregory Whitehead, eds. *Wireless Imagination: Sound, Radio, and the Avant-Garde*. Cambridge, MA: MIT Press, 1994. 331-71.
Crisell, Andrew. *Understanding Radio*. 2nd ed. London: Routledge, 1994.
Dahlhaus, Carl. *Esthetics of Music*. William Austin, trans. Cambridge: Cambridge Univ. Press, 1982.
—. *Analysis and Value Judgment*. Siegmund Levarie, trans. New York: Pendragon, 1983.
Esslin, Martin. "Samuel Beckett and the Art of Broadcasting". *Encounter* 45.3 (1975): 38-46.
—. "Beckett's *Rough for Radio*". *Journal of Modern Literature* 6 (1977): 95-103.

—. "Telling it How it Is: Beckett and the Mass Media". Joseph H. Smith, ed. *The World of Samuel Beckett*. Baltimore: Johns Hopkins Univ. Press, 1991. 204-16

Feldman, Morton. "Samuel Beckett, Words and Music". London: Universal Edition, 1987.

—. *Give My Regards to Eighth Street: Collected Writings of Morton Feldman*. B.H. Friedman, ed. Cambridge, MA: Exact Change, 2000.

Ferneyhough, Brian. *Collected Writings*. James Boros and Richard Toop, eds. Amsterdam: Harwood Academic Publishers, 1995.

Frost, Everett C. "Fundamental Sounds: Recording Samuel Beckett's Radio Plays". *Theatre Journal* 43.3 (1991): 361-76.

—. "The Note Man on the Word Man: Morton Feldman on Composing the Music for Samuel Beckett's *Words and Music* in *The Beckett Festival of Radio Plays*". Bryden, ed. 47-55.

Knowlson, James. *Damned to Fame: The Life of Samuel Beckett*. London: Bloomsbury, 1996.

Kostelanetz, Richard. "John Cage as a *Hörspielmacher*". Richard Kostelanetz, ed. *Writings about John Cage*. Ann Arbor: Univ. of Michigan Press, 1996. 213-21.

Lacoue-Labarthe, Phillipe. *Musica Ficta (Figures of Wagner)*. Felicia McCarren, trans. Meridian: Crossing Aesthetics Series. Stanford: Stanford Univ. Press, 1994.

Laws, Catherine. "Morton Feldman's *Neither*: A Musical Translation of Beckett's Text". Bryden, ed. 57-85.

Nancy, Jean-Luc. "Vox Clamans in Deserto". Nathalia King, trans. *The Birth to Presence*. Brian Holmes et al, trans. Stanford: Stanford Univ. Press, 1993. 234-47.

Prieto, Eric. *Listening In: Music, Mind, and the Modernist Narrative*. Stages 19. Lincoln: Univ. of Nebraska Press, 2002.

Wilcher, Robert. "'Out of the Dark': Beckett's Texts for Radio". James Acheson and Kateryna Arthur, eds. *Beckett's Later Fiction and Drama: Texts for Company*. London: Macmillan, 1987. 1-17.

Worth, Katherine. "Words for Music Perhaps". Bryden, ed. 9-20.

Musical and Verbal Counterpoint in Thirty Two Short Films About Glenn Gould

Deborah Weagel, Albuquerque

> The human voice is a musical instrument affiliated with the reed family. In the film, *Thirty Two Short Films About Glenn Gould*, the voice is frequently treated as an instrument, and the spoken word is integrated into a variety of complex contrapuntal settings. For example, in one of the short films, "The Idea of North: A Radio Documentary by Glenn Gould", three voices sound and interact to create a counterpoint that is analogous to music. As these voices interrelate, Gould (as performed by Colm Feore), who is already familiar with the broadcast, acts as though he is conducting the verbal music. His gestures acknowledge subtle nuances and he treats the interplay and layering of words as though they were intricately composed musical notes. In this essay, I draw upon both the film and the screenplay to illustrate a variety of ways in which the spoken word is integrated into a contrapuntal fabric.

> I do believe most of us are capable of a much more substantial information intake than we give ourselves credit for.
> – Glenn Gould (*Glenn Gould Reader* 393)

Glenn Gould (1932-1982) was known internationally as a pianist and was admired by many for his interpretation of Johann Sebastian Bach's music. In 1955, when still in his early twenties and relatively unknown, he recorded Bach's *Goldberg Variations* in Columbia Records' 30th Street Studios in New York City. The release of this first album made the Canadian pianist world-famous. Later he recorded *The Well-Tempered Clavier*, a nine-year project, which was completed in 1971. This accomplishment was also a sensation and exhibited Gould's sensitivity to and understanding of contrapuntal music. In response to a second recording of the *Goldberg Variations* in 1981, Samuel H. Carter writes: "I think of Glenn Gould as an artist of strong intentionality. He shapes and molds a musical line in its breadth and in its detail with breathtaking awareness" (Bach, *Goldberg Variations,* liner notes). The producer Paul Myers explains that "Gould possessed a phenomenal keyboard technique, which was an essential to his recording methods" (Bach, *Well-Tempered Clavier I,* liner notes 15). He adds that when Gould recorded the first part of *The Well-Tempered Clavier*:

> [H]e would make ten or fifteen takes of a particular prelude or fugue. Nearly every one of them would be note-perfect, but each was completely different, not only in tempo or dynamics but also in 'registration', voicing of musical lines, and emotional content. It was extraordinary to hear each version emerge as he considered it anew. (15)

Gould was passionate about contrapuntal music, and claimed it was the only music that truly interested him. Nancy Canning writes that Gould told a friend he would "wander about the house much of the time with perhaps two radios and a television set all on in different rooms at once" (21). This habit illustrates Gould's fascination with hearing multiple ideas, musical and/or verbal, simultaneously. Therefore, it is not surprising that when François Girard and Don McKellar wrote a screenplay that celebrates the life and accomplishments of Gould, counterpoint of various kinds was included as an integral part of the work. This essay presents an analysis of these contrapuntal textures and focuses on music and the spoken word. It specifically explores the manner in which the spoken word is treated like music in certain passages of the film[1].

The term "counterpoint" originates from the Latin word, *contrapunctus,* which comes from *contra punctum* and means 'against note' ("Counterpoint", 551). The term was first used in the fourteenth century in relation to specific rules regarding musical lines that occurred simultaneously. As time progressed, the various rules changed, and after 1600 the term "counterpoint" came to have different connotations and meanings[2]. The following general definition is provided in *The New Harvard Dictionary of Music:*

---

[1] I would like to thank Heather Alvarez for suggesting I analyze *Thirty Two Short Films About Glenn Gould* in order to research counterpoint from a musico-literary perspective.

[2] For example, in a general sense, the term "counterpoint" became associated with the writing of strict composition, which involved both polyphonic and homophonic part writing. It was also used in connection with only polyphonic compositions. Some musicians used the term quite specifically in reference to vocal polyphony prior to 1600 and the instrumental polyphony of Bach. In the twentieth century, some theorists made a distinction between polyphony and counterpoint, defining the former as the utilization of equal voices, and the latter as a technique in which voices were dealt with in terms of varied significance (*New Grove* 561).

Counterpoint is a feature of all music in which combinations of two or more simultaneously sounding pitches are regularly employed. The term and its adjective form contrapuntal, however, are often used to distinguish from one another musical textures in which each of the several lines sounding together retains its character as a line and textures in which one line predominates and the remainder are clearly subservient, retaining little or no distinct character as lines. In this sense, a fugue of Bach is contrapuntal whereas a nocturne of Chopin is not [...]. (205)

Sometimes counterpoint is associated with the linear aspect of music in contrast with harmony, which is often affiliated with music's vertical component. However, both counterpoint and harmony are basically interconnected. Contrapuntal writing achieved a particularly rich vitality in the late Baroque period, as exemplified in the works of Bach. There are two general types of counterpoint found in Bach's works: the first deals with the melodic parts that share a certain equality, as can be found in a fugue, and the second is concertante continuo polyphony that includes a continuo bass and unequal melodic parts.

Musical counterpoint that is associated with Bach occurs throughout *Thirty Two Short Films About Glenn Gould*. The form of the film is structured after Bach's *Goldberg Variations,* which consist of an opening aria, thirty variations, and a reprise of the opening aria. Gould's own recordings of Bach's contrapuntal work are heard throughout the film. For example, in the first short film entitled, "Aria", Gould's performance of the opening aria of *The Goldberg Variations* is heard. The film concludes with Prelude No. 1 from *The Well-Tempered Clavier,* and the during the credits Contrapuntus No. 9 from Bach's *The Art of the Fugue* is performed with Gould at the organ. Other contrapuntal recordings by Gould are sandwiched in between the opening and closing pieces, e.g., Bach's Two Part Invention No. 13, his Prelude from the *English Suite* No. 5, and more selections from *The Goldberg Variations* and *The Well-Tempered Clavier*. The music is not limited to that of Bach. Composers such as Richard Wagner, Ludwig van Beethoven[3], Sergey Prokofiev, Alexander Scriabin, Paul

---

[3] In the short film, "Variation in C Minor", one variation from Beethoven's *32 Variations in C Minor* is played. So 'thirty two' is a significant number in the film.

Hindemith, Arnold Schoenberg, and even Gould himself are included[4]. There is, however, a strong emphasis on Bach and his musical counterpoint.

In the film, Girard and McKellar incorporate another type contrapuntal texture that was very significant to Gould: a counterpoint with words. Gould was particularly intrigued with the medium of radio and created documentaries for that medium that became known as "contrapuntal radio" (*Glenn Gould Reader* 376)[5]. His *Solitude Trilogy* comprises three sound documentaries that explore counterpoint with the spoken word: "The Idea of North" (1967), "The Latecomers" (1969), and "The Quiet in the Land" (1977)[6]. "The Idea of North" consists of five spoken voices with the sound of a train acting as the basso continuo. In "The Latecomers", multiple characters speak both individually and simultaneously with the sound of the sea as the basso continuo[7]. "The Quiet in the Land" incorporates nine spoken voices in addition to singing by members of the Mennonite Children's Choir, the congregation of the Kitchener-Waterloo United Mennonite Church, and Janis Joplin. It includes other sounds and music as well. In the case of all three documentaries, Gould painstakingly works with recorded voices and sounds, and 'composes' contrapuntal 'music' using predominantly spoken words. The last of the three documentaries is particularly contrapuntal with its "multi-layered structure" (*Solitude Trilogy,* liner notes). The counterpoint incorporates "provocative statements: from the simple, effective sounds of a car (not a horse and buggy) pulling up on a gravel road outside a church tolling, which opens the documentary, to a

---

[4] Gould wrote String Quartet, Op. 1, and in the film the first movement is performed by The Bruno Monsaingeon Quartet. The entire piece is available on the compact disc, *Glenn Gould: The Composer.*

[5] In the short film, "Solitude", some of the radio documentaries are discussed.

[6] Some of Gould's other radio documentaries include: *Arnold Schoenberg: The Man Who Changed Music* (1962); *Stokowski: A Portrait for Radio* (1971); *Casals: A Portrait for Radio* (1974); and *Richard Strauss: The Bourgeois Hero* (1979). Robert Hurwitz writes: "There is a great deal of counterpoint in the Schoenberg documentary: at one point, for example, Krenek and Cage speak simultaneously while a Gregorian chant and the music of Guillaume Dufay, Guillaume de Machaut and Karlheinz Stockhausen are all mixed together (and clearly heard) in the background" (258). Howard Fink writes that Gould's contrapuntal documentaries were inspired by "Schoenberg's spoken-word compositions" (38).

[7] Gould specifically refers to both the train and the sea as basso continuos (*Glenn Gould Reader* 377).

contemporary rock singer tempering the social fabric of this strictly disciplined and isolated" Mennonite community (liner notes)[8].

The documentary that is most emphasized in *Thirty Two Short Films* is "The Idea of North". In fact, the short film that depicts the prologue to this particular documentary is entitled, "The Idea of North: A Radio Documentary by Glenn Gould". In it the human voice is treated like a musical instrument, and the spoken word is integrated into a variety of complex contrapuntal settings[9]. In the short film, a recording of three voices sounds, and these voices interact to create a counterpoint that functions similarly to music, according to a passage from the scene in the screenplay:

> The voice – Schroeder, a nurse – is describing her fascination with the North. Vallee's voice mixes with Schroeder's, and the two blend into an expressive counterpoint. Gould brings in a third voice, Phillips, which joins the other two. Surprisingly, each voice finds its place in the mixture, and a fragile balance holds them together. The words detach themselves, taking on new meanings; in juxtaposition they become music. (93)

As these voices interrelate, Gould, who is already familiar with the broadcast, acts as though he is conducting the verbal music. His gestures acknowledge the "minutest nuances" (94), and he treats the interplay and layering of words as though they were intricately composed musical notes. Here the screenplay reflects Gould's practice, according to a witness, Bob Phillips. In the short film, "Crossed Paths", Phillips, who appears as himself, recounts a time when Gould interviewed him for "The Idea of North":

> It was a very penetrating interview, the most intelligent questions I think I'd ever heard about the North from experts, laymen or anything else, questions that required rather long answers. And as I would start to speak, or make a point, he would register his feelings not by voice but by a smile but all the time **he was using his hands and conducting**. And this was perhaps slightly off-putting when you're trying to think deep thoughts but, because I had no idea of what this was all about, but **he**

---

[8] Gould wrote introductions for the first two documentaries ("The Idea of North" and "The Latecomers"), and both are published in the liner notes, as well as in *The Glenn Gould Reader*. Gould did not write an introduction for the third documentary, "The Quiet in the Land". The author of the liner notes for this documentary is unidentified.

[9] In his seminal book, *Music and Literature: A Comparison of the Arts,* Calvin Brown writes: "The human voice itself is a wind instrument of the reed family, and each voice has its own recognizable timbre – just as, less obviously, each piano or violin has its individual sound." (38) So in this respect, the spoken word is produced by a musical instrument.

continuously was just waving his arm, then sort of bring up this idea and so on. **I was his orchestra for that hour.** (80; my emphases)

As Gould worked on the documentary in the studio, he became in a sense a composer of the spoken word as music. In the essay, "The Music Itself: Glenn Gould's Contrapuntal Vision", Edward W. Said writes: "Counterpoint is the total ordering of sound, the complete management of time, the minute subdivision of musical space, and absolute absorption for the intellect." (48) Gould ordered the sounds, words, time, and space in "The Idea of North" and sometimes worked for hours to create a few minutes of the documentary. Robert Hurwitz explains that putting together "these programs was long and difficult, and like most studio work, tedious" (258). In working on "The Idea of North", Gould realized at a certain point that he would need about one hour and twenty-five minutes airtime to present the material he had assembled. However, he had been allotted only one hour and brainstormed to figure out what could be deleted or changed. After successfully editing the piece down to around one hour and twelve minutes, he finally said to himself, "Look, we really could hear some of these people speaking simultaneously – there is no particular reason why not." (*Glenn Gould Reader* 376)

The five characters included in the documentary – Marianne Schroeder, Frank Vallee, Robert (Bob) Phillips, James Lotz, and Wally Maclean – were all interviewed separately. During the making of the piece they did not meet or interact in any way. Gould explains that the "dramalike juxtapositions [...] were achieved through some careful after-the-fact work with the razor blade on tape [...]" (393). He writes further:

> The point about these scenes, I think, is that they test, in a sense, the degree to which one can listen simultaneously to more than one conversation or vocal impression. It's perfectly true that in that dining-car scene not every word is going to be audible, but then by no means every syllable in the final fugue from Verdi's *Falstaff* is, either, when it comes to that. Yet few opera composers have been deterred from utilizing trios, quartets, or quintets by the knowledge that only a portion of the words they set to music will be accessible to the listener – most composers being concerned primarily about the totality of the structure, the play of consonance and dissonance between the voices [...]. I would like to think that these scenes can be listened to in very much the same way that you'd attend the *Falstaff* fugue. (393)

Just as composers are concerned with the underlying structure of a musical composition, so was Gould aware of the form of his work. He writes that he wanted "to create a structure in which one could feel free to have different approaches and responses" (376) to whatever problems emerged. With this goal in mind, he sketched out the scenes and decided to have the following form: a prologue, five scenes, and an epilogue. (See Gould's graph of the prologue in figure 1. See also figure 2 for a graph of Gould's work on "The Latecomers"[10].) This is the structure that became set in his mind and on paper and remained, with minor changes. He refers to the prologue as "a sort of trio sonata" (393), and as mentioned, considers the sound of the train to be the "basso continuo" (393) in this composition created mostly with spoken words.

Figure 1: Glenn Gould's Graph of the Prologue to "The Idea of North"
Reproduced Courtesy of the Estate of Glenn Gould

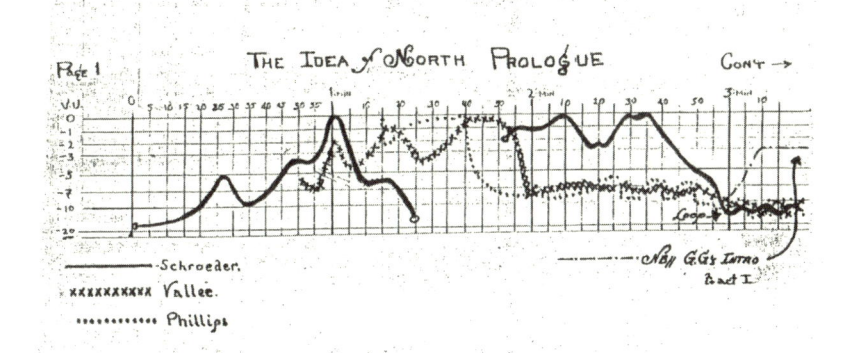

---

[10] I acknowledge the help of Jeannine Barriault in obtaining a copy of these documents from the Glenn Gould *fonds* at the National Library of Canada. I also thank Malcolm Lester for granting permission on behalf of the Estate of Glenn Gould to include them in this essay. The National Library of Canada has a useful website with information on Gould. Cf. http://www.nlc-bnc.ca/glenngould/ (accessed July 6, 2004). The two graphs, which include the last names of some of the participants, illustrate one way in which Gould visually worked through his ideas of contrapuntal relationships for his documentaries.

Figure 2: A Graph by Glenn Gould for the Radio Documentary, "The Latecomers"
Reproduced Courtesy of the Estate of Glenn Gould

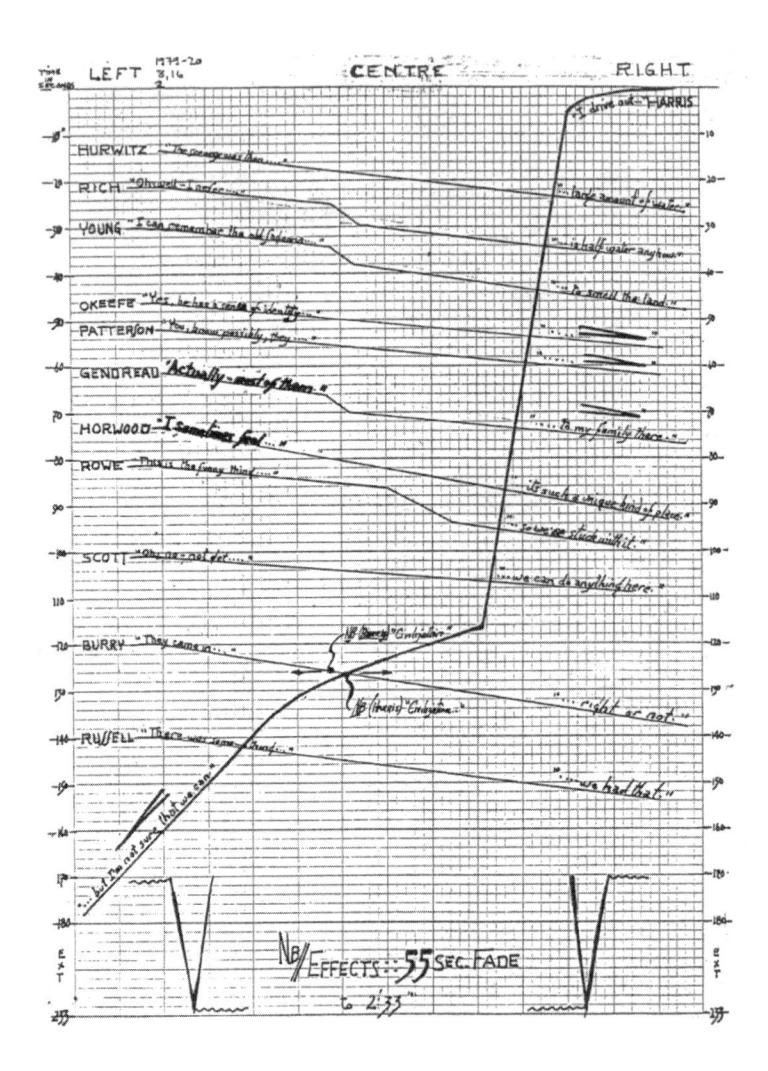

There are, however, limitations to the analogy made between musical and verbal counterpoint. Eric Prieto writes that:

> the application of concepts from one art to objects from the other is an inherently metaphorical act. The very fact that works of literature use words, and not tones, means that no literal transfer between the two is possible. Short of the actual superimposition of music and text – as in song, opera, and the like – there is just no way to get over that threshold of metaphoricity. (52)

Prieto states further that "the test of a good musical metaphor" involves "the same test that applies for any other kind of metaphor: the quantity and quality of information imparted, the extent to which the metaphor affords new ways of seeing" (53-54).

Certain questions can be posed in relation to Gould's radio documentaries. Gould compares a scene from his "The Idea of North" to the final fugue in Giuseppe Verdi's *Falstaff*. If the words in the *Falstaff* fugue were spoken in rhythm without specified pitch, and without the interaction and added texture of the orchestra, would the result be chaos? It seems that Verdi was most concerned with the voice as an instrument in the fugue and in the complex contrapuntal relationship of multiple voices and instruments. The emotion and passion of this climactic passage, coupled with intricate musical counterpoint, appear to be more important than the diction and comprehension of the actual words being sung. In this particular setting, the specified pitches and their relationships are crucial to each other, both from a vertical (harmonic) and horizontal (melodic) standpoint. Thus, in relating this operatic passage to the dining-car scene in Gould's "The Idea of North", we participate in a "metaphorical act", and as Prieto suggests, "no literal transfer between the two is possible". Bruno Monsaingeon writes that although a literal transfer is not possible, there are strong connections between Gould's radio documentaries and music:

> Although the immensely complex "contrapuntal documentaries" Gould made for radio may not appear to be music in the conventional sense, they are, nonetheless, true musical compositions in the structural sense, exploiting all the rhythmic, contrapuntal, and harmonic parameters of the spoken voice, and they can produce purely musical enjoyment even for the non-English-speaking listener who does not understand their textual contents (is this, incidentally, not true of most opera lovers?). (Gould, *Glenn Gould: The Composer* liner notes 7)

However, it can also be asked: what is the significance of Gould's metaphor? How does it help us to hear differently? *The New Harvard Dictionary of Music* states that "melodies relate to each other in counterpoint, with the result that a perceptual balance is struck between the individualities of the lines and their combination", and that "the ear's attention will ideally be focused now on one line, now on the other, and simultaneously on both" (205). If the spoken word of one individual is likened to a melodic line, and if we consider the combination of two people speaking simultaneously, we too can focus on one person's voice now, and then on another, and simultaneously on both[11]. So the process of hearing two or more people speak concurrently resembles the process of hearing multiple musical melodies performed at the same time. Gould has shown us how to listen to the spoken word presented in a contrapuntal texture and to reflect upon the musical qualities of that experience. Through the musical metaphors found in his radio documentaries, he helps us to hear the 'music' in the world around us[12].

This leads to another question: can 'any' occurrence of simultaneous conversations be viewed as verbal counterpoint, as a type of musical metaphor? In Gould's case, with his world-renowned expertise in performing and interpreting musical counterpoint, it is not a far stretch to label his contrapuntal documentaries 'musical', particularly when some of them include music. However, if a person were to sit at a dinner party and hear multiple conversations simultaneously, could this be called verbal counterpoint? Could it be considered a 'musical' experience? I assert that it could potentially be a musical experience, in a metaphorical sense, for those who take the time and effort to hear general pitch, timbre, rhythm, tempo, harmony, and counterpoint. Furthermore, all of the words spoken do not necessarily need to be perfectly understood. Just as Verdi celebrates the voice as an instrument in his *Falstaff* fugue more than he seems to be concerned about the words being understood, the spoken words in a contrapuntal setting do not necessarily need to be perfectly comprehended either. In Gould's "The Idea of North", the texture and interaction of the voices and other sounds, such as the train, take

---

[11] Brown writes: "It is, of course, a matter of frequent occurrence for two or more persons to talk at the same time, and at a party where there are several conversations going on at once it is perfectly possible to station oneself between two groups and follow two conversations simultaneously." (39)

[12] John Cage was also instrumental in helping the public hear 'music' in ordinary sounds and silence in such pieces as *4'33"*.

precedence over the actual words being spoken. However, the words are not completely arbitrary either. As mentioned, each person who participated in the project was interviewed, and Gould took great pains to coordinate the words that dealt with a particular theme: solitude.

Girard and McKellar seem to be very much in tune with Gould's obsession with counterpoint that involves more than musical notes. They recognize Gould's fascination with verbal counterpoint not only in the short film, "The Idea of North", but in "Truck Stop" as well. In this short film, multiple voices occur simultaneously in a way that is analogous to music. In the film, Gould sits alone at a table in a truck stop diner. The following passages from the screenplay describe the setting:

> The atmosphere in the restaurant is calm but full of voices. A dozen simultaneous conversations create a low rumble in the room. A single voice cuts through the mass of voices and Gould turns to look. At another table, three truckers – one about fifty, the others younger – are sitting across from one another. We focus on this conversation, and soon the rumble of voices dies away artificially so that we can hear more clearly. [...] Gould's attention is drawn to the beleaguered waitress at the counter. She is calculating bills and trying to deal with a troublesome but harmless regular sitting next to her. Their voices are superimposed onto the first trucker's, and are often heard simultaneously. This blend of voices begins to form a rhythmic, contrapuntal pattern. (86)

> Gould leaves this conversation before it ends and turns to face two older truckers who are playing pool. We slowly move towards them. Their conversation is also added to the oddly musical blend of voices in the room. We see the small gestures of Gould's hands playing across the top of his table as if he were conducting this 'vocal symphony'. (87-88)

The contrapuntal conversations involved in this film are in both French and English and add to the work's Canadian flavor. The screenplay calls for multiple voices that create "a low rumble in the room" (86) at the beginning of the verbal counterpoint and a "room rumbling with many voices" (89) at the end. This "low" background rumbling can be considered a basso continuo of sorts, over which other voices are more prominently featured in this musical scene. In the film, Gould interprets the experience as musical, as can be seen by his gestures, by which he acts as though he were subtly conducting the voices. In this case, Girard and McKellar skillfully assist the viewer to hear the 'music' and verbal counterpoint that exist in a common diner.

One might ask how the spoken word differs from the written word in regard to a musical type of counterpoint. As mentioned above, Gould associates Verdi's *Falstaff,* or opera in general, with "The Idea of North". Musical counterpoint can also be achieved with the written word but must be approached differently. For example, in the screenplay, voices in "The Idea of North" that are to sound concurrently are grouped together on the written page as follows:

>   **S 1**
>   intriguing; because, then, I could see the outlines
>   **V 2**
>   *themselves as more sceptical-----[fade]*
>   **P 3**
>   various capacities. Sure the North has changed my
>   life; I can't   (95)[13]

Each line is read separately, but with the understanding that these lines are meant to be heard at the same time. This passage in some ways is like a musical score, in which words and music can be analyzed separately, but are intended to be performed simultaneously.

Furthermore, with the written word there is a descriptive element in which the contrapuntal relationship is explained. This is represented in the screenplay in the passages above from "Truck Stop". Descriptions such as these detail the manner in which counterpoint takes place: "[t]heir voices are superimposed onto the first trucker's, and are often heard simultaneously. This blend of voices begins to form a rhythmic, contrapuntal pattern" (86); and, "[t]heir conversation is also added to the oddly musical blend of voices in the room" (88). While this example is drawn from a screenplay that is intended to be realized in a film, similar cases occur in literature. For example, a passage in Part 2 of Albert Camus's *L'étranger* represents verbal counterpoint in a very dynamic and intense way. When Marie visits Meursault in prison, there are prisoners on one side of the room, and visitors are on the other side, opposite them. During this scene, multiple conversations occur simultaneously, and Camus refers to a "bass continue", as can be found in the following passage:

> La plupart des prisonniers arabes ainsi que leurs familles s'étaient accroupis en vis-à-vis. Ceux-là ne criaient pas. Malgré le tumulte, ils parvenaient à s'entendre en parlant très bas. Leur murmure sourd,

---

[13] **S I** is Schroeder, voice 1; **V 2** is Vallee, voice 2; and **P 3** is Phillips, voice 3.

parti de plus bas, formait comme une **basse continue** aux conversations qui s'entrecroisaient au-dessus de leurs têtes. (115-116; my emphasis)[14]

This passage 'describes' the way that counterpoint takes place. If this scene were spoken or performed, it would be possible to actually hear the conversations occurring concurrently[15].

Finally, I would like to address the issue of radio versus film. In the short films, "The Idea of North" and "Truck Stop", there is not only spoken word, but, as in live opera, a visual scene. When a person sees *Thirty Two Short Films,* the individual is listening to the music, words, and other sounds, as well as watching images on the screen. Film contains a visual component that is not available with radio. Listening to Gould's radio documentary, "The Idea of North", is a different experience from listening to the prologue and viewing related images on the screen. In "Truck Stop", one sees the diner and various people talking, with Gould in the midst of it all. Girard and McKellar use images in a brilliant way that enable them to employ what film critic Harvey Roy Greenberg defines as a "paucity of words" (2) to present a portrait of Gould. When words are used, they are often incorporated in a contrapuntal, musical manner.

---

[14] Two translations are presented here:

"Most of the Arab prisoners and their families had squatted down facing each other. They weren't shouting. Despite the commotion, they were managing to make themselves heard by talking in very low voices. Their subdued murmuring, coming from lower down, formed a kind of **bass accompaniment** to the conversations crossing above their heads." (trans. Ward 74; my emphasis)

"The native prisoners and their relations on the other side were squatting opposite each other. They didn't raise their voices and, in spite of the din, managed to converse almost in whispers. This murmur of voices coming from below made a sort of **accompaniment** to the conversations going on above their heads." (trans. Gilbert 91; my emphasis)

In Matthew Ward's English translation, "basse continue" is translated as "bass accompaniment" (74). Stuart Gilbert's translation uses simply "accompaniment" (91). Although all these definitions are musical, *basse continue* is often specifically associated with contrapuntal textures, and is therefore important to the passage. The two English translations could apply to a variety of musical styles. Interestingly, Camus, like Gould, admired Bach. In fact, Camus's second wife, Francine Faure, was a pianist who specialized in performing the music of Bach.

[15] For a more detailed analysis of some of the counterpoint in Camus's novel, cf. my essay, "Musical Counterpoint in Albert Camus' *L'étranger*".

On the other hand, in radio (and this is certainly true in literature that is not illustrated), the listener (or reader) is free to create and imagine the scenery, characters, and landscape in a very individual way. Interestingly, Gould genuinely appreciated radio and seemed to prefer to create his own images as he listened to both music and the spoken word. Howard Fink writes that Gould was "a child of the radio generation of the 1930s and 40s" (36), and "that he was an avid radio listener, especially to radio dramas of all kinds" (36). There was a certain abstraction to the radio that intrigued him. In an interview with John Jessop, Gould said, "I was fascinated with radio theatre because it seemed to me somehow more pure, more abstract, and, in a certain sense, it had a reality for me that, later on, when I became familiar with conventional theatre, that kind of theatre always seemed to lack." (*Glenn Gould Reader* 374) He seemed to enjoy the challenge of inventing his own mental images to go along with the sounds provided[16].

In conclusion, *Thirty Two Short Films* is successful in portraying both the musical and verbal counterpoint that Gould found so compelling. It also includes "a complex tapestry of sight and sound which cunningly embodies its subject's consuming passion for counterpoint" (Greenberg 1). The film incorporates interart metaphors that enhance and embellish our understanding of art in general. Furthermore, the film emphasizes the manner in which complex contrapuntal musical textures can be achieved with the spoken word. The film and some of Glenn Gould's radio documentaries aid in expanding not only the capability and possibilities of what can be achieved with spoken words, but also our definition of music. The line between what is traditionally labeled music and non-music is blurred, and 'music' can be further extended to include solely spoken words in a contrapuntal setting.

I acknowledge the Office of Graduate Studies, the Graduate and Professional Student Association, and the Department of English at The University of New Mexico for financial assistance that enabled me

---

[16] One might say that Gould's inclination to carry on interviews and conduct business with people on the telephone, rather than in person, may be that he preferred to imagine the people with whom he conversed as opposed to actually seeing them. There was a certain abstraction in this experience that seemed to be intriguing to him. An interview is depicted in the short film, "Motel Wawa", in which Gould responds to questions by interlocutor, Elyse Mach, on the telephone.

to present a version of this paper at the fourth conference of the International Association for Word and Music Studies in Berlin, Germany, 2003.

References

Bach, Johann Sebastian. *The Goldberg Variations, BWV 988.* Glenn Gould, perf. CD. CBS, 1982.
—. *The Well-Tempered Clavier, Book I.* Glenn Gould, perf. CD. Sony, 1993.
—. *The Well-Tempered Clavier, Book II.* Glenn Gould, perf. CD. Sony, 1993.
Brown, Calvin S. *Music and Literature: A Comparison of the Arts.* Hanover: Univ. Press of New England, 1948/1987.
Cage, John. *4'33".* New York: Henmar, 1960.
Camus, Albert. *L'étranger.* Paris: Gallimard, 1942.
—. *The Stranger.* Matthew Ward, trans. New York: Vintage, 1988.
—. *The Stranger.* Stuart Gilbert, trans. New York: Vintage, 1946.
Canning, Nancy. "Glenn Gould's Contrapuntal Radio: Bach to the Future". *Ear Magazine* 14.5 (1989): 18-23.
"Counterpoint". *The New Grove Dictionary of Music and Musicians.* Stanley Sadie and John Tyrrell, eds. 2nd ed. London: Macmillan, 2001.
Fink, Howard. "Glenn Gould's Idea of North: The Arctic Archetype and the Creation of a Syncretic Genre". *GlennGould* 3.2 (1997): 35-42.
Girard, François, dir. *Thirty Two Short Films About Glenn Gould.* Videocassette. Rhombus, 1993.
Girard, François and Don McKellar. *Thirty Two Short Films About Glenn Gould: The Screenplay.* Toronto: Coach House, 1995.
Gould, Glenn. *Glenn Gould Radio Documentaries: Pablo Casals, Leopold Stokowski.* CD. CBC, 2001.
—. *The Glenn Gould Reader.* Tim Page, ed. New York: Vintage, 1984.
—. *Glenn Gould: The Composer.* CD. Sony, 1992.
—. *Glenn Gould's Solitude Trilogy: Three Sound Documentaries.* CD. CBC, 1992.
—. String Quartet, Op. 1. Great Neck, NY: Barger and Barclay, 1956.
Greenberg, Harvey Roy. "Thirty Two Short Films About Glenn Gould". *The Silver Screen on the Couch: Film Reviews by Harvey Roy Greenberg, MD.* http://doctorgreenberg.net/32shortfilms.htm. Accessed July 6, 2004.
Hurwitz, Robert. "Towards a Contrapuntal Radio". McGreevy, ed. 253-263.
McGreevy, John, ed. *Glenn Gould: By Himself and His Friends.* Toronto: Doubleday, 1983.
Prieto, Eric. "Metaphor and Methodology in Word and Music Studies". Suzanne M. Lodato, Suzanne Aspden, Walter Bernhart, eds. *Word and Music Studies: Essays in Honor of Steven Paul Scher and on Cultural Identity and the Musical Stage. Proceedings of the Third International Conference on Word and Music Studies at Sydney, 2001.* Word and Music Studies 4. Amsterdam: Rodopi, 2002. 49-67.

Randel, Don Michael, ed. *The New Harvard Dictionary of Music.* Cambridge: Belknap/Harvard Univ. Press, 1986.
Said, Edward W. "The Music Itself: Glenn Gould's Contrapuntal Vision". McGreevy, ed. 45-54.
Verdi, Giuseppe. *Falstaff.* Sir Georg Solti, cond. CD. Decca, 1989.
Weagel, Deborah. "Musical Counterpoint in Albert Camus' *L'étranger*". *Journal of Modern Literature* 25.2 (Winter 2001/2002): 141-145.

Notes on the Contributors

Stephen Benson is Lecturer in Contemporary British Literature at the University of East Anglia. His work on twentieth-century literature and music has appeared in *Narrative*, *The Journal of Commonwealth Literature*, *Critical Survey* and *New Comparison*. *Literary Music*, a book focusing in particular on the representation of music in contemporary fiction, is forthcoming from Ashgate. Other work includes *Cycles of Influence: Fiction, Folktale, Theory* (Wayne State Univ. Press, 2003).

Michael Halliwell studied literature and music in South Africa and completed his operatic studies at the London Opera Centre and with Tito Gobbi in Florence. He pursued a career in opera as principal baritone for the Netherlands Opera, the Nuremburg Opera, and the Hamburg State Opera, as well as giving guest performances in opera and recitals in many European countries. Since 1996, he has been Graduate Co-ordinator of Performance at the Sydney University Conservatorium of Music. He was appointed Chair of Vocal Studies and Opera in 2000 and is currently Pro-Dean. He still performs regularly in opera, concert, radio and television and released a CD of vocal settings of Kipling's Barrack-Room Ballads in 2001. A CD of Boer War songs will be released in 2005. He has lectured and published widely on music and literature, and his research speciality is operatic transformations of the novel. His study, *Opera and the Novel: The Case of Henry James*, was published in January, 2005.

Lawrence Kramer is Professor of English and Music at Fordham University (New York) and co-editor of the journal *19th-Century Music*. He is the author of numerous articles and seven books on the interrelations of music, literature, history, and culture. Recent titles include *Opera and Modern Culture: Wagner and Strauss* (2004), *Musical Meaning: Toward a Critical History* (2001), and *Franz Schubert: Sexuality, Subjectivity, Song* (1998).

Suzanne M. Lodato, Vice-President of the WMA, is on the Scholarly Communications program staff at The Andrew W. Mellon Foundation. Her research interests concern the music of Richard Strauss, particularly his lieder; vocal music (opera and art song) of the nineteenth and early twentieth centuries; and literary/musical relationships. She edited WMS volume 4, and her articles on song and song cycle analysis appear in WMS 1 and 3. Her essay on Richard Strauss's choral works was published in the *Strauss Companion* (2003), and she has authored entries for *The New Grove History of Music and Musicians* and the *Reader's Guide to Music: History, Theory, and Criticism*.

David L. Mosley is a faculty member in philosophy at Bellarmine University and the University of Louisville. He is author of *Gesture, Sign, and Song: An Interdisciplinary Approach to Schumann's Eichendorff Lieder, Op.39* and is currently at work on a book exploring the role of resonance in the philosophical thought of Friedrich Nietzsche.

Eric Prieto is an Associate Professor of French at the University of California at Santa Barbara. He is the author of *Listening In: Music, Mind, and the Modernist Narrative* (University of Nebraska Press, 1992). His primary research interests are in postcolonial Francophone literature and the relations between music and literature. Among his most recent publications are articles on "Alexandre Stellio and the Beginnings of the Biguine" (*Nottingham French Studies*) and "Michel Leiris and Jazz" (*International Journal of Francophone Studies*).

Jürgen Thym is Professor Emeritus of Musicology at the Eastman School of Music (University of Rochester). Having taught there since 1973 and serving as chair of the musicology department from 1982 to 2000, he contributed to the field in three distinct areas: 1) as translator of music theory treatises (Kirnberger, *Die Kunst des reinen Satzes in der Musik*, with David Beach, Yale University Press 1983; Schenker, *Kontrapunkt*, with John Rothgeb, Schirmer Books 1987, Musicalia 2001); 2) as editor of several volumes in the Arnold Schoenberg Gesamtausgabe, with Nikos Kokkinis, Schott/Universal Edition, 1984-94; and 3) as author of numerous essays on text-music relations in the German Lied, partly in collaboration with Ann C. Fehn. Currently, he is working on *Construction of Freedom*, an edition and translation of selected writings of the Italian composer Luca Lombardi (to be published by Koerner-Verlag, Baden-Baden) and on *Of Poetry and Song: Approaches to the Nineteenth-Century German Lied*, a book gathering articles by Rufus Hallmark, Harry E. Seelig, Fehn and himself (to be published by University of Rochester Press).

David Francis Urrows holds degrees from Brandeis University, the University of Edinburgh, and Boston University, where he received his doctorate in 1987. He is Associate Professor in the Department of Music at Hong Kong Baptist University, where he teaches music history, analysis, and aesthetics. Dr. Urrows has published many articles on topics ranging from the history of the Western sacred music in China to contemporary choral music and choral composers. He is co-author of *Randall Thompson: A Bio-Bibliography* (1991), and is also the editor of a critical edition of the works of the nineteenth-century German-American composer, Otto Dresel. The first volume, *Otto Dresel: Collected Vocal Music*, appeared in 2002. The second volume, containing Dresel's chamber works, is in preparation.

Deborah Weagel holds degrees in art and design (BA, Brigham Young University), music theory and composition (MM, University of New Mexico), and French (MA, University of New Mexico). She is currently a doctoral student in English at the University of New Mexico, where her areas of interest include interdisciplinary studies, (auto)biography, feminism/gender studies, and postcolonial literature. Her book, *Interconnections: Essays on Music, Art, Literature, and Gender*, is being published in Calcutta, India, and two of her compositions for solo piano will be included in the appendix. Her essays have been published in the *Journal of Modern Literature, Samuel Beckett Today/Aujourd'hui, The Rocky Mountain Review of Language and Literature,* and *CLCWeb: Comparative Literature and Culture*. In addition, her article. "Shedding Light on Jean-Delphin Alard: 19th-Century Violinist, Pedagogue, and Composer", is forthcoming in *VSA Papers,* the journal of the Violin Society of America and the Catgut Acoustical Society. She is currently working on a second collection of her own essays that deal with music, art, literature, and gender.

Werner Wolf is Professor of English and General Literature at the University of Graz, Austria, and member of the executive board of the WMA. His main areas of research are literary theory, especially narratology and literary self-referentiality, functions of literature, eighteenth- to twenty-first-century English fiction, eighteenth- and twentieth-century drama, and intermedial relations between literature and other media, notably music and the visual arts. His extensive publications include *Ästhetische Illusion und Illusionsdurchbrechung in der Erzählkunst* (1993), *The Musicalization of Fiction: A Study in the Theory and History of Intermediality* (1999), and numerous articles on intermediality. He is also co-editor of WMS 1, 3 and 5.

EcoMedia.

Sean Cubitt

Amsterdam/New York, NY 2005. X, 168 pp.
(Contemporary Cinema 1)

ISBN: 90-420-1885-2 €	35,-/ US $ 44.-

For the last twenty years ecology, the last great political movement of the 20th century, has fired the imaginations not only of political activists but of popular movements throughout the industrialised world. *EcoMedia* is an enquiry into the popular mediations of environmental concerns in popular film and television since the 1980s. Arranged in a series of case studies on bio-security, relationships with animals, bioethics and biological sciences, over-fishing, eco-terrorism, genetic modification and global warming, *EcoMedia* offers close readings of Peter Jackson's *The Lord of the Rings*, Miyazake's *Princess Mononoke*, *The Perfect Storm*, *X-Men* and *X2*, *The Day After Tomorrow* and the BBC's drama *Edge of Darkness* and documentary *The Blue Planet*. Drawing on the thinking of Flusser, Luhmann, Latour, Agamben and Bookchin, *EcoMedia* discusses issues from whether animals can draw and why we like to draw animals, to how narrative films can imagine global processes, and whether wonder is still an ethical pleasure. Building on the thesis that popular film and television can tell us a great deal about the state of contemporary beliefs and anxieties, the book builds towards an argument that the *polis*, the human world, cannot survive without a three way partnership with *physis* and *techne*, the green world *and* the technological.

USA/Canada: 906 Madison Avenue, UNION, NJ 07083, USA.
Call toll-free (USA only)1-800-225-3998, Tel. 908 206 1166, Fax 908-206-0820
All other countries: Tijnmuiden 7, 1046 AK Amsterdam, The Netherlands.
Tel. ++ 31 (0)20 611 48 21, Fax ++ 31 (0)20 447 29 79
Orders-queries@rodopi.nl						www.rodopi.nl
Please note that the exchange rate is subject to fluctuations

Le Chant de l'arabesque.
Poétique de la répétition dans l'œuvre de Claude Simon.

Stéphanie Orace:

Amsterdam/New York, NY 2005. 335 pp.
(Faux Titre 263)

ISBN : 90-420-1965-4   € 67,-/ US $ 94.-

Deux constats appliqués à l'œuvre de Claude Simon sont au fondement de cette étude. En premier lieu, il convient de donner toute sa force à la conception simonienne de l'écriture comme fabrication ; en second lieu, de mesurer l'ampleur des échos tissés de livre en livre et qui érigent lentement le « portrait d'une mémoire ». Embrassant l'ensemble des romans simoniens, nous nous proposons d'analyser les enjeux de ces retours, aux manifestations protéiformes. Intimement liée à la poétique romanesque, la répétition ne l'est pas moins de l'imaginaire ; jamais reprise stricte à l'identique, elle implique différence et variation. Se donnent alors à voir nombre de tensions constitutives qui travaillent l'ensemble scriptural, de la phrase à l'œuvre entière. Dès lors, si la syntaxe tout autant que la structure tendent à la circularité, ce retour parfait que dessine le cercle est bientôt compliqué : il se tord, se distend, se déploie. Nous voulons suivre cette arabesque et nous mettre à l'écoute de son chant.

USA/Canada: 906 Madison Avenue, UNION, NJ 07083, USA.
Call toll-free (USA only)1-800-225-3998, Tel. 908 206 1166, Fax 908-206-0820
All other countries: Tijnmuiden 7, 1046 AK Amsterdam, The Netherlands.
Tel. ++ 31 (0)20 611 48 21, Fax ++ 31 (0)20 447 29 79
Orders-queries@rodopi.nl   www.rodopi.nl
Please note that the exchange rate is subject to fluctuations

The Yearbook of the Research Centre for German and Austrian Exile Studies 6

Arts in Exile in Britain 1933-1945:
Politics and Cultural Identity.

Edited by Shulamith Behr and Marian Malet.

ISBN: 90-420-1786-4   € 76,-/ US $ 95.-
Amsterdam/New York, NY 2005. 377 pp.

This volume focuses on the contribution of refugees from Nazism to the Arts in Britain. The essays examine the much neglected theme of art in internment and address the spheres of photography, political satire, sculpture, architecture, artists' organisations, institutional models, dealership and conservation. These are considered under the broad headings 'Art as Politics', 'Between the Public and the Domestic' and 'Creating Frameworks'. Such categories assist in posing questions regarding the politics of identity and gender, as well as providing an opportunity to explore the complex issues of cultural formation. The volume will be of interest to scholars and students of twentieth-century art history, museum and conservation studies, politics and cultural studies, in addition to those involved in German Studies and in German and Austrian Exile Studies.

USA/Canada: 906 Madison Avenue, UNION, NJ 07083, USA.
Call toll-free (USA only)1-800-225-3998, Tel. 908 206 1166, Fax 908-206-0820
All other countries: Tijnmuiden 7, 1046 AK Amsterdam, The Netherlands.
Tel. ++ 31 (0)20 611 48 21, Fax ++ 31 (0)20 447 29 79
Orders-queries@rodopi.nl   www.rodopi.nl
Please note that the exchange rate is subject to fluctuations